IMAGES
of America

LAKE BOON

I0806169

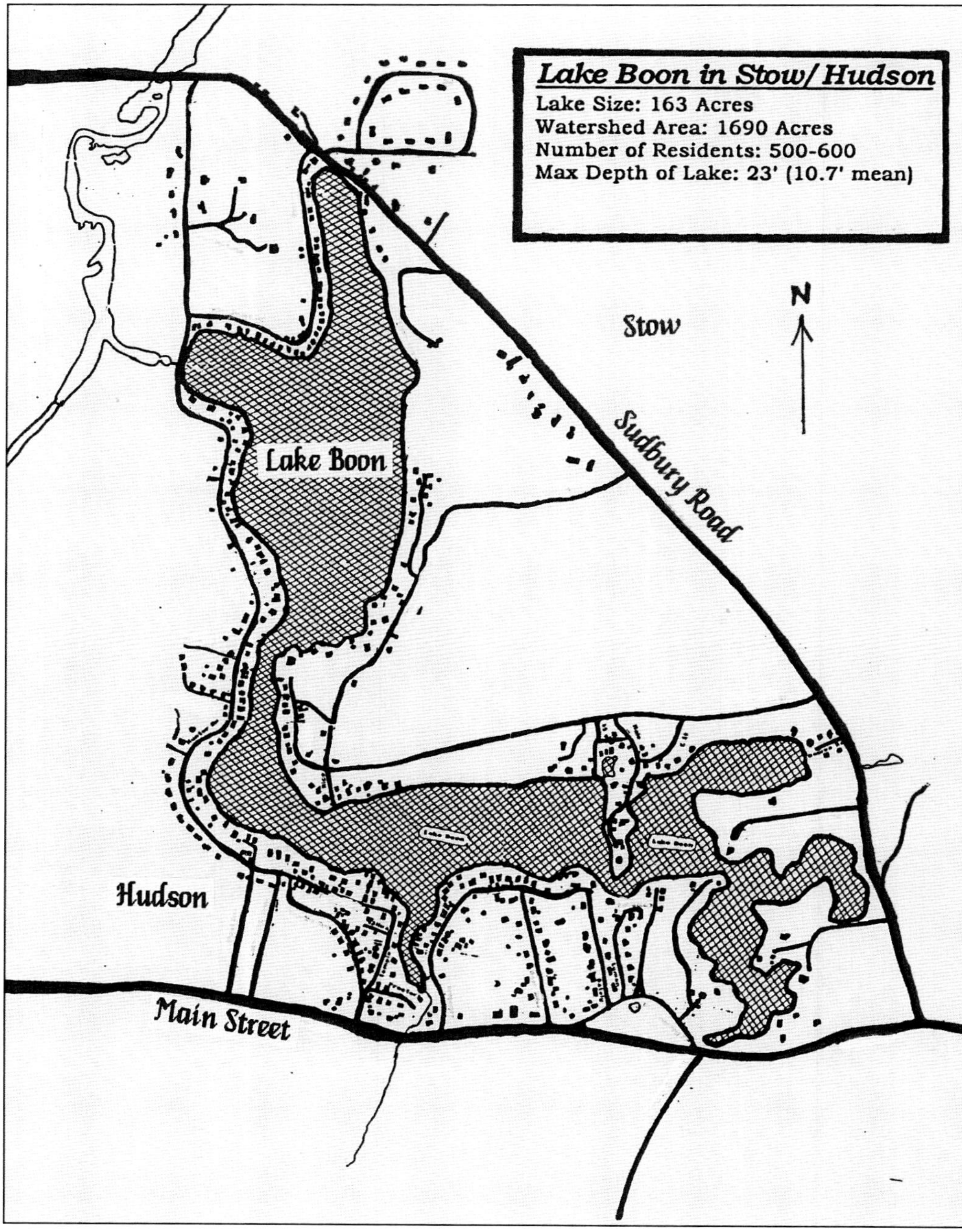

Cover Photograph: **Elko Villa Cottage in the 1920s.** This very elaborate cottage featured a two-story porch with a grand staircase leading down to the lake, a stone dock, and a motor launch for leisure lake travel. The cottage also featured a boathouse with its own small porch. It is still standing at 194 Barton Road in Stow, Massachusetts. (Berry photograph.)

IMAGES
of America

LAKE BOON

Lewis Halprin and Alan Kattelle

ARCADIA
PUBLISHING

ISBN 978-0-7385-6436-4

Published by Arcadia Publishing
Charleston, South Carolina

Printed in the United States of America

Library of Congress Catalog Card Number: 2008939195

For all general information contact Arcadia Publishing at:
Telephone 843-853-2070
Fax 843-853-0044
E-mail sales@arcadiapublishing.com
For customer service and orders:
Toll-Free 1-888-313-2665

Visit us on the Internet at www.arcadiapublishing.com

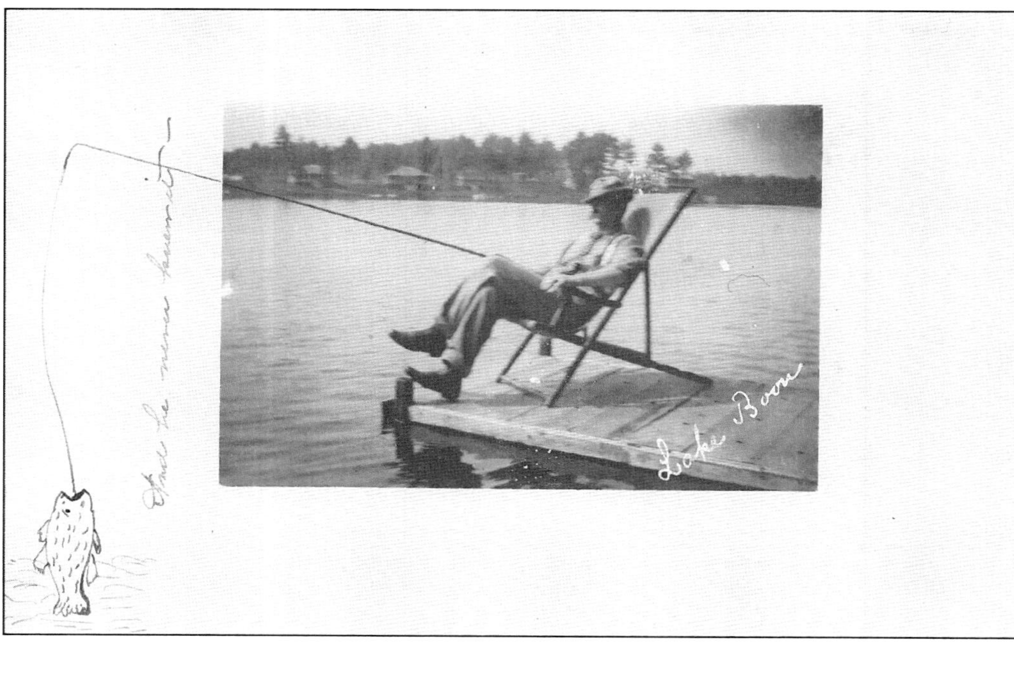

Contents

Acknowledgments

In the memory of all the people who came to Lake Boon during the summer in the early 1900s. For just three months out of the year, they formed a close community that had fun both in and out of the water. Then in the fall, they went back to their humdrum lives for the rest of the year. May we share their pleasure through these pictures and stories.—Lew Halprin.

My father, Laurence W. Kattelle (1890–1982), spent his boyhood and young adulthood summers on Lake Boon, and throughout his life he maintained an active interest in the history of the lake and its environs. In gratitude for his legacy, I dedicate my efforts on this book to his memory.—Alan Kattelle.

Image Credits

Throughout the text, certain images are followed with the following photograph credits:

(Berry) Fifty images created by the Marlborough Massachusetts photographer Alexander Berry at various dates from approximately the 1890s to the 1930s using a large view camera that made 5-by-7-inch glass-plate negatives. These photographs are from the Richard Conard collection.

(Conard) Two images from the postcard collection of Richard Conard of Wayland, Massachusetts.

(Gelpke) A map drawn by Richard Butler, uncle of Dick Gelpke, a Lake Boon resident.

(Halprin) Twenty-one images from the collection of Lewis Halprin, a Lake Boon resident and one of the compilers of this book.

(Hudson) Eight images from the collection of the Hudson Historical Society.

(Jackson) Twelve images from the collection of Paul Jackson of Wilmington, Delaware, a summer resident of Lake Boon.

(Kattelle) Fourteen images from the collection of Alan Kattelle, a Lake Boon resident and one of the compilers of this book.

(Parker) Three images from the collection of Alda and Lee Parker of Hudson, Massachusetts.

(Phalan) Seven images from the collection of Lake Boon postcards owned by Neal Phalan of Lake Boon, Massachusetts.

(Raina) Ten images from the collection of Ken Raina, president of the Lake Boon Association and a Lake Boon resident.

(Stow) Nine images from the Ancient Documents Collection of the Town of Stow.

INTRODUCTION

Lake Boon was originally formed by a melting glacier thousands of years ago, and for most of its life it was a simple body of water hiding in the woods. But in the late 1800s, it suddenly took on a very exciting life as a summer resort. Several fortunate things happened to bring this about: The mill complex in the nearby town of Maynard depended on the Assabet River to turn the wheels of its machinery. But the Assabet would get very slow in the summer and was not always a reliable source to generate energy. To help get over such dry spells, it was decided to build a dam at the outlet of Lake Boon in order to impound a sizable amount of water. The water would then be released into the river whenever the river was low so that the mills always had waterpower.

However, toward the end of the 1800s, practical ways were found to use electricity, and it started to replace waterpower as a means to run machinery. This meant that the nearby mills no longer depended on the fickle flow of the Assabet River to run their machinery. The water impounded within Lake Boon was now unnecessary. With the year-round height of the water staying constant, and its shoreline remaining fixed, recreational use of the lake began.

Two different railroad lines reached from Boston to points west, and passed very close to Lake Boon. As a result, the lake had two railroad stations serviced by many trains each day to and from Boston. Since roads in the early 1900s were not very good, and auto travel was in its infancy, the railroads provided a very convenient way to reach the lake. Those who worked in Boston could commute weekly, or even daily, by train.

The distance from Boston, after train service was established, was neither too far nor too close, but just the right distance to attract many Boston residents to spend the summer at the shores of Lake Boon.

The community at Lake Boon grew rapidly. First there were tents and very small cabins used by the adventurous during the summer. Then the cabins became larger as whole families spent the summer at the lake. As the more well-to-do came to the lake, their cabins became large and elaborate, both inside and out. Then, to service the summer folk, small shops, two post offices, meeting rooms, churches, small department stores, drugstores, and a hotel were built. Quite a few "clubs" were established, some of which were strictly for single young men.

Transportation around the lake during its early adventurous days was mostly by boat. The roads were unpaved, and most of the summer folk came to the lake by train and therefore didn't have a car or horse for getting around. Beginning in 1911, Laurence W. Kattelle operated a regularly scheduled boat, the *Princess*, around the lake, stopping at several main docks to pick up or drop off passengers, or stopping at any dock if flagged down. Canoes and rowboats were very popular and were used as alternate means of transportation. Many cabins had large signs on top of their roofs so boaters could identify the cabins that they wished to visit.

One of the people who came to the lake frequently was a local photographer, Alexander Berry. He came with his 5-by-7 inch glass-plate view cameras in the early 1900s and took many photographs of the lake and its people. Fortunately for us, these photographs survived and are now in the collection of a local historian, Richard Conard. They are featured in this book and show how the vacationers at Lake Boon had fun—we see them boating, swimming, hunting, and having parties. The photographs show the clothing styles, mostly full-length and formal, even when swimming. Many styles of shelter can be seen, from simple tents, small cabins, three-story summer lodges, and little shops, to meeting halls and even a full-size hotel.

It turned out Lake Boon was an active vacation spot at the same time that postcards were a very popular way to send notes through the mail, especially if you were on vacation. As a result, at least 150 different postcards featuring Lake Boon scenes are known to have been produced during that time, most of which are in the postcard collection of lake resident Neal Phalan, who is sharing them with us through this book.

Lake Boon is also fortunate in still having as nearby residents, descendants of those that lived at the lake during its most active period. These include Alan Kattelle, the co-compiler of this book who has contributed a wealth of information about the early lake days, Paul Jackson, whose family was one of the first to build at the lake, and the many families who opened their memories and closets and shared with us their family's pictures, stories, and trivia.

Today, lake activity has changed. Gone are the genteel ladies being decorously paddled along in silent canoes and the elegant mahogany launches with inboard engines quietly cruising. In their place are daring water-skiers and raucous jet-skis. The quaint cabins with their summer vacationers have grown into full-size winterized houses occupied year-round.

But wait! All is not lost. Those days can still be resurrected, at least in our minds. How? First, sit down in your favorite easy chair, or maybe out on your porch or dock, then let this book carry you back to the early part of the 1900s and the time when Lake Boon was justifiably known as a jumpin' place.

Enjoy your trip.
Lew & Alan

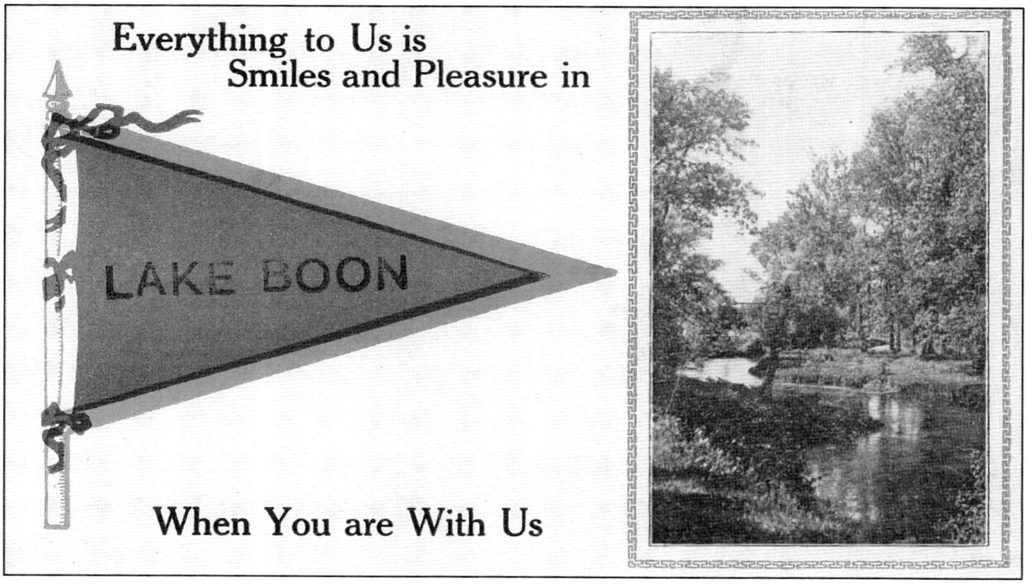

One

Fascinating Beginnings

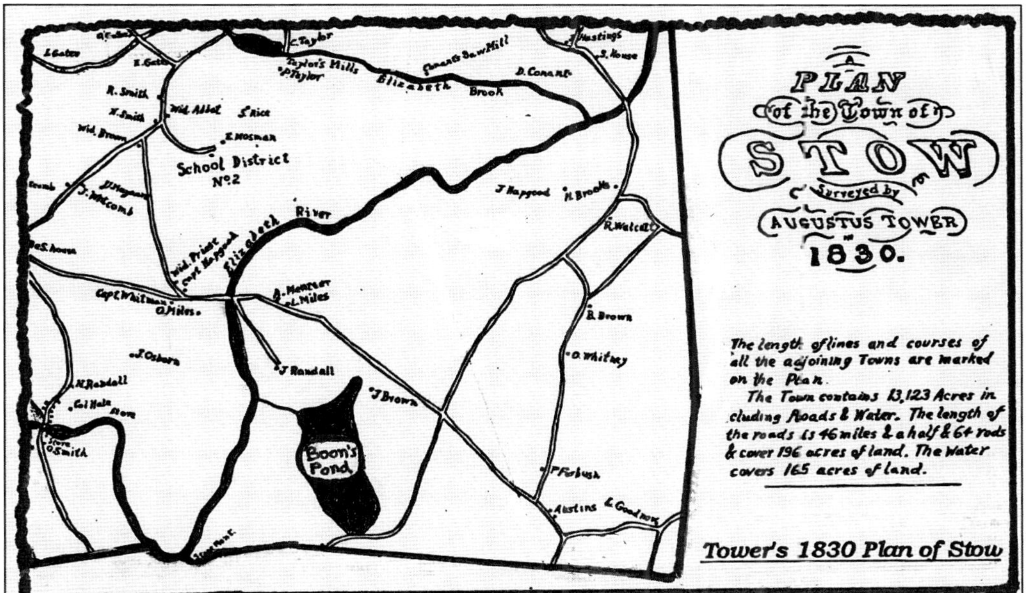

A Portion of 1830 Map Showing Original Lake Boon. Lake Boon, called Boon's Pond back in the mid-1880s, was only a single-basin body of water, fed chiefly by springs and with an outlet into the Assabet River (then called the Elizabeth River). The original lake (pond) was located entirely in the southwest corner of the town of Stow, Massachusetts, as shown by this 1830 map, clearly illustrating its single-basin status at that time. After the lake was enlarged, the new lake lay partly in Stow and partly in the adjoining town of Hudson.

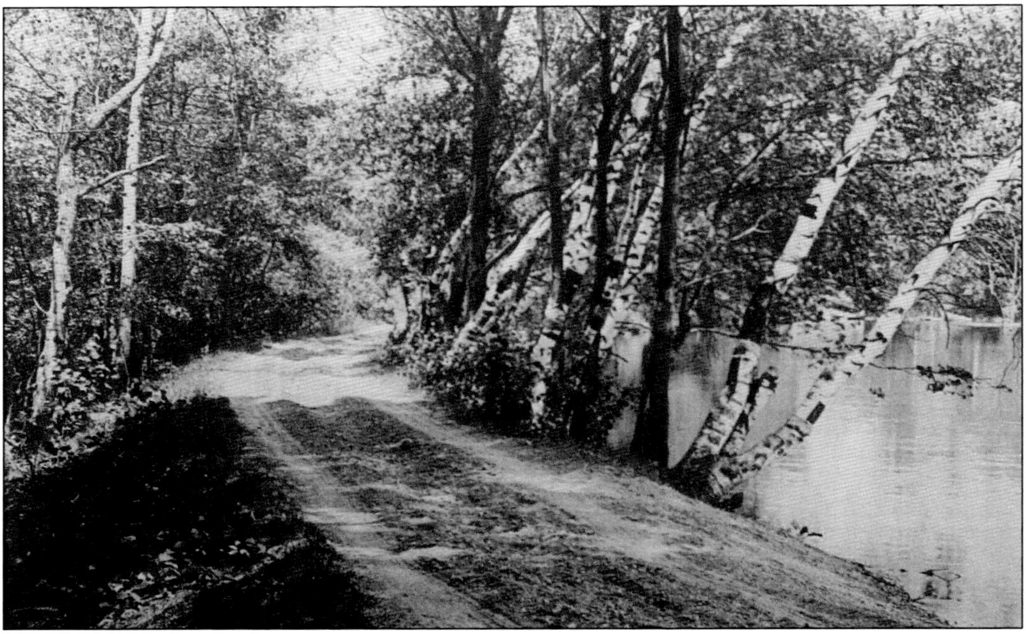

The Dam at the End of Lake Boon. Around 1870, a dam was installed where Lake Boon flowed into the Assabet River in order to impound water within the lake. The dam raised the level of the water and caused the lake to expand from a single basin into three basins, each separated by a short narrow section. The contained water was then released whenever the river was low, for use by the water-driven machinery in the woolen mill located downstream in nearby Maynard.

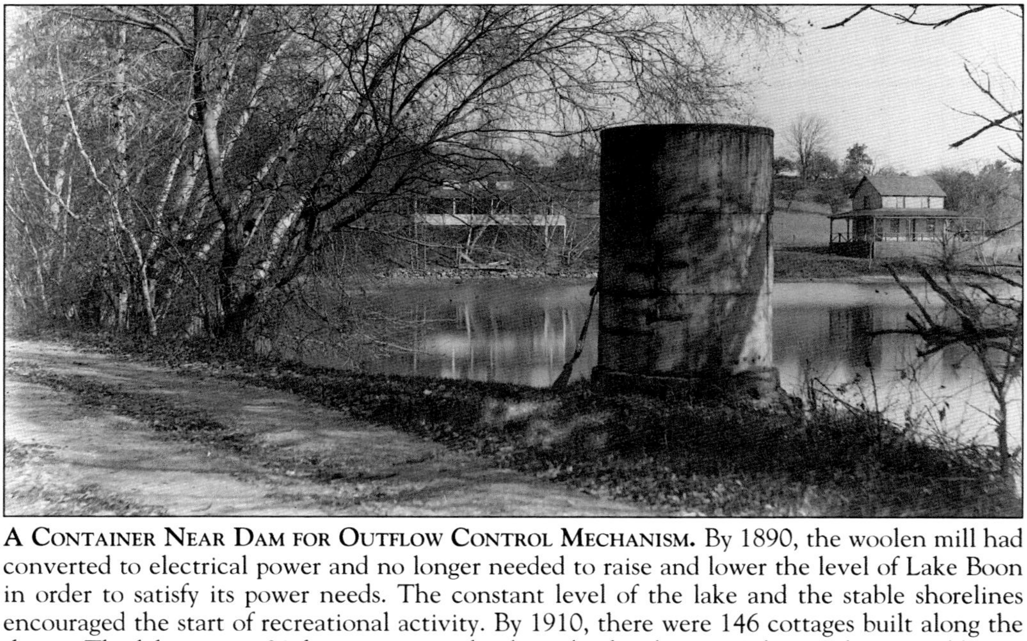

A Container Near Dam for Outflow Control Mechanism. By 1890, the woolen mill had converted to electrical power and no longer needed to raise and lower the level of Lake Boon in order to satisfy its power needs. The constant level of the lake and the stable shorelines encouraged the start of recreational activity. By 1910, there were 146 cottages built along the shores. The lake is now 21 feet maximum depth in the first basin, 10 feet in the second basin, and 6 feet in the third basin. (Berry.)

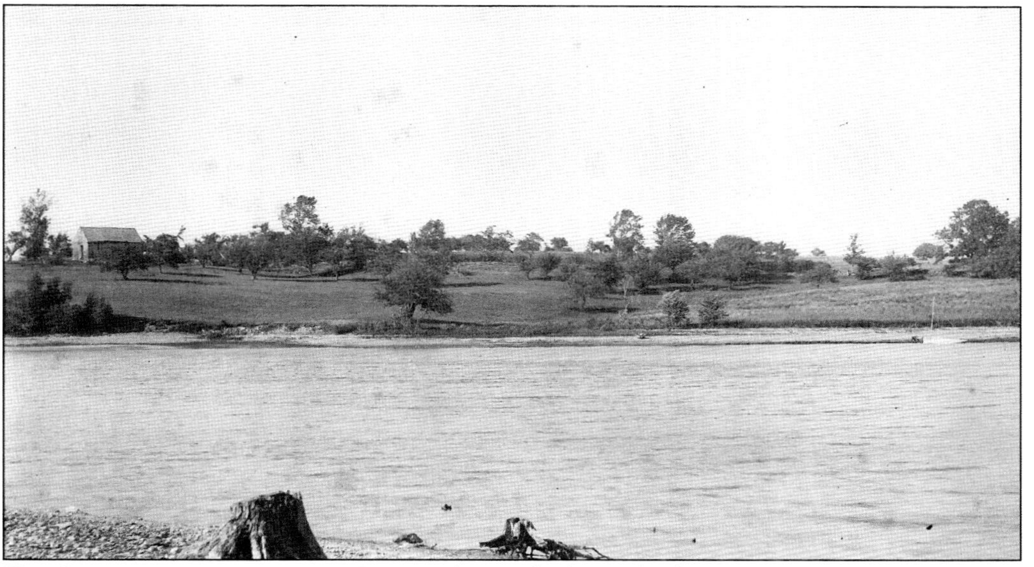

THE SHORELINE OF EARLY LAKE BOON. The north shore of Lake Boon is shown here in 1890, shortly after the lake reached its current depth and its current shoreline. The barn is that of the Mead Homestead (later owned by Jerome Barton). No recreational cabins were present along the shoreline at that time. (Stow.)

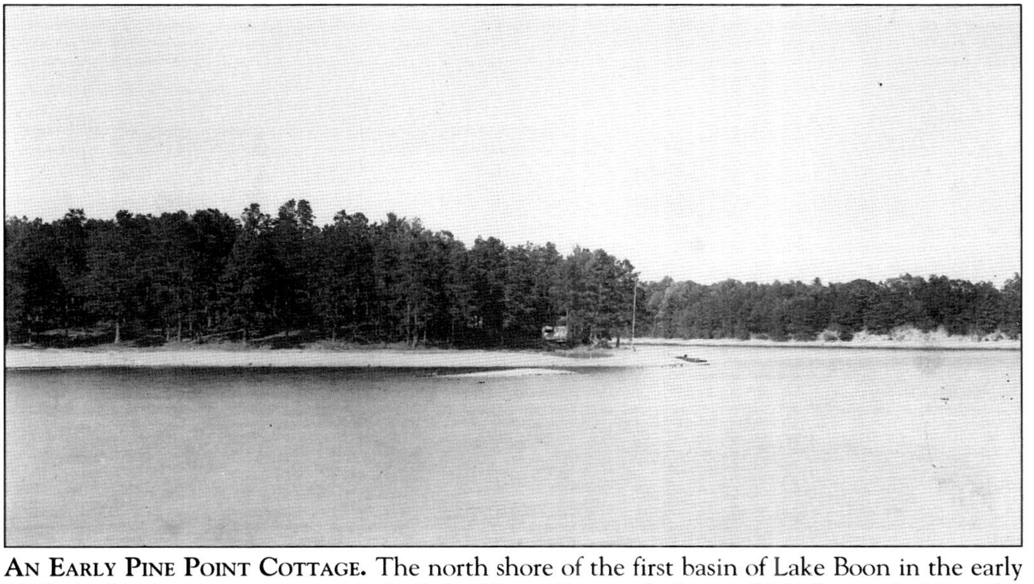

AN EARLY PINE POINT COTTAGE. The north shore of the first basin of Lake Boon in the early 1890s had only one cottage on it, built by Capt. Thomas Jackson of Marlborough. Note the sand bar that extended into the lake just off the point. (Stow.)

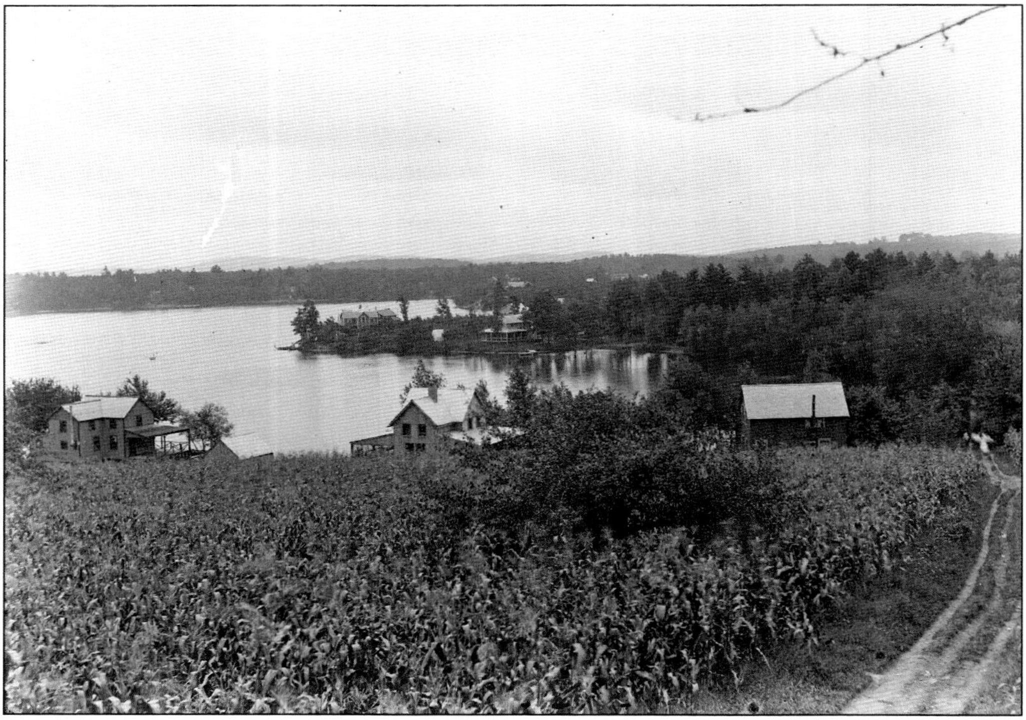

The Corn and Cottages Grow Together. This photograph shows the view from Boon Hill at the north portion of the lake and early cottages along the shore. West Point cottage is shown in the top center, Tufts cottage is at the left, and the original Moondyne cottage is at the right. The corn crop is growing on the old Barton farm. Barton Road is shown at the far right. (Berry.)

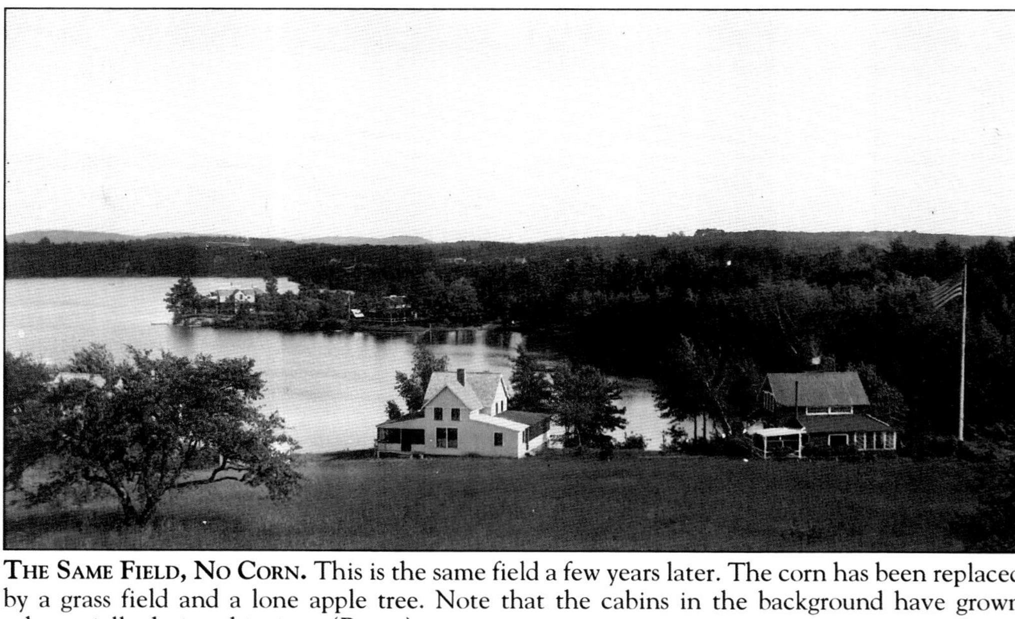

The Same Field, No Corn. This is the same field a few years later. The corn has been replaced by a grass field and a lone apple tree. Note that the cabins in the background have grown substantially during this time. (Berry.)

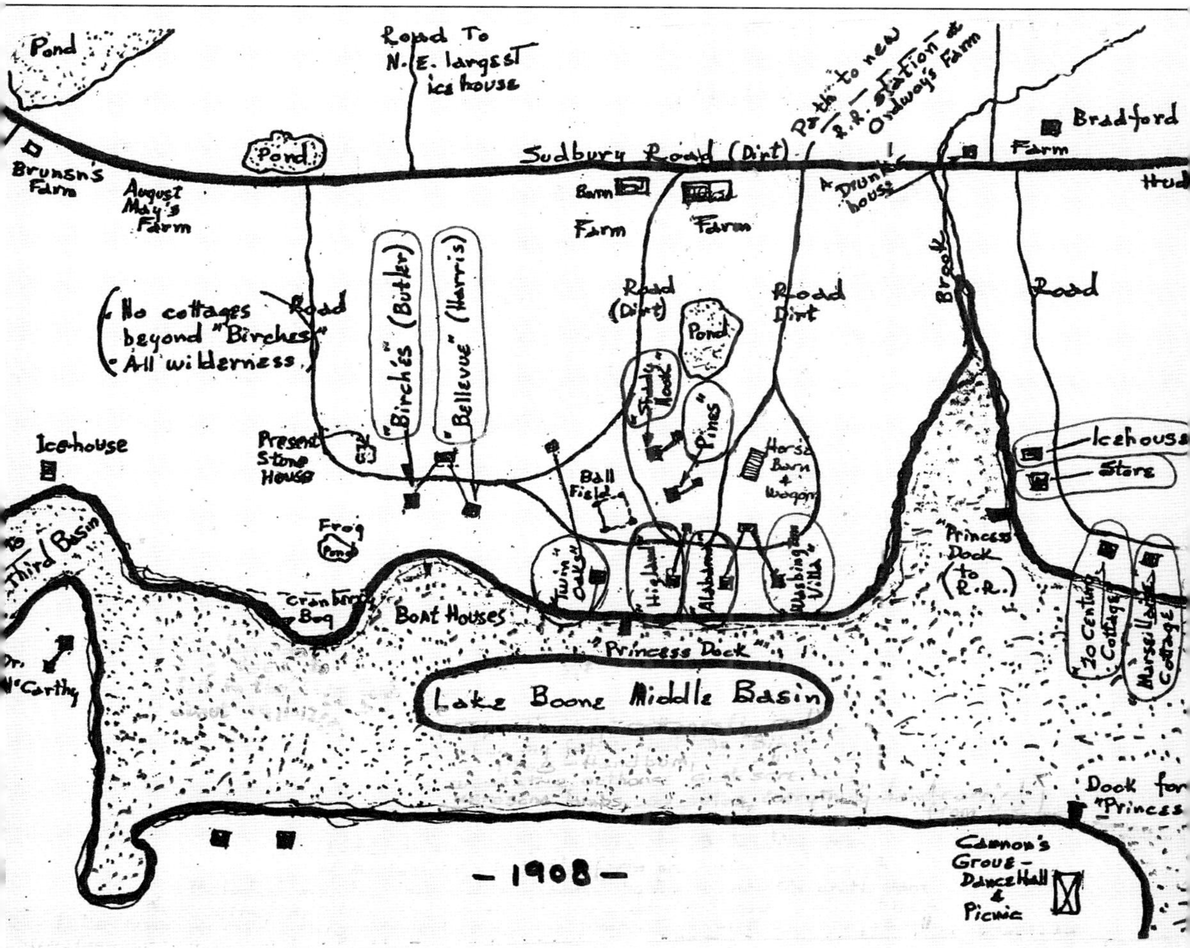

A Lakeside Cabin Venture. Lakeside was one of the first groups of cabins built on the second basin of the lake. It was a co-op venture by eight business men of Marlborough, who bought the farm on the main road in 1908, including land on the south side of the second basin of the lake. They built eight cottages all alike (except in two sizes) and built a ball field for their own use. All furnishings were bought eight of each (icebox, boats, etc.). This map was drawn by Richard Butler in 1920, whose father owned the "Birches" cottage. The following are comments he made in recollections written for his family in 1982: Hand pumps were used for all water, wood stoves for all cooking and heating, outhouses (no indoor toilets), cloth screening, kerosene lamps (no electricity), no autos, and everything had to be hand-carried from the railroad. Originally the deep-woods came directly to the edge of the lake with the cottages nestled among them. The Birches (Butler) had a large birch clump of five trees from one stump. About 1932, the trains started a fire near the large icehouse near White Pond and with the wind blowing toward the lake, it devastated all the trees and burned the Birches. At that time, all the roads outside town, except the main road (Hudson-Sudbury Road), were the typical rural roads of three ruts with grass between.

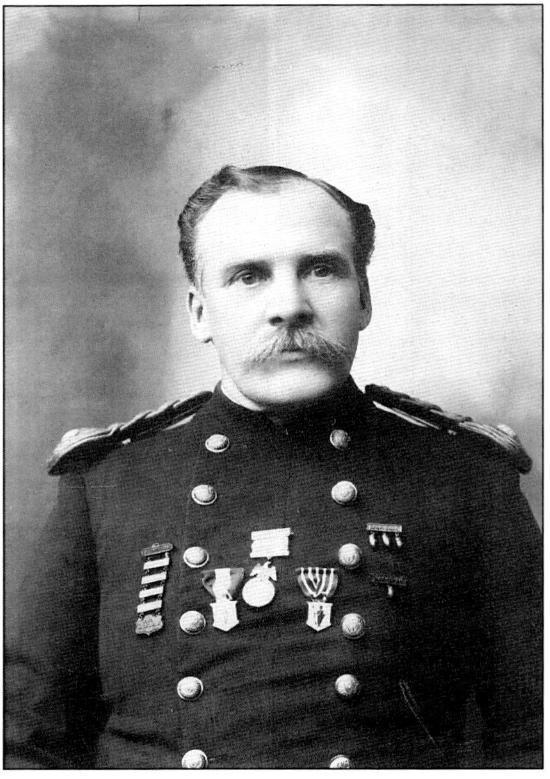

CAPTAIN T.E. JACKSON. Capt. Jackson led the Marlborough Volunteer Army Company in the Spanish-American War. After returning from that war as a local hero, he started building cabins and cottages on the recently formed Lake Boon. The first one was for his own family; called "Pine Point," it is still standing and is considered the oldest cottage remaining on the lake. (Jackson.)

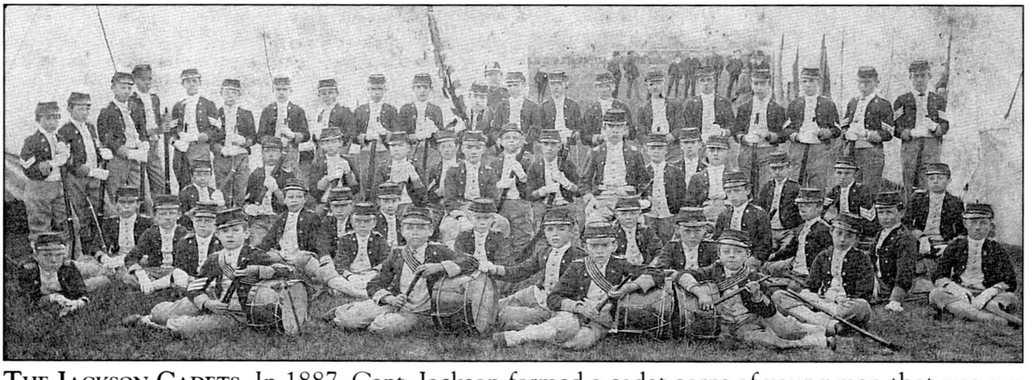

THE JACKSON CADETS. In 1887, Capt. Jackson formed a cadet corps of young men that was run in military style. The encampment was at Lake Boon for its first five years before moving to the Framingham area. (Jackson.)

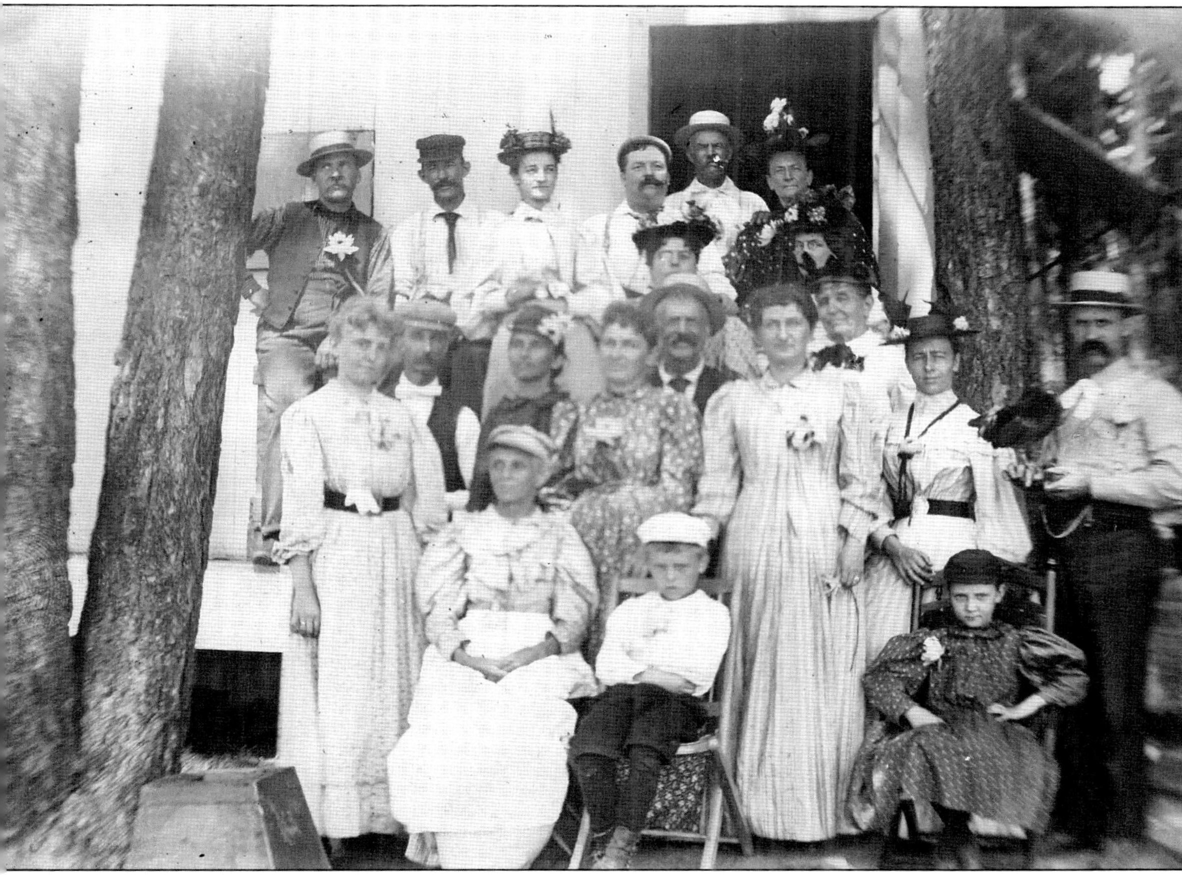

The Jackson Family, 1893. One of the first cottages on Lake Boon was at Pine Point on the north part of Lake Boon's first basin. T.E. Jackson (upper left) originally pitched a tent at this site, then built a small cottage (partially shown in the background). Here the family is gathered at their Lake Boon site to enjoy a day in the woods. The Jackson cottage at Pine Point was later expanded into the large house that is still standing at this same spot. (Jackson.)

The family members in this photograph are identified from left to right as follows: (first row) Addie Jackson, Leroy Jackson, and Flossie Jackson; (second row) Ina Jackson, Joe Warren, Hattie Proctor, Mrs. T.E. Jackson, Sarah Ward, Lizzie Trull, and Fred Trull (with Bantom rooster); (third row) Joe Jackson and Harriet Rogers; (fourth row) Mrs. Pickering and Mrs. Joe Warren; (top row) T.E. Jackson, Will Ward, Mabel Warren, Will Pickering, Henry Miles, and Lyd Miles.

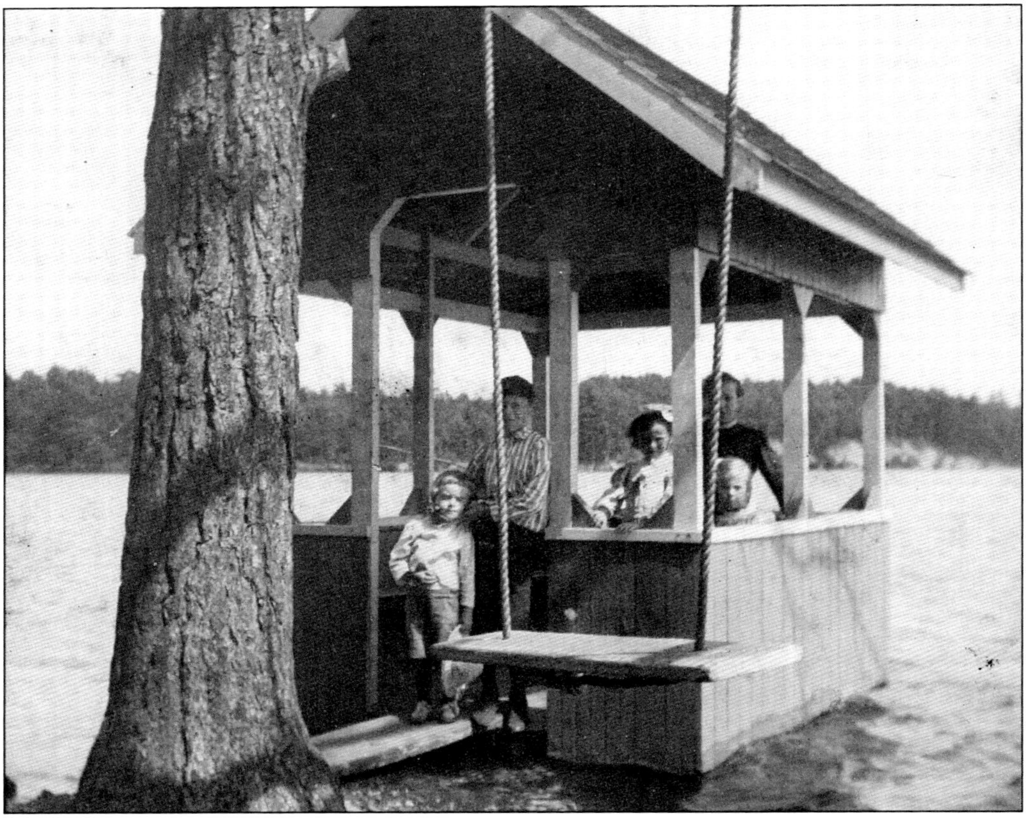

A Summer House at Pine Point. The Jackson cottage at Pine Point, on the northern part of Lake Boon, sported a little "summer house" on the water's edge at the very tip of Pine Point. The lake could be viewed from three sides, and there was always a breeze. (Jackson.)

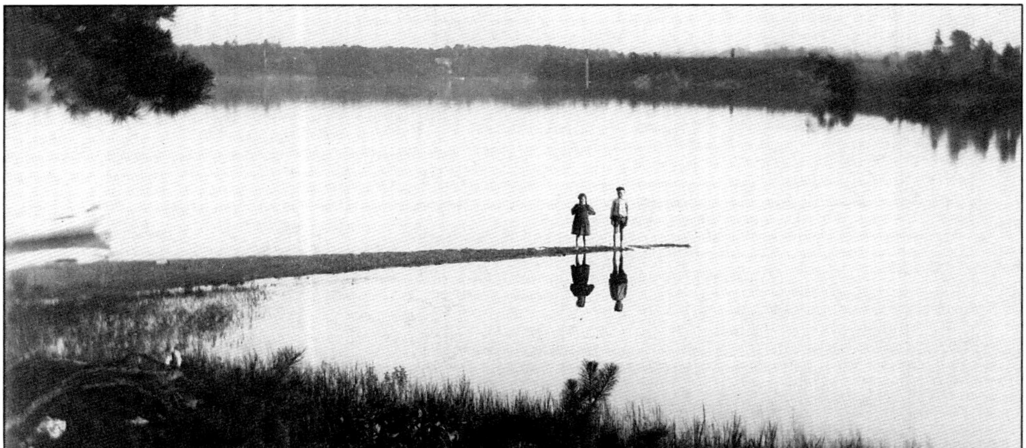

The Sand Bar on Lake Boon. Near Pine Point there is a shallow spot in the lake's first basin that in the early days of the lake was above water and allowed one to walk quite a ways out onto the lake. The sand bar is currently underwater, but occasionally, a motor boat that comes around the bend at Pine Point will be abruptly reminded that it is still there. (Jackson.)

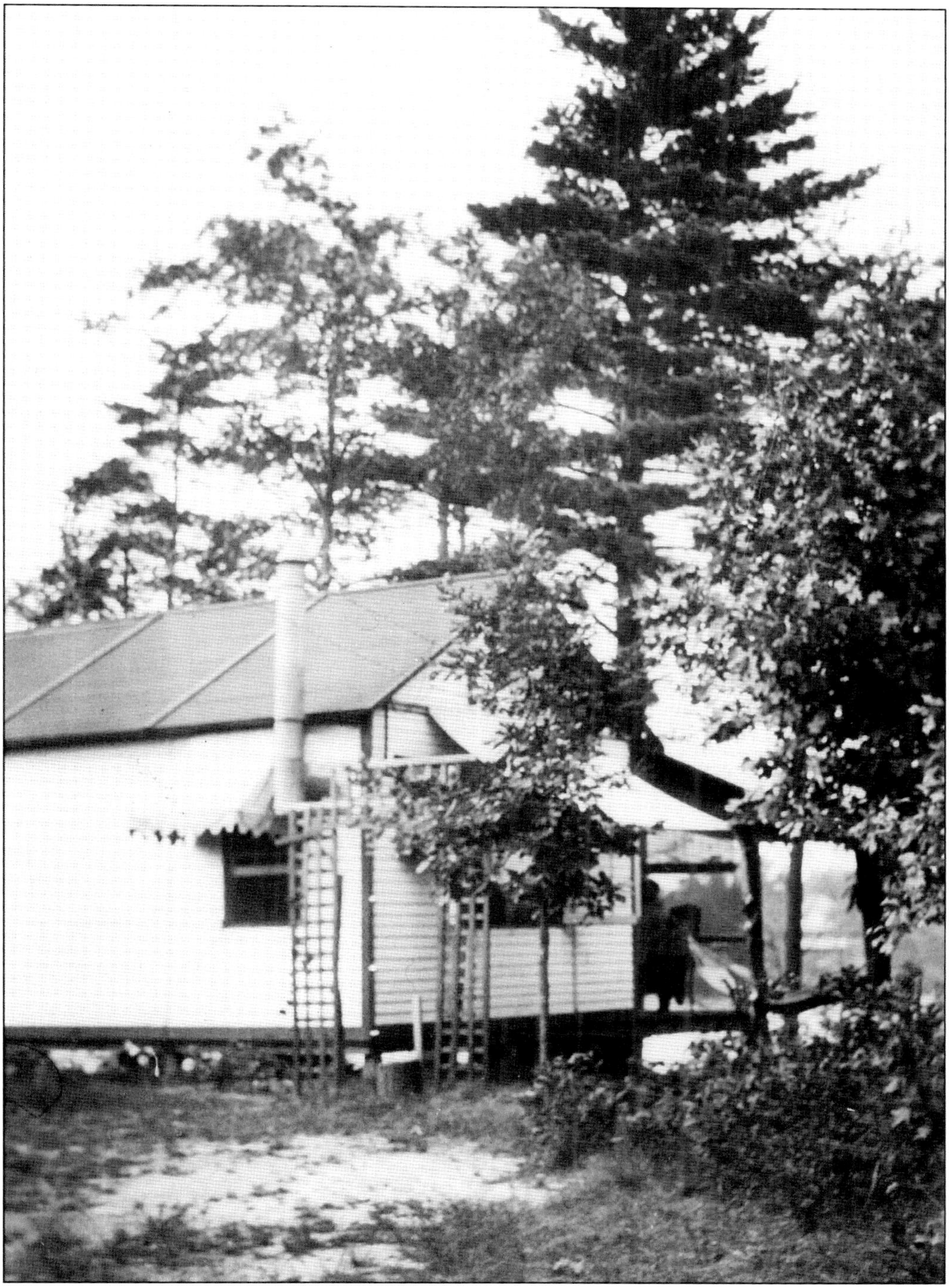

A Small Cottage in the Woods. These are typical of the small cottages that were originally built around the lake. This particular cottage was a "Hogdson House," a very early pre-fabricated house erected about 1924 by L.W. Kattelle for his sister, Fannie Kattelle. Note that the lake can be seen through the space under the cottage. (Kattelle.)

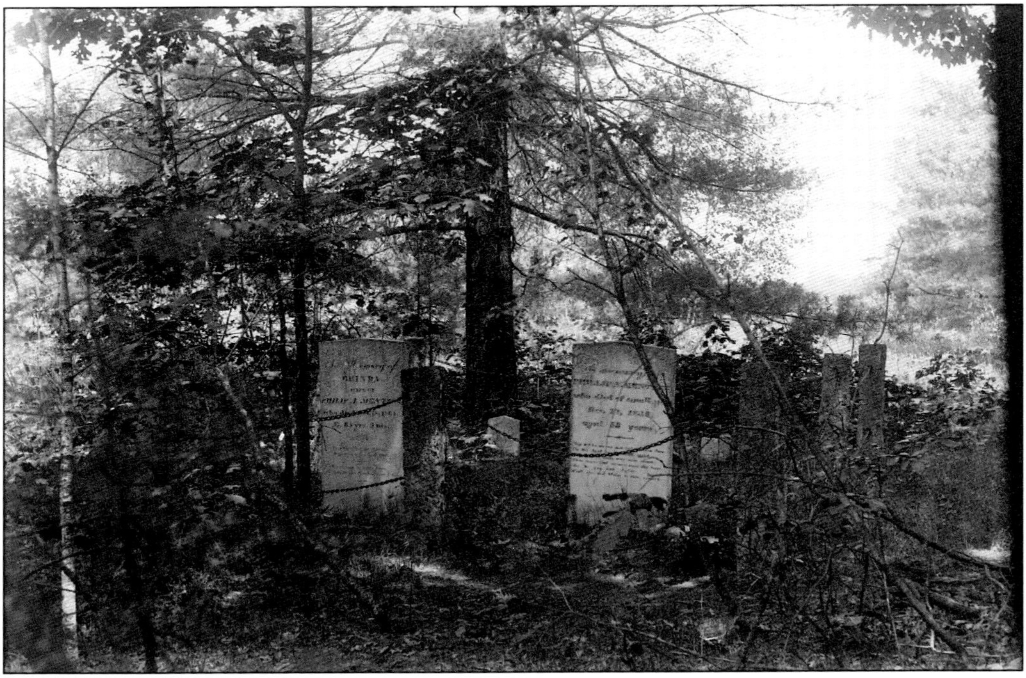

Mentzer's Grave. A nearby farmer, Phillip N. Mentzer, died of smallpox, and it is said that the townsfolk were so afraid of catching it themselves that they did not allow his body to be buried in the town cemetery. A small private cemetery was established on the edge of his farm, near the corner of Sudbury Road and Pine Point Road where he and, later, others in his family were buried. (Berry.)

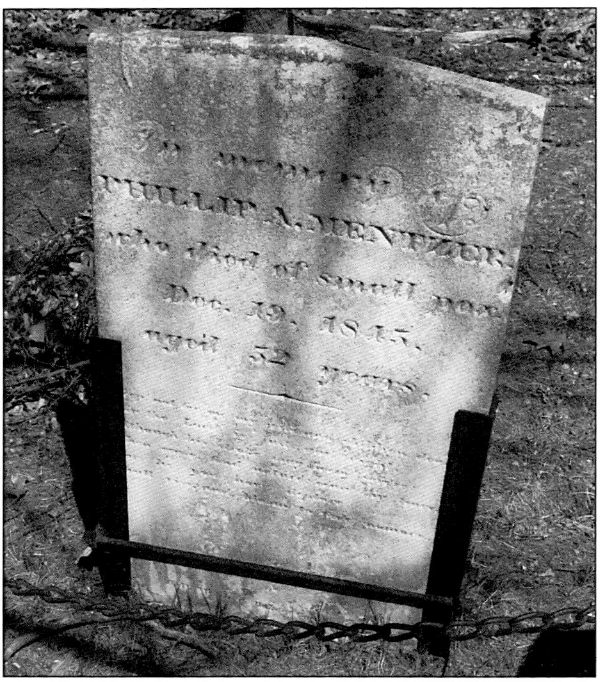

Mentzer's Grave Still With Us. A development of homes called "Wildwood" has grown up around Mentzer's grave, which is now at the corner of Lakewood Road and Wildwood Road. The gravestones are well maintained by the residents of the development. (Halprin.)

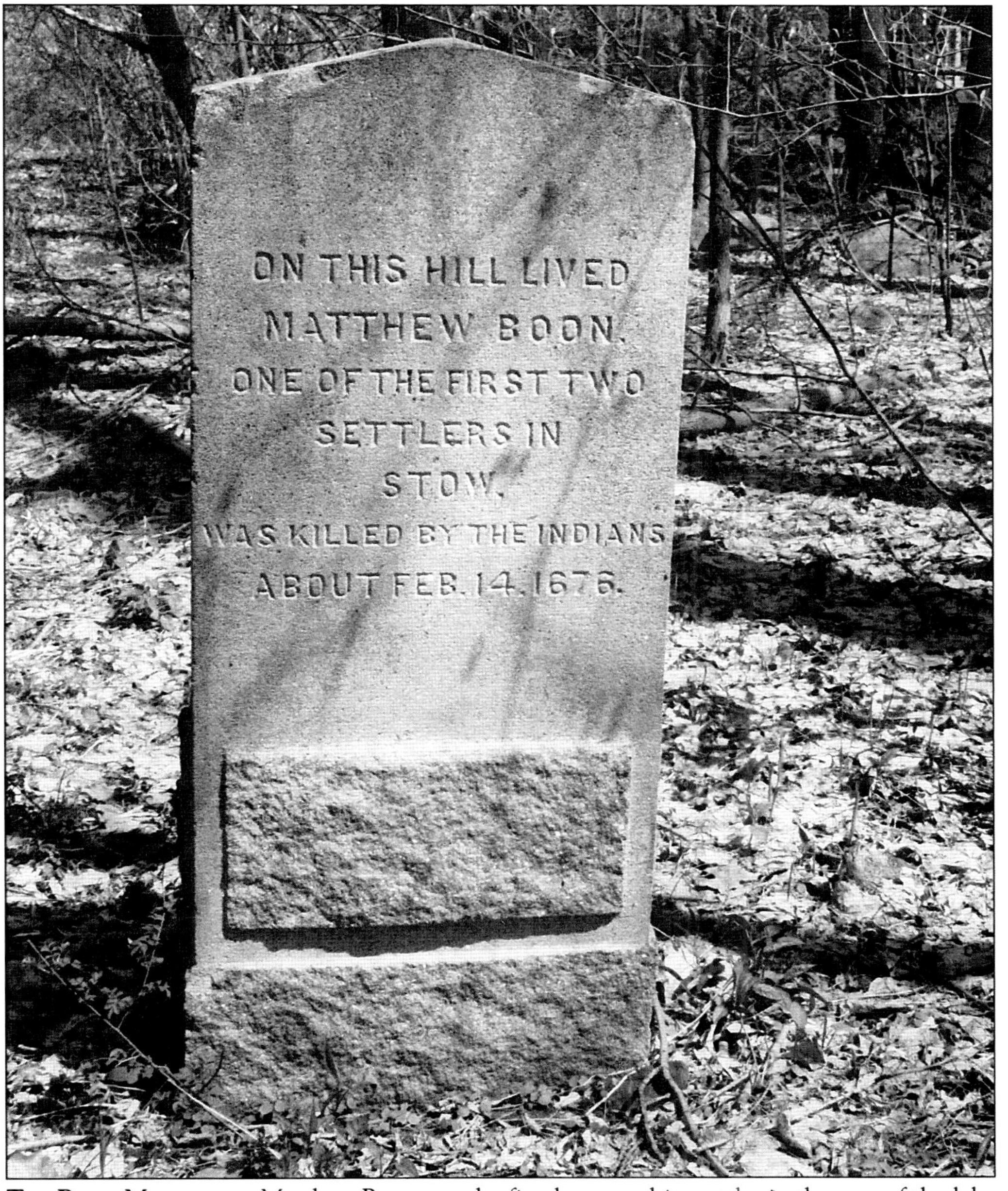

THE BOON MONUMENT. Matthew Boon was the first known white settler in the area of the lake in the mid-1600s. He built a cabin for himself and his family on what is now Boon Hill just north of the lake. He was killed by Native-American warriors during King Philip's War. This monument was erected at the site of his cabin in 1883 and reads:

"On this hill lived
Matthew Boon
one of the first two
settlers in Stow.
Was killed by the Indians
about Feb. 14, 1676." (Halprin.)

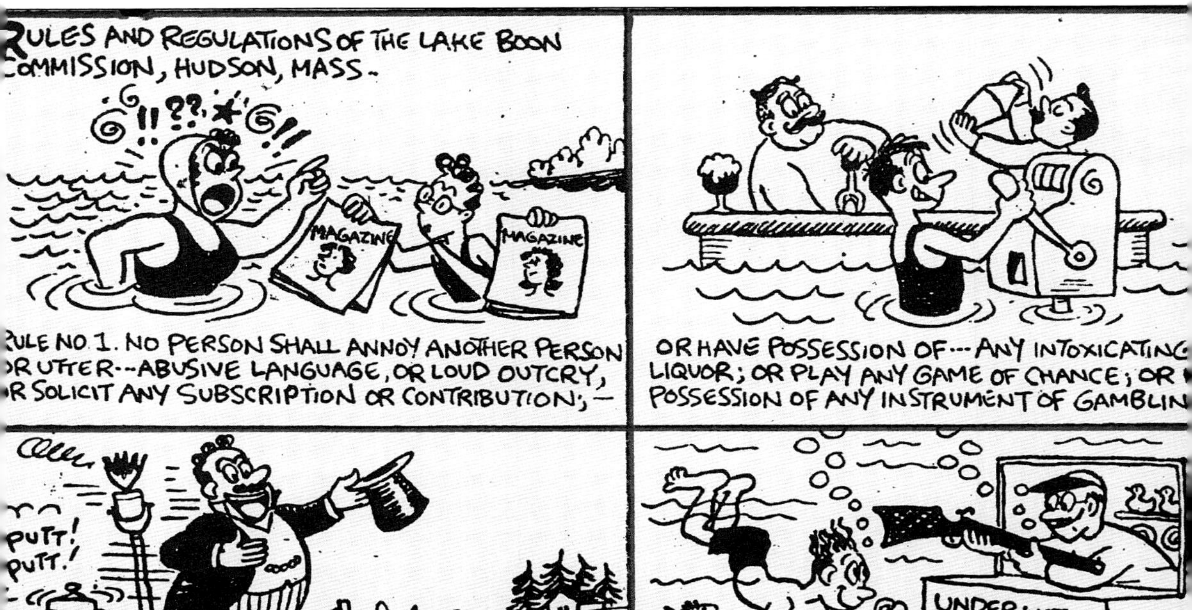

The Rules of the Lake. As the recreational use of the lake grew, the Commonwealth recognized the need for rules governing lake usage. By a 1941 act of the Great and General Court, they established the Lake Boon Commission, empowered to enforce certain rules and regulations, two of which were lampooned in this 1942 cartoon in a Boston paper. (Kattelle.)

Additional rules often were imposed on groups of cabins by the owner of the land on which they were built. For instance, the cabins on Pine Point Road (these are all now year-round houses) still have the following rules attached to their property deeds:

1. No garbage, swill, tin ware, broken crockery, ashes, etc., shall be placed upon or buried on this land.
2. No odor shall be allowed to escape from any closet, sink or cesspool.
3. No drainage from sinks, closets or cesspools shall be allowed to enter the lake.
4. No washing of clothing shall be allowed in the lake.
5. Nothing shall be done, which shall in any way raise the rate of fire insurance on our land.
6. No fires shall be allowed on any of the lots unless permission in writing be obtained of the fire warden.
7. All noise, loud talking or singing, must cease at 10:30 p.m. except on Saturdays and then at midnight.
8. No clubs shall be allowed the use of any cottage except by written permission.

Two

The Many Shapes and Sizes of Cottages

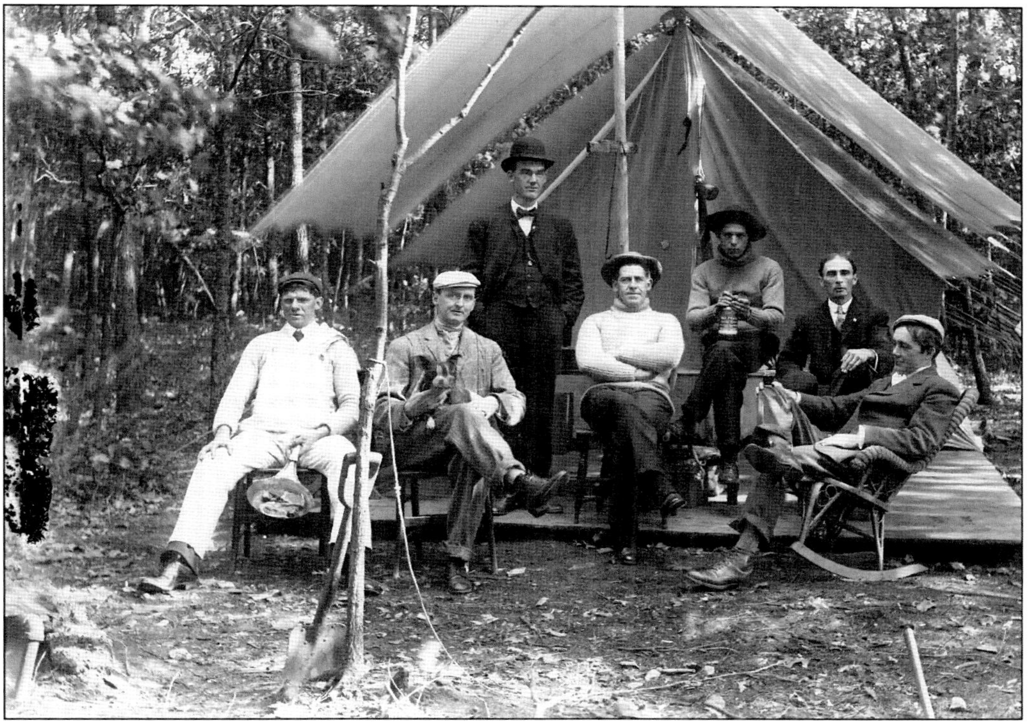

The Tent Settlers. Once Lake Boon's shoreline was settled, and rail and streetcar lines made the area accessible, people from nearby towns started to use the lake for recreational purposes. Most started out by just pitching tents. This picture shows a group of men sharing a sunny afternoon in the woods by the lake. (Berry.)

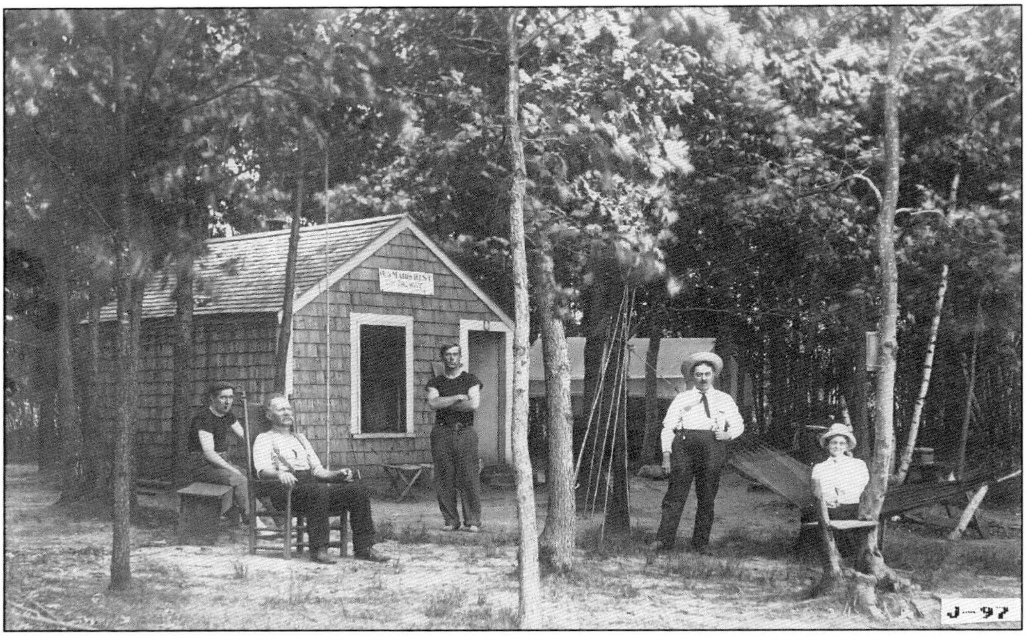

The Cabin in the Woods. After tents, the next step would be to build a little cabin that provided better protection against the elements, and, of course, invite a lot of friends over to share nature with you. This cabin, called "Old Maid's Rest," was built by Tim Ordway, probably in the early 1900s, and came with a choice of indoor or outdoor sleeping. (Jackson.)

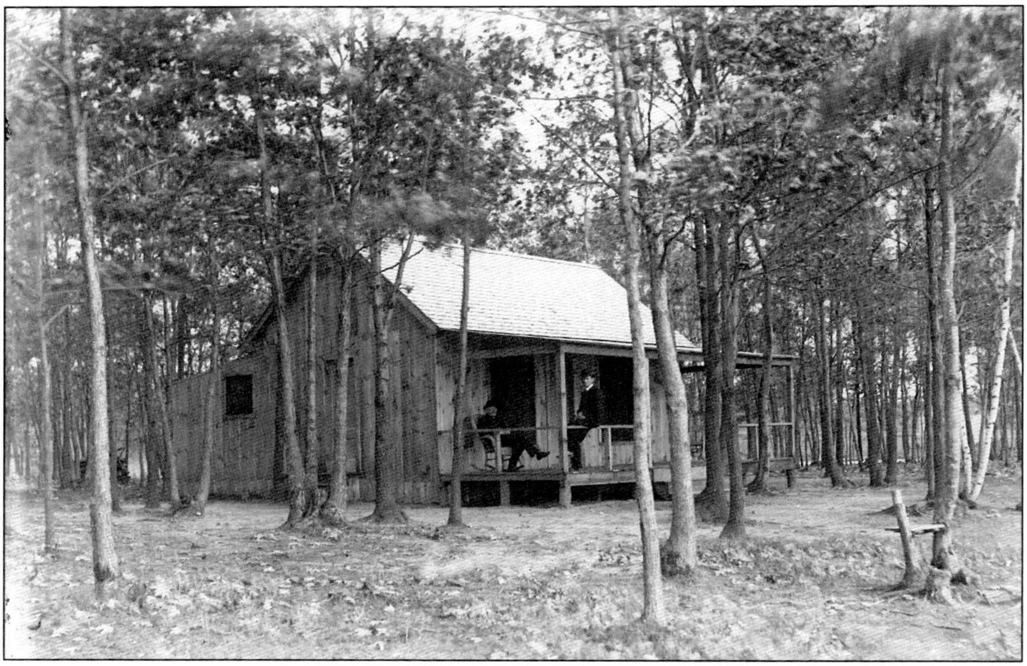

A Fancier Cabin. This one-room cabin became more elaborate with a comfortable and covered front porch, and what is probably an attached and enclosed "out-house" at the rear. There was no source of heat within the cabin, nor the outhouse! (Berry.)

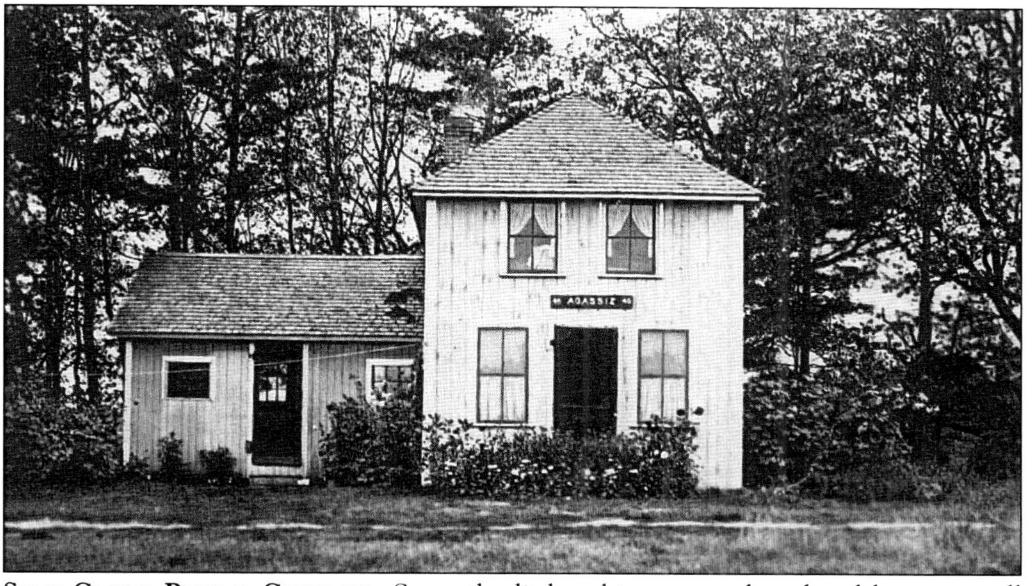

Some Cabins Become Cottages. Soon, the little cabins were enlarged and became small cottages. This cottage, called Agassiz, was particularly fancy. It contained an upstairs sleeping loft, a fireplace for heating and possibly cooking, and even a clothes dryer (an outside clothesline). (Parker.)

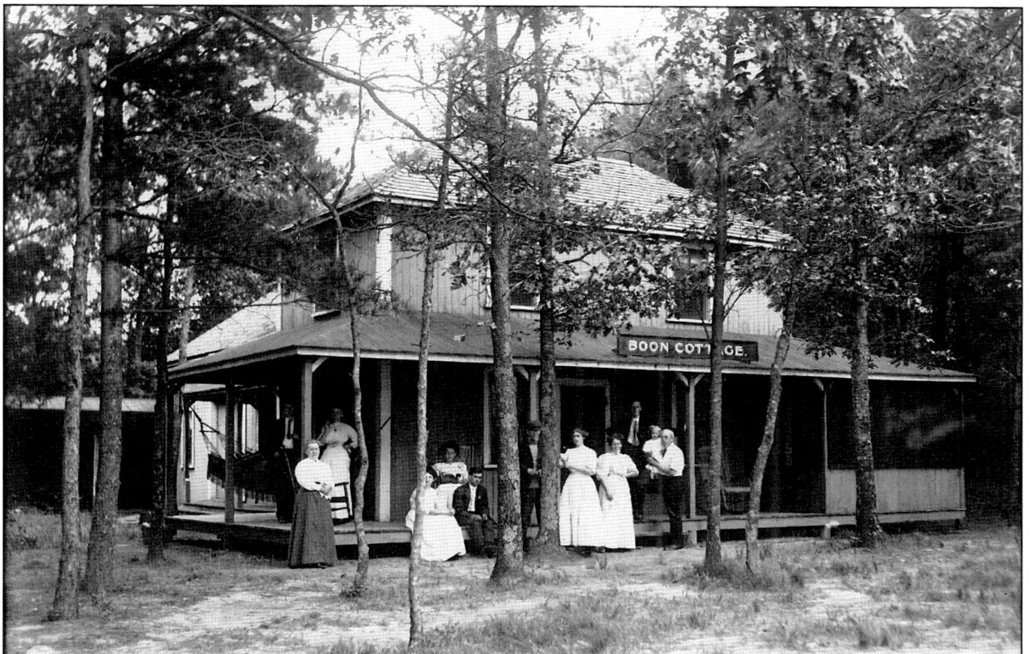

The Cottage Sprouts a Porch. After a cottage was built, the first "imprcvement" was always a porch. This one, called Boon Cottage, one of the Parker cottages on the east side of the lake, not only had a front porch, but it extended around to both sides as well. Part of the porch is enclosed with screens for enjoying pleasant bug-free evenings. (Berry.)

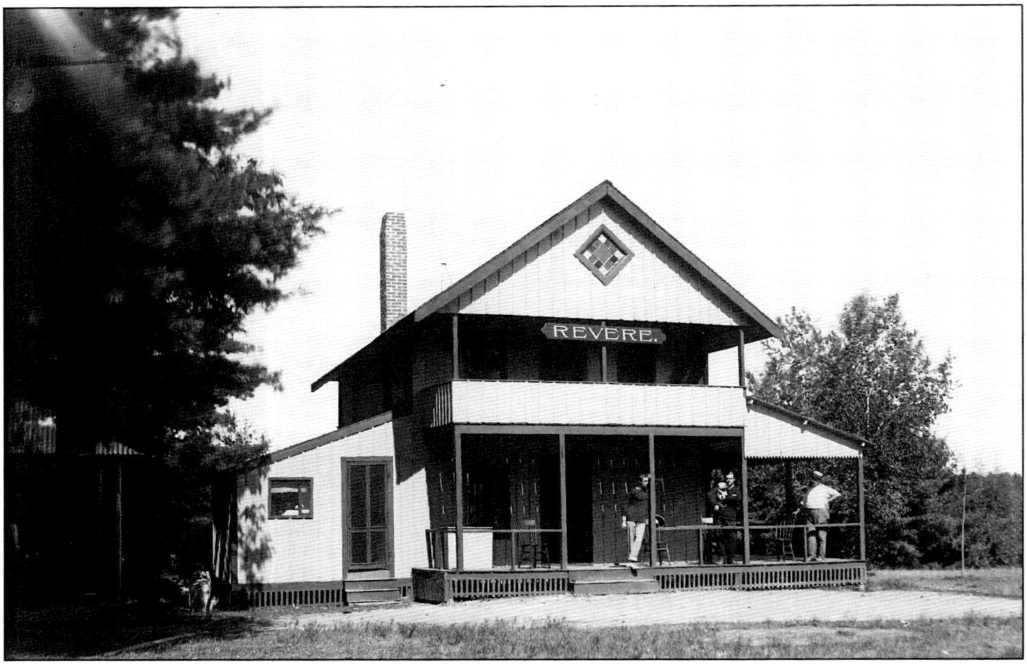

REVERE. The porch is lined with fishing poles, waiting for its occupants to engage in their favorite sport. (Berry.)

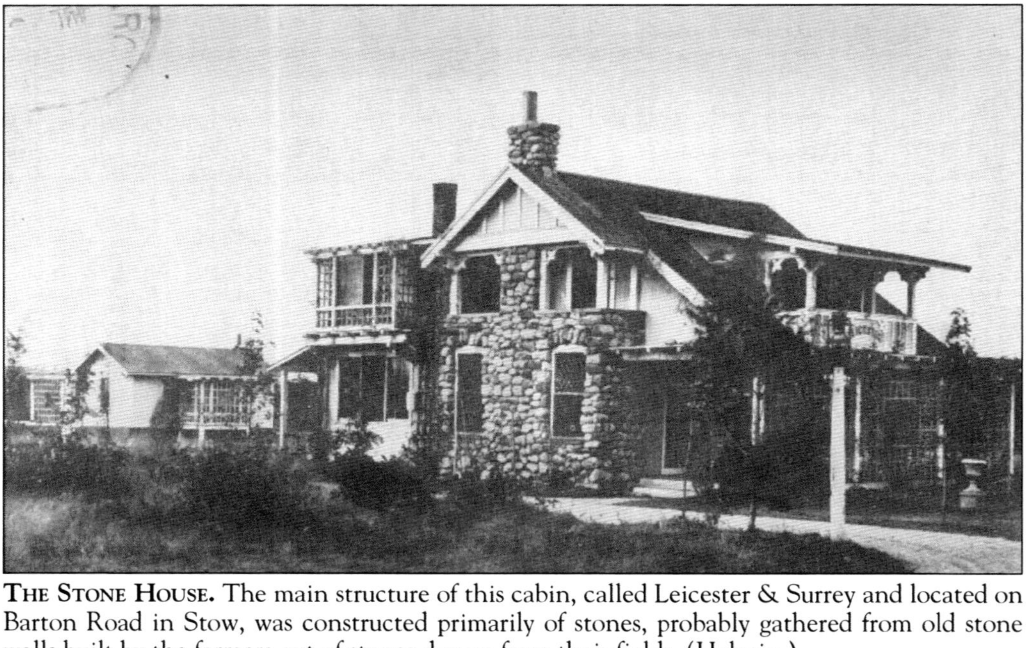

THE STONE HOUSE. The main structure of this cabin, called Leicester & Surrey and located on Barton Road in Stow, was constructed primarily of stones, probably gathered from old stone walls built by the farmers out of stones dug up from their fields. (Halprin.)

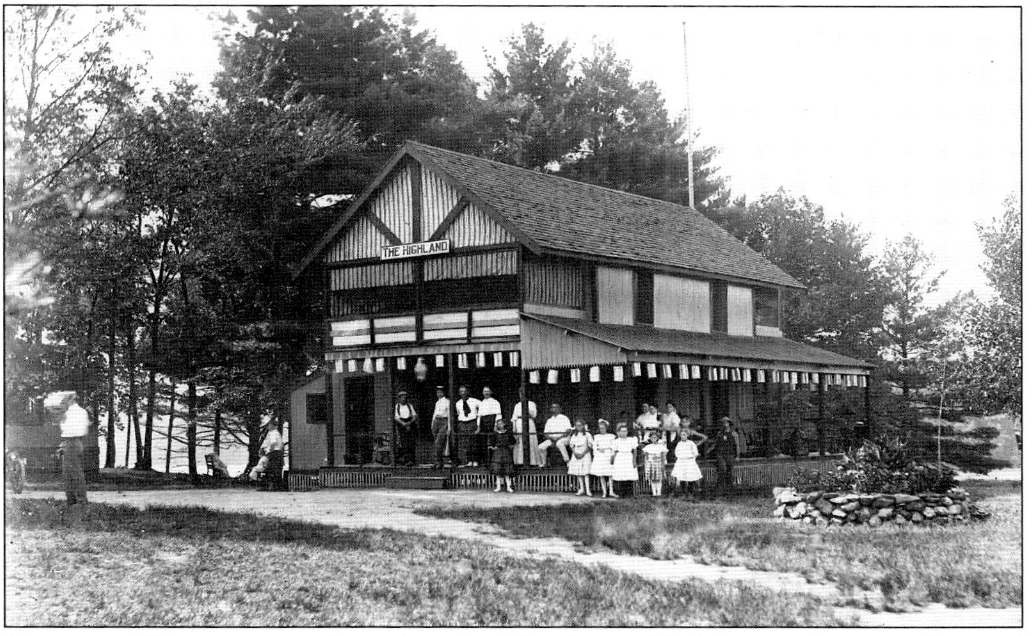

HIGHLAND. This cottage was located south of the dam and had Japanese lanterns all around the bottom porch, as well as a large front porch on the second floor with barber-stripe shades. (Berry.)

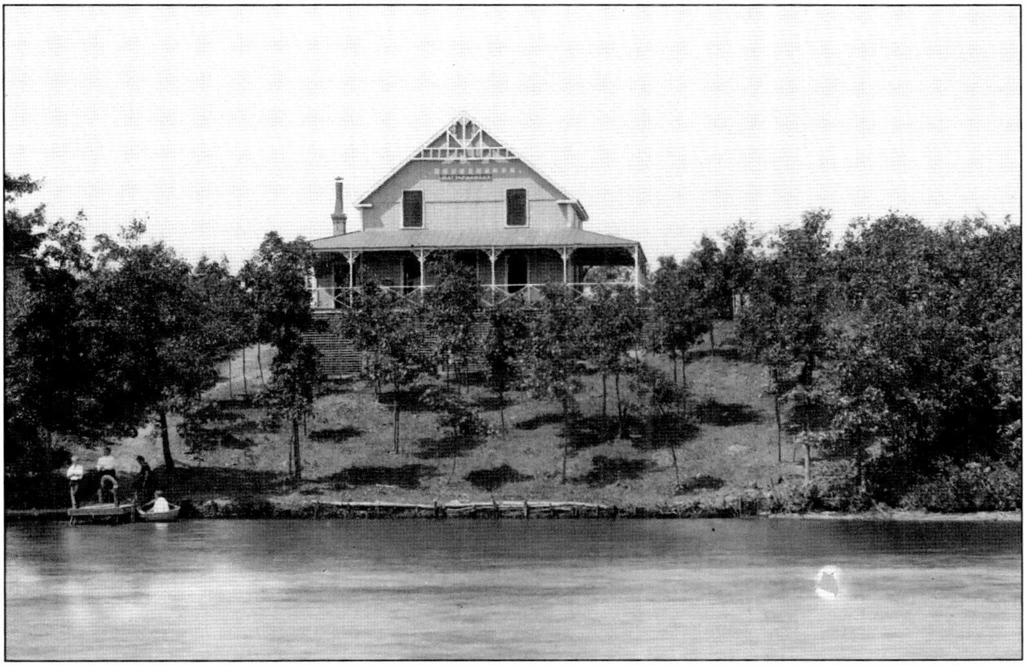

MATTAPANNOCK. Perched high on a slope near the lake, this cottage with a large porch provided sweeping views of the lake as well as comforting breezes during hot afternoons. Its design featured elaborate scroll work at the gable end of the main roof as well as on each porch roof support. (Berry.)

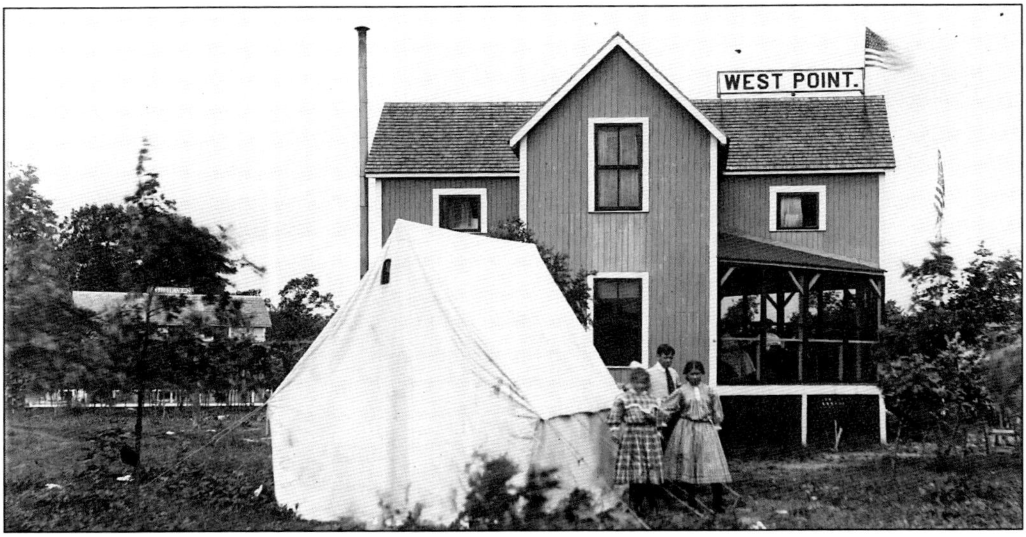

West Point. The tent in the foreground probably provides the children with their own "cabin" during the summer. It is located on Barton Road near the dam. (Berry.)

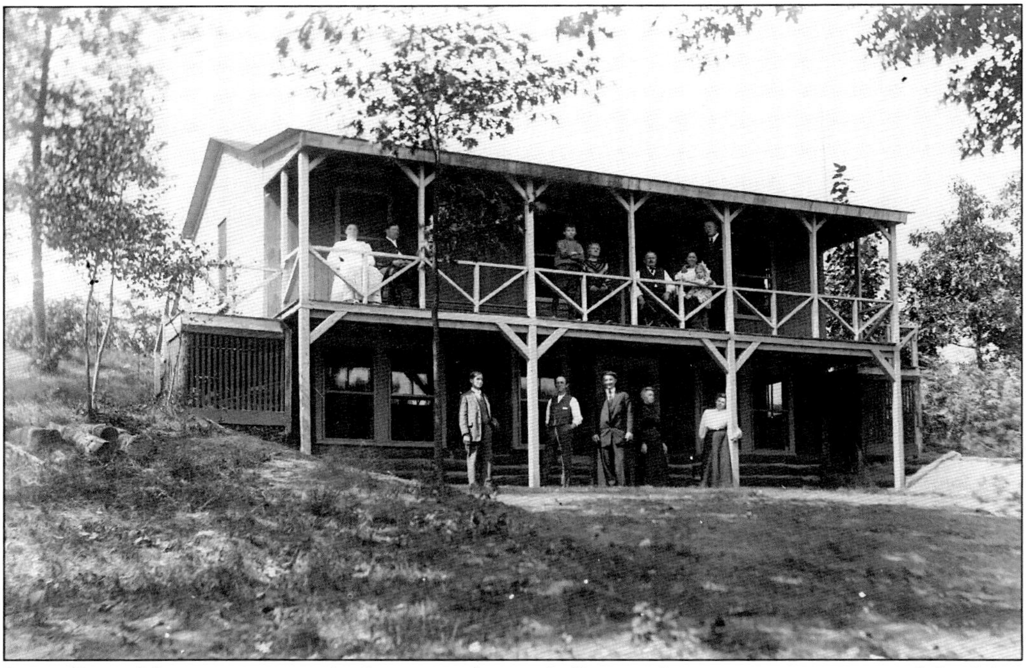

Lone Pine. This cottage was built into a sloping hill providing a two-story view of the lake, shown here being enjoyed by an extended family. (Berry.)

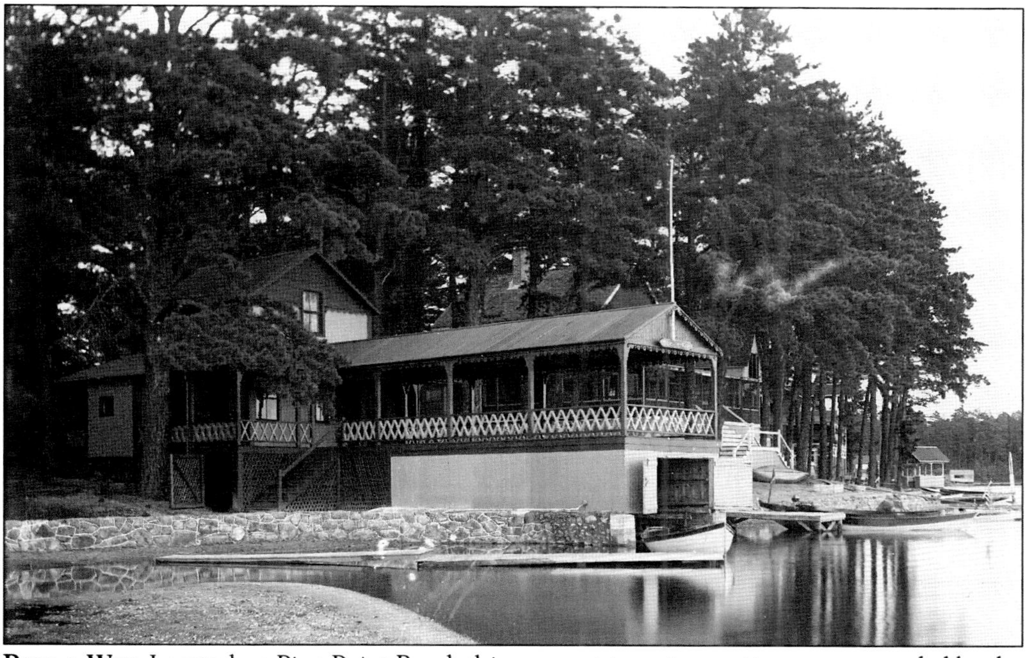

Bide-a-Wee. Located on Pine Point Road, this compact two-story cottage was expanded by the addition of a very large and handsome-looking porch that extended out over the lake. Sitting on this porch was like sitting on a wide covered dock. Boats could be floated directly into the protection of the boathouse that was built under the porch. (Berry.)

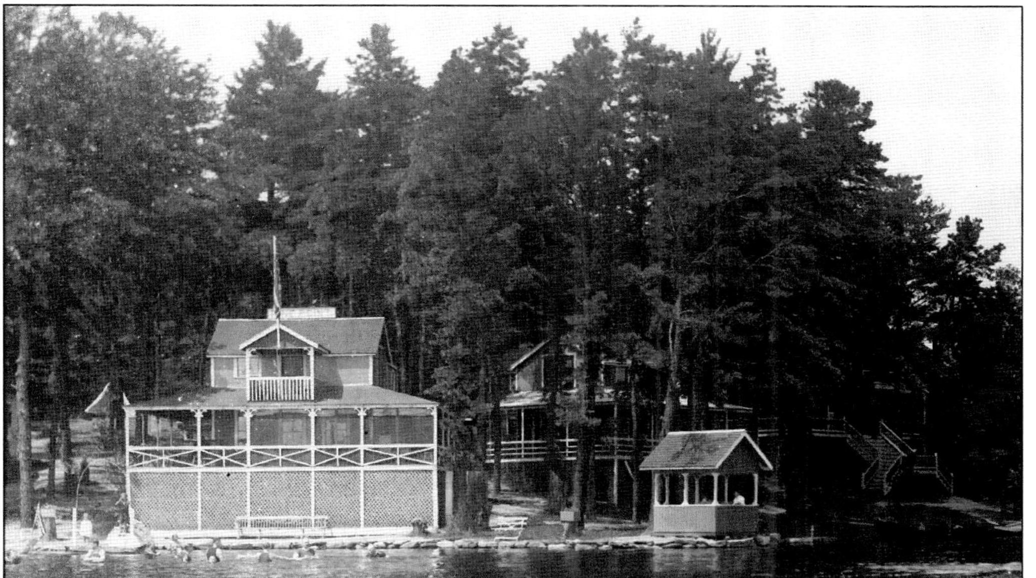

Pine Point. This was one of the first full-size cottages on the lake and was built by Capt. T.E. Jackson in 1888. It is located on Pine Point Road at a point where the road makes a very sharp bend. The little gazebo structure showing at the edge of the lake is right at the point of this bend and provides a great panoramic 270-degree lake view. (Berry.)

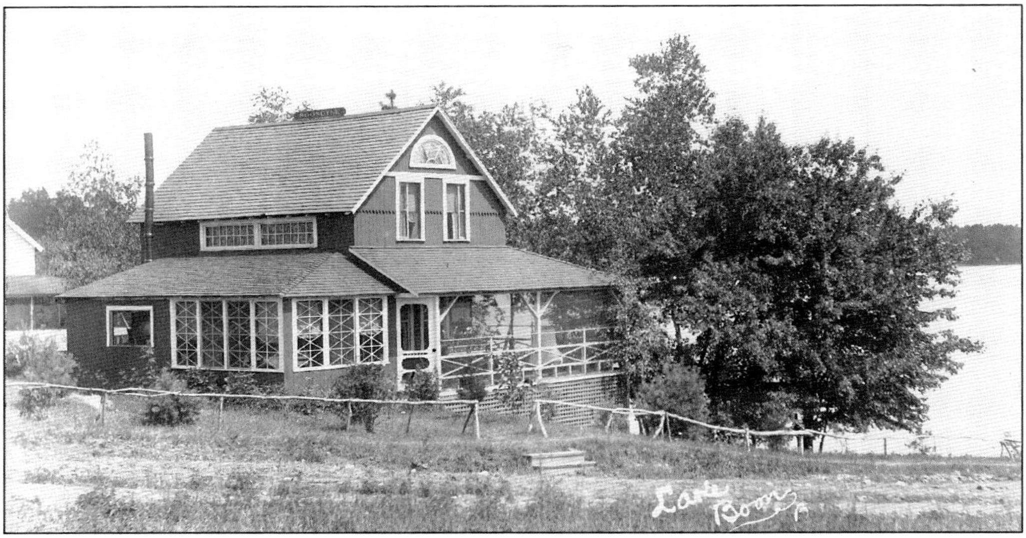

Moondyne (Growing). Located at the corner of Pine Point and Barton Roads, the original Moondyne (shown on the top of p. 12) started out as a simple two-room cabin on the northwest corner of the lake, near the dam. By the time this photograph was taken, a second story was added probably containing sleeping lofts, then several porches were added, and one of them was closed in. A split-rail fence surrounds what is now a cottage. (Phalan.)

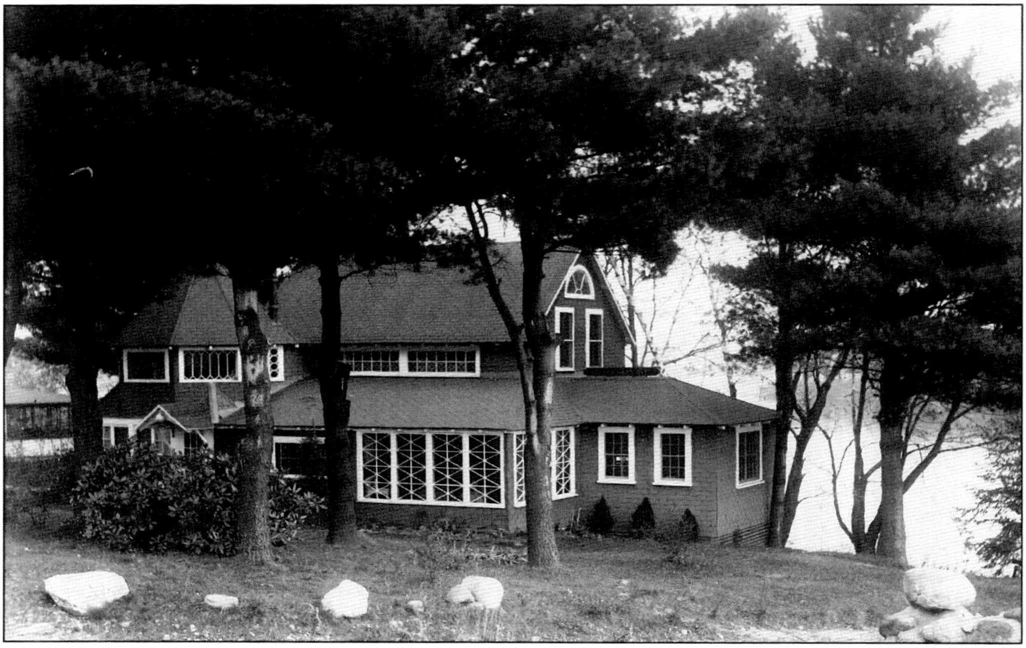

Moondyne (Current). But that was not the end of the remodeling. The west side porch was closed in and enlarged to make another bedroom, a new entryway was added facing the street, and an interesting cupola was built above the entryway that provided a sweeping view of the lake and the neighboring pine woods. This elegant cottage still commands its place as the western kingpin of the row of Pine Point cottages (along with Hanson's Beach on the western end and Pine Point in the middle). (Berry.)

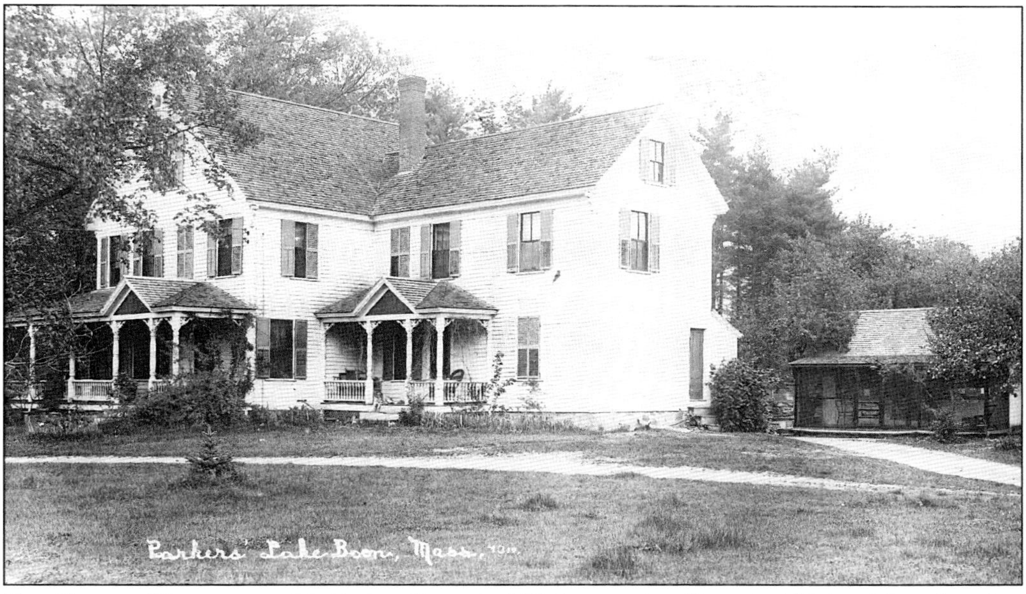

The Parker Homestead. J.J. Parker (born in 1834) moved to Stow in 1864 and bought what became known as the Parker farm, located on Sudbury Road on the east side of the lake (before the lake was expanded to its current dimensions). His farmhouse burned to the ground in 1894 and was replaced by this house (labor and materials totaled $1,500). He lived in this house as did several additional generations of the Parker family for over 100 years. (Phalan.)

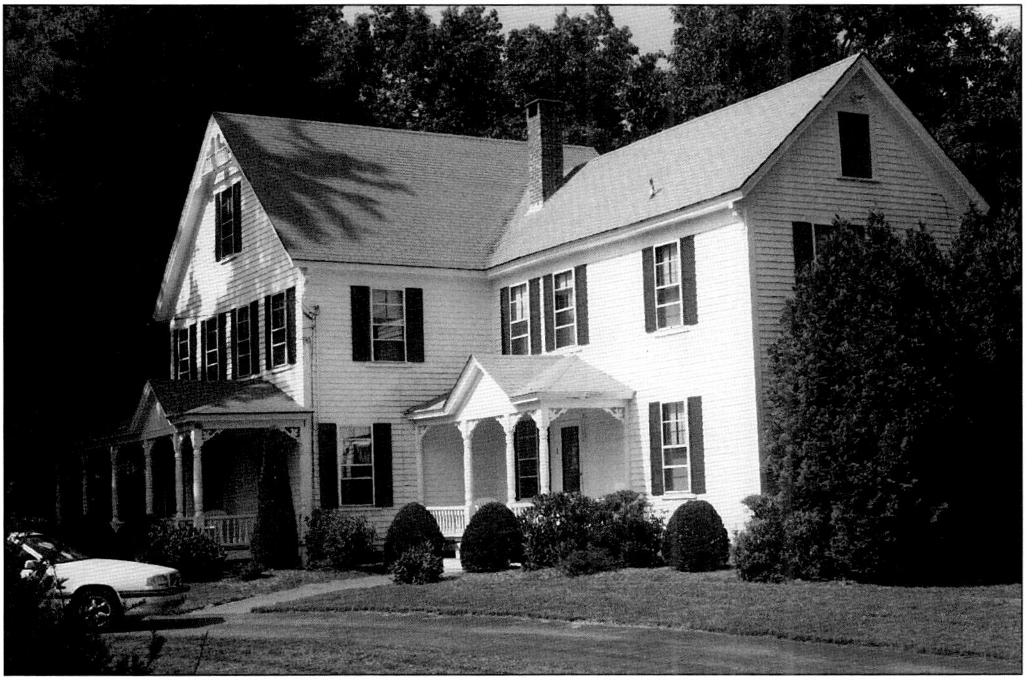

Under New Ownership. The old Parker homestead is no longer owned by the Parker family. Its last Parker resident, Emma Parker, was born in this house and died on her 97th birthday. It is well maintained by its new owner and still retains its charm.

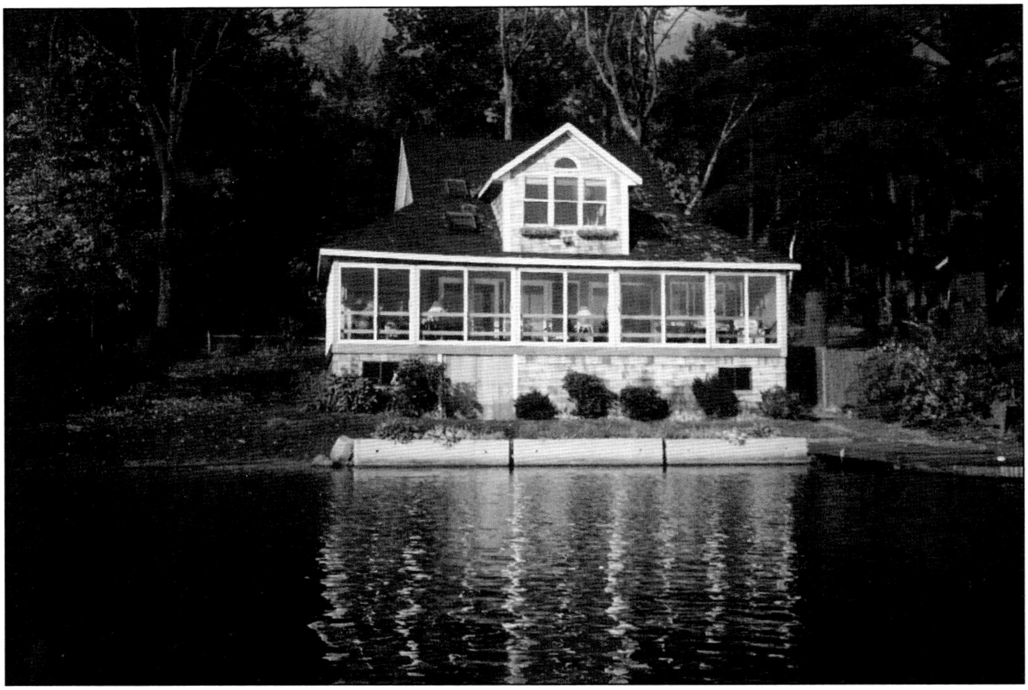

Deborah. This beautiful cottage built next to a shimmering Lake Boon now features a totally enclosed wrap-around porch, which in earlier photographs was an open porch. (Halprin.)

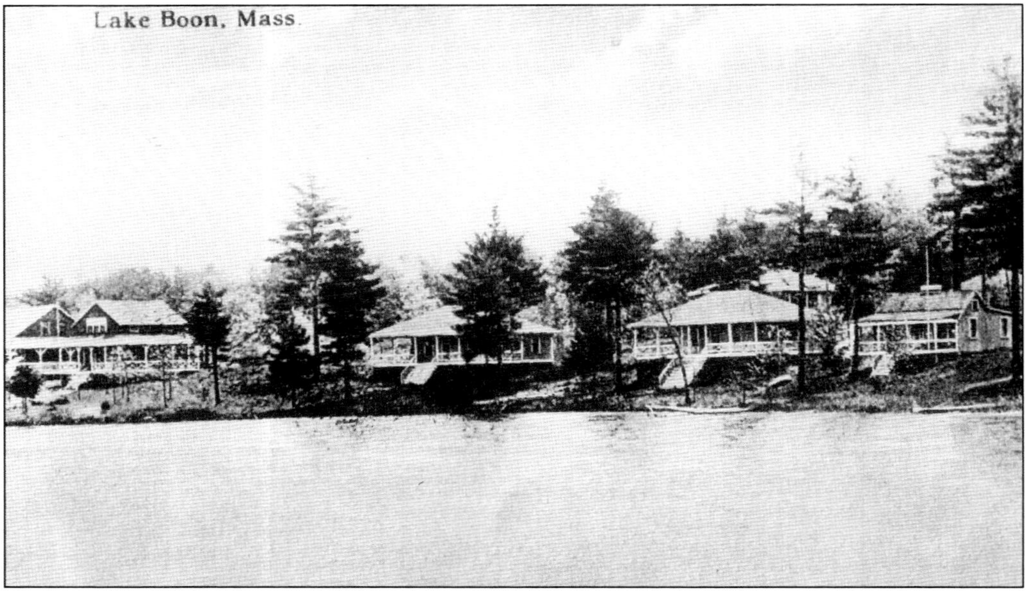

A Cottage Collage. In some areas around the lake, especially where the bank had a shallow slope, cottage development was very dense. Many of the cottages were built on 1/5-acre lots. These cottages are in the second basin of the lake near Boon Cove. (Phalan.)

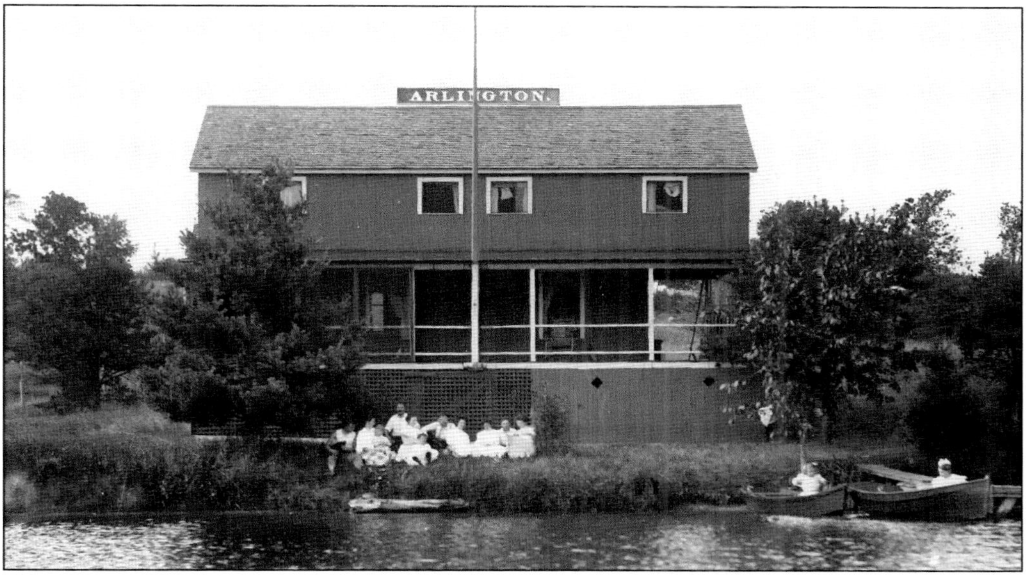

Arlington. A family enjoys the lake on a sunny day in front of Arlington cottage on the north side of the lake (now 84 Pine Point Road). The date is about 1910. (Berry.)

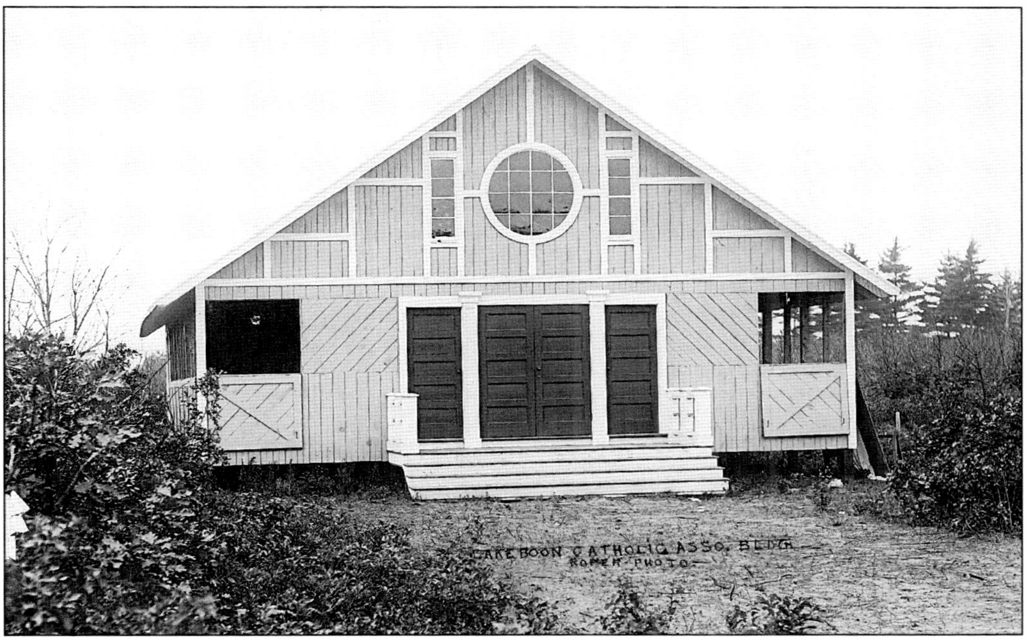

Association Hall. This building, located off Barton Road, was built around 1909 by a group of St. Bridget's parishioners (from nearby Maynard) for conducting Catholic services at the lake on Sundays. Services were provided during the summers until about 1961, when St. Isidore's Parish in Stow was built. To make room for larger crowds, the side porches were later closed up and the hall was made wider on each side. The building no longer exists. (Phalan.)

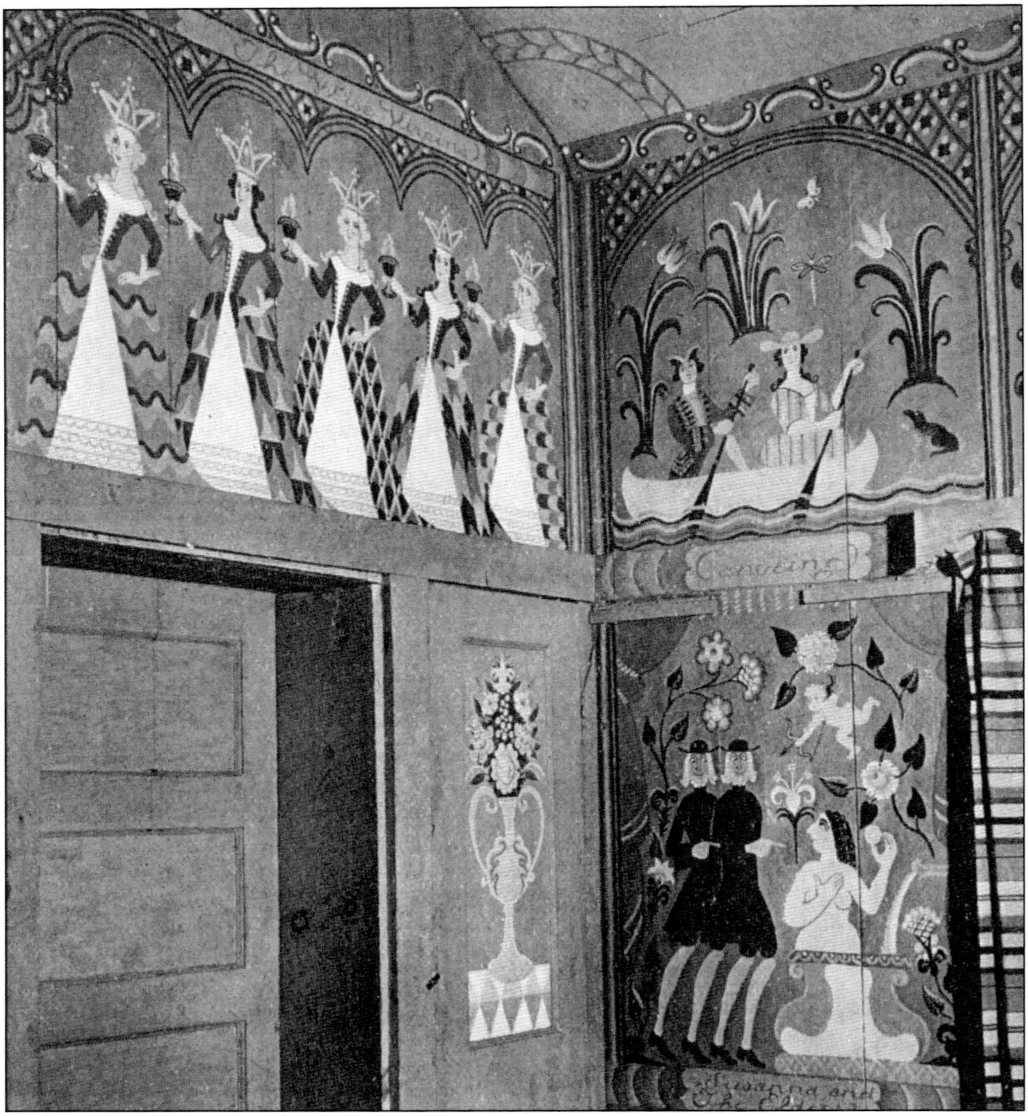

Chamberlain House, Living Room. Down at the southern end of the lake stands a modest-looking house, originally built for Mr. and Mrs. Henry Chamberlain, now occupied by their nephew and his wife, Alan and Natalie Kattelle. When the house was nearing completion, an artist and stage designer friend, Claggett Wilson, asked if he could decorate the living room. The delightful result, in a style known as "Swedish Primitive," is shown above. The artist's principal theme was the joys of country living, tempered with scenes from the Old Testament. Shown here are "Susannah and the Elders" (below) and "The Wise Virgins" with their lamps filled and burning (over the door). "The Foolish Virgins," with glum expressions and extinguished lamps, are on the other side of the fireplace (not shown). (Kattelle.)

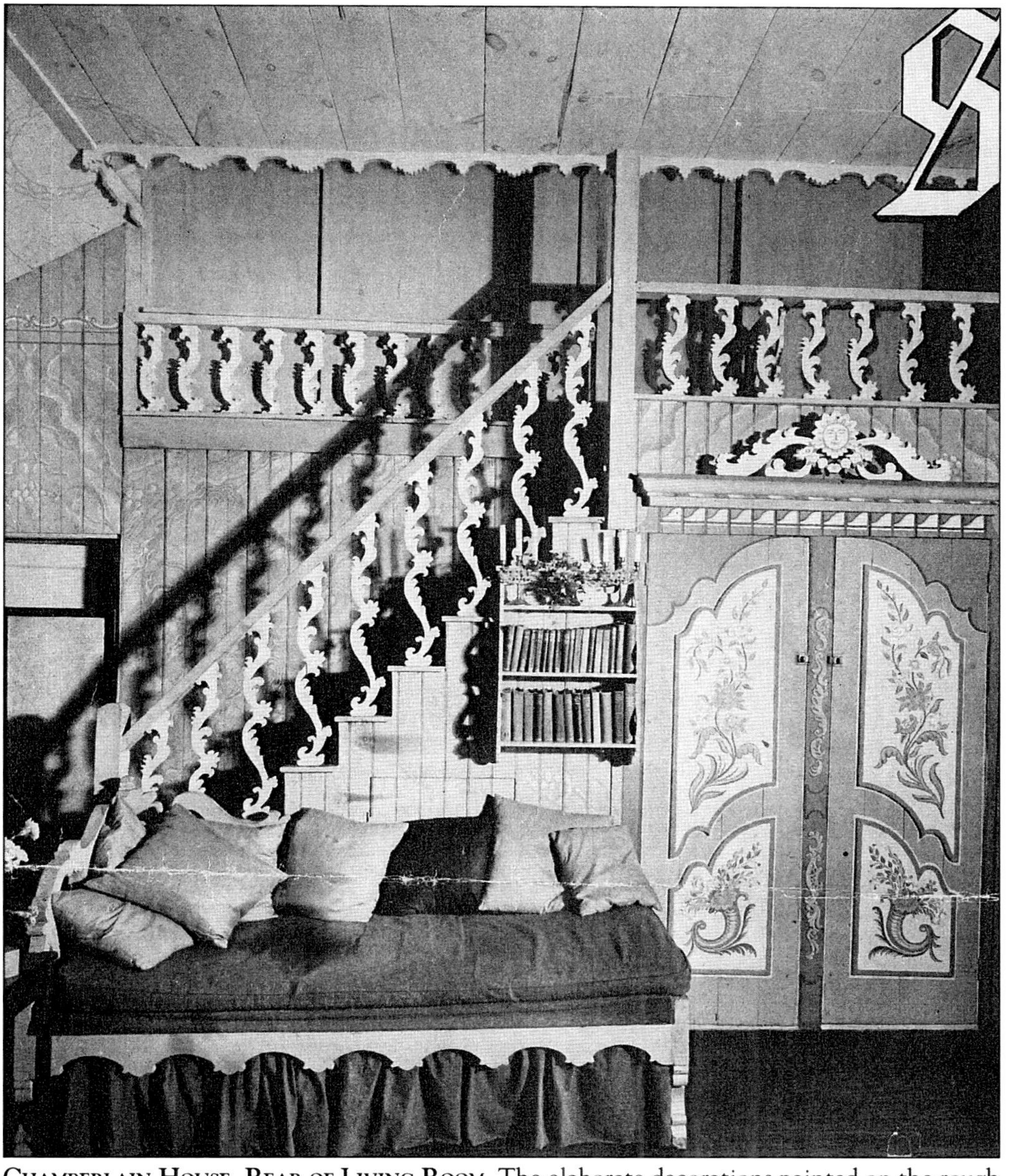

Chamberlain House, Rear of Living Room. The elaborate decorations painted on the rough wood paneling in the living room extend to the back of the room as well. The jigsaw balusters that grace this staircase to a tiny guest bedroom was done by a local farmer, Alfred Ordway, who did carpentry and delivered ice when not tending to his farm. (Kattelle.)

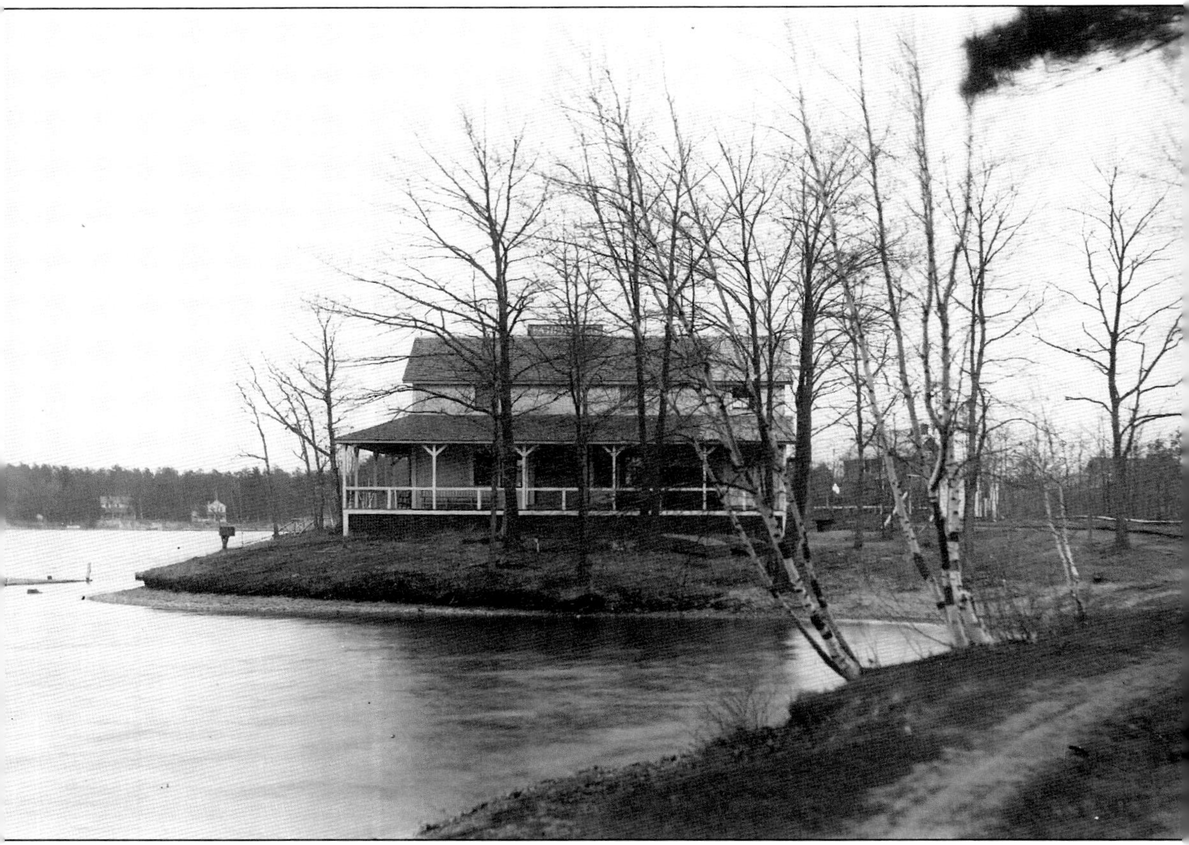

FAIRHAVEN. The cottage Fairhaven was originally a hunting and fishing camp on the Assabet River near Bailey's Brook (the little stream that connects Lake Boon and the Assabet River). At that time, the cottage was called "Fur, Feather & Fin." During the winter in the early 1890s, the cottage was cut into three parts, dragged on the ice of the Assabet River up to the Sudbury Road bridge, then hauled by mules to the Hanson Beach area. It was then dragged over the Lake Boon ice to its current location and reassembled. The dirt road on the right is Barton Road. The picture was taken from the lake's dam. (Berry.)

Three

How People Came and Went

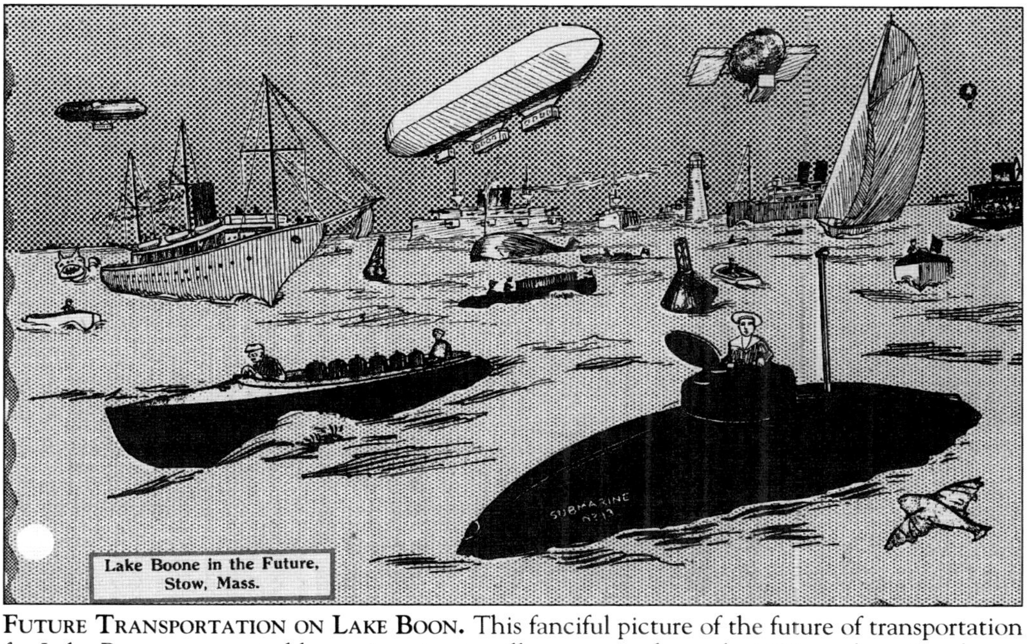

Future Transportation on Lake Boon. This fanciful picture of the future of transportation for Lake Boon was created by an imaginative illustrator in the early 1920s and reprinted on a 1979 Metropolitan Area Planning Council's report on Lake Boon's water quality.

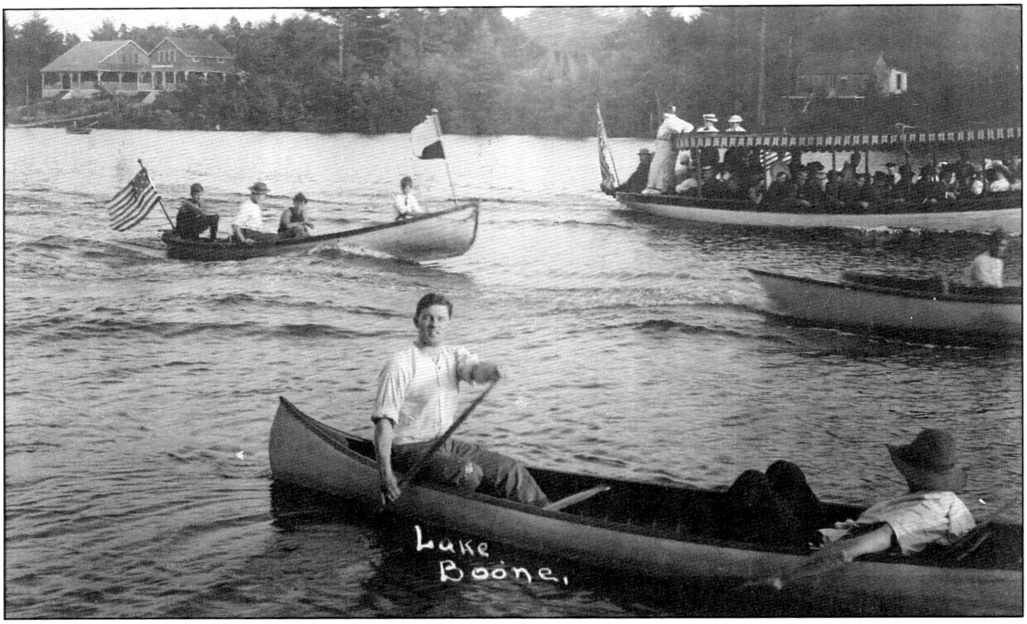

PICK YOUR MEANS OF TRANSPORTATION. Because the roads around the lake were chiefly dirt roads designed for horse and buggy, and because most lake visitors did not come with their cars, transportation around the lake was mostly by walking or by boat. This picture shows the very popular canoe, several private motor launches, and the *Princess* public transportation boat making its rounds. (Phalan.)

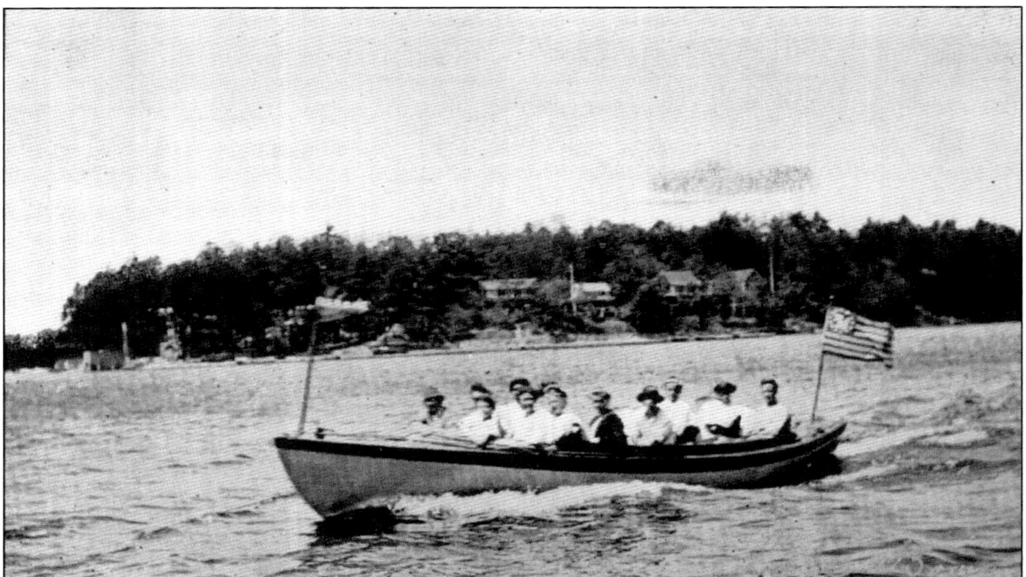

GETTING A QUICK VIEW OF THE LAKE. This 12-person gasoline-powered motor launch speeds its occupants around a slightly choppy lake for an exciting tour of shoreline. (Halprin.)

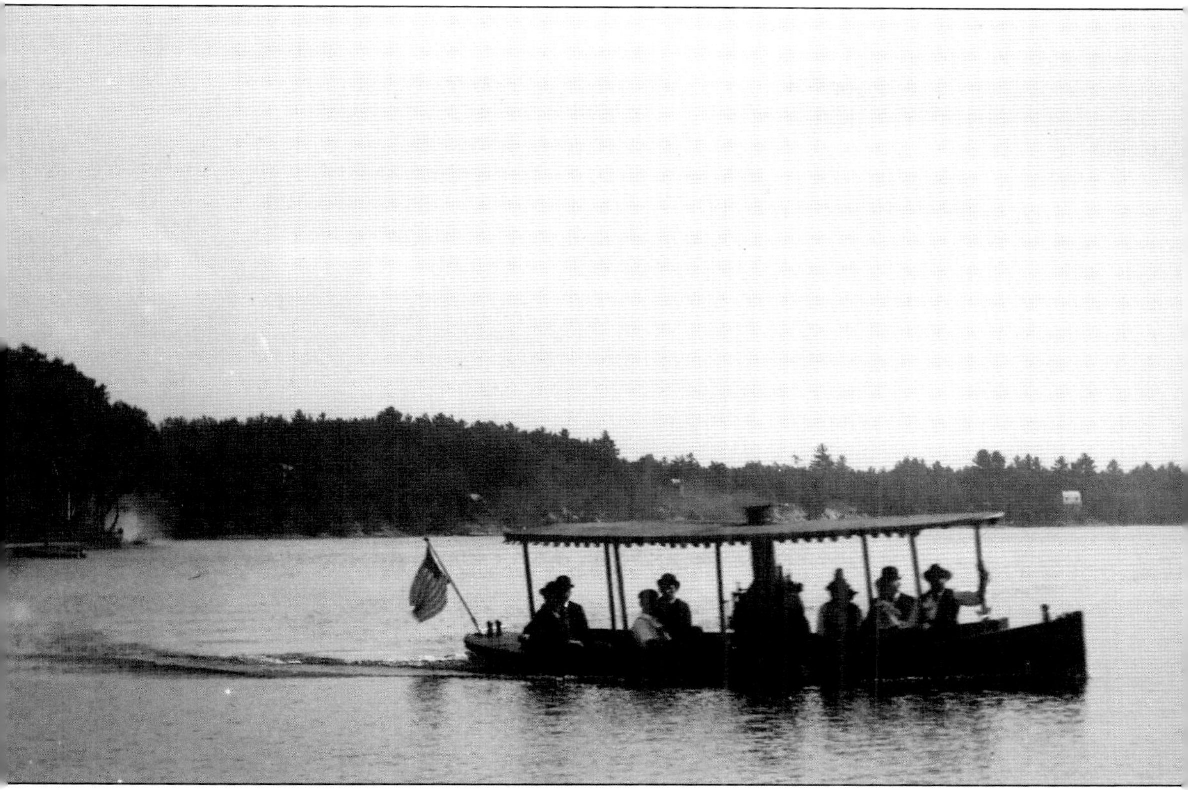

The *Cleo*—the Lake's Only True Steamboat. The first boat to provide transportation on Lake Boon was the *Cleo*. The boat was owned by a Mr. Canning, who owned several acres of land on the lake called Indian Point.

On Indian Point, he provided picnic grounds with tables, benches, and swings, and sold light "tonics" such as ginger ale, root beer, and sarsaparilla. Picnickers would come from Boston by train on the Boston and Maine's Marlborough Branch to a flag station called Whitman Crossing. Then they would take a five-minute walk to the lake from the station, then a 1-mile steamboat ride on the *Cleo* to the picnic grounds. During the day, there would be a ride offered around both basins of the lake for 10¢ a head.

The *Cleo* was 25 feet long with a canopy top and seated 25. It was powered by steam and was very dependable, smooth running, and quiet. But it was also hot, smoky, and very slow. It was replaced in about 1900 by the *Princess*, a gasoline-powered boat. (Berry.)

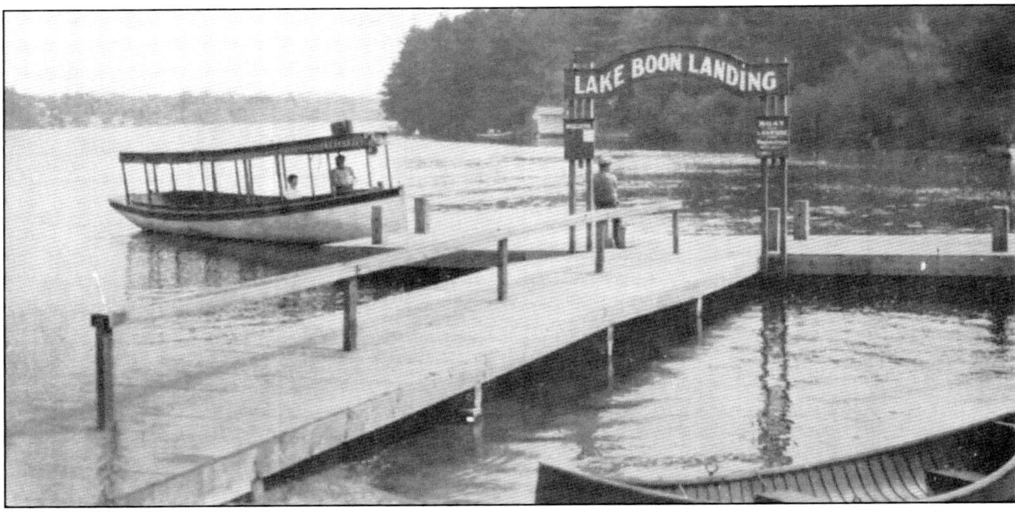

THE *PRINCESS* AT ITS MAIN DOCK. This dock, near Hanson's Beach on Sudbury Road at Pine Point Road, was the connection to either the motor boat landing on the Assabet River that took passengers to Maynard, or the Boston and Maine Marlborough Branch Rail Road station, both a five-minute walk away. (Halprin.)

LAKE BOON — TIME TABLE — BOAT "PRINCESS"

WEEK DAYS A. M.

Lake Boon Ldg. Lv.	†*7.15	*8.20	*8.55	*9.30	10.00	*10.45	†11.50		
Cove Landing	†*7.30				*10.10		†*12.00		
Lakeside	*7.32				*10.12		*12.02		
Lake Boon Ldg. Ar.	*7.50	8.50	9.25	†10.00	*10.30	11.15	*12.25		

P. M.

Lake Boon Ldg. Lv.	*12.45	*1.45	2.15	2 50	†*3.40	*4.45	†5.30	*6.20	*7.00
Cove Landing	†*1.00			*3.00	†*3.55		†*5.50		
Lakeside	*1.02			*3.02	*3.57		*5.52		
Lake Boon Ldg. Ar.	†*1.20	2.15	2.45	*3.20	†*4.20	5.15	†*6.05	6.50	7.30

SUNDAYS A. M. — P. M.

							P. M.		
Lake Boon Ldg. Lv.	†*8.15	9.30	*10 40	11.40			†*12.25	1.45	2.25
Cove Landing		9.40	10.50						†2.35
Lakeside		9.45	10.52						2.37
Lake Boon Ldg. Ar.	8.45	10.30	†11.15	*12.10			1.00	†2.15	†2.55

P. M.

Lake Boon Ldg. Lv.	2.55	*3.35	4.15	†*4.45	*5.20	5.55	*6.30		

THE *PRINCESS* SCHEDULE. By 1911, business on the *Princess* flourished. There were now about 150 cottages on the lake, and new ones were being built every year. Train service was good and many men commuted to Boston all summer. To get them to their trains and to encourage use of the boat during the day, Laurence Kattelle established a regular schedule of arrivals and departures at designated locations. This is the 1911 schedule. (Jackson.)

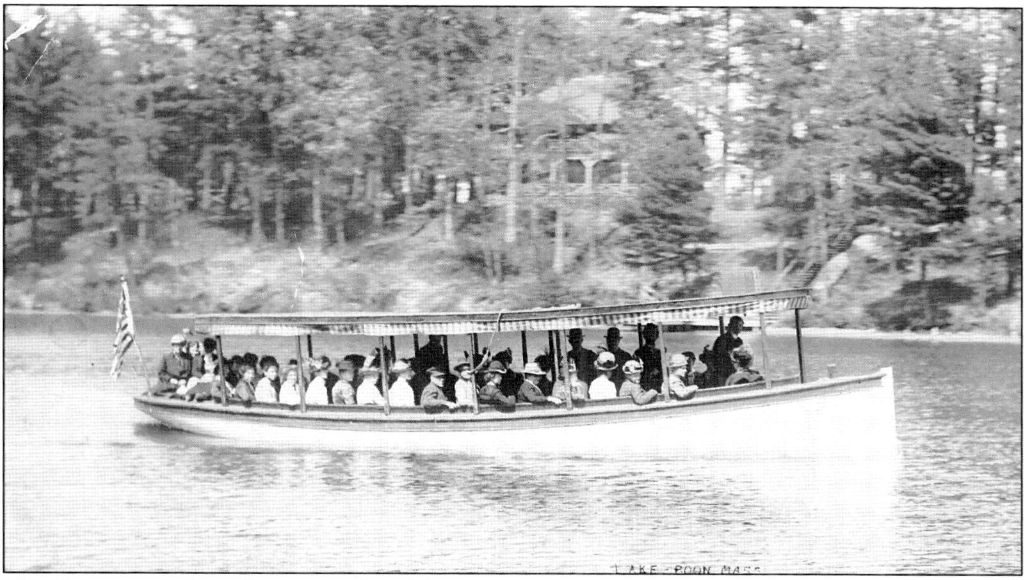

THE *PRINCESS*. The *Cleo* was replaced by the *Princess* in 1910. It was built at Riverside on the Charles River. It contained a two-cylinder, four-cycle engine, was 35 feet long, had a 10-foot beam, and seated 50 passengers. Stanchions every 5 feet supported a roof and side curtains, which were rolled up in fine weather but gave protection when it rained. The new boat was trucked up to the lake and put into service during the summer of 1900. It ceased operations in 1927. (Halprin.)

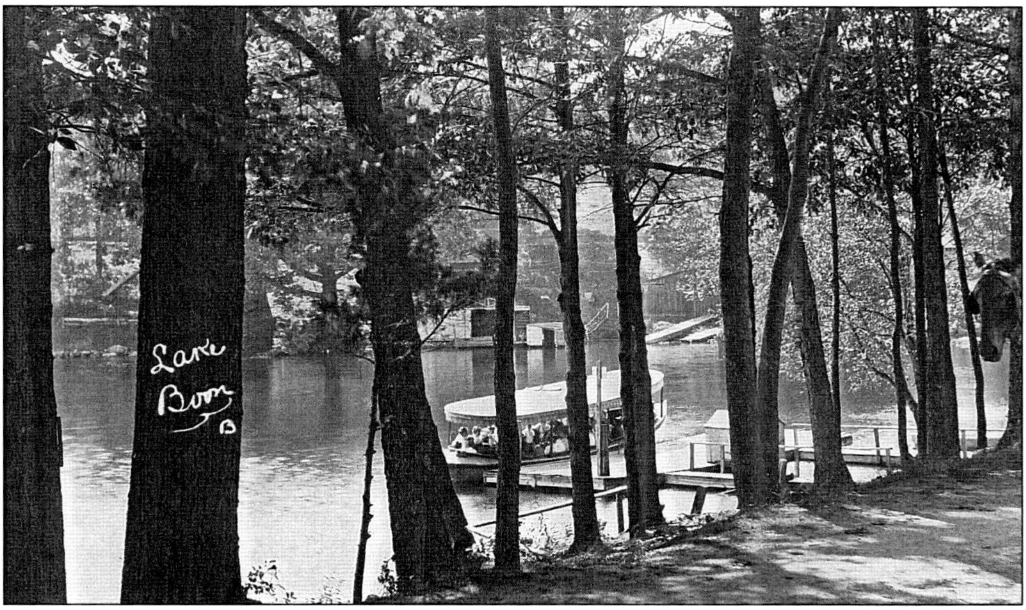

ANOTHER STOP FOR THE *PRINCESS*. A horse watches through the trees as the *Princess* makes a stop at one of its scheduled docks on the lake. (Conard.)

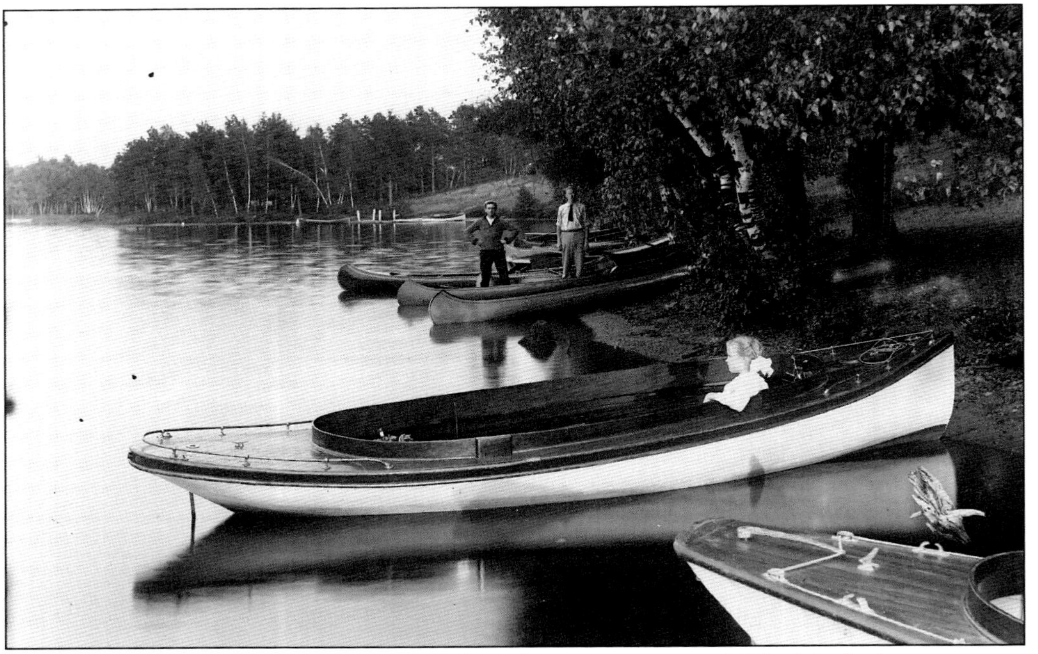

CANOES AND BOATS. The *Princess* was not the only way to get around. The lake had many canoes parked along its shoreline, as well as small rowboats and gasoline-powered motorboats. (Berry.)

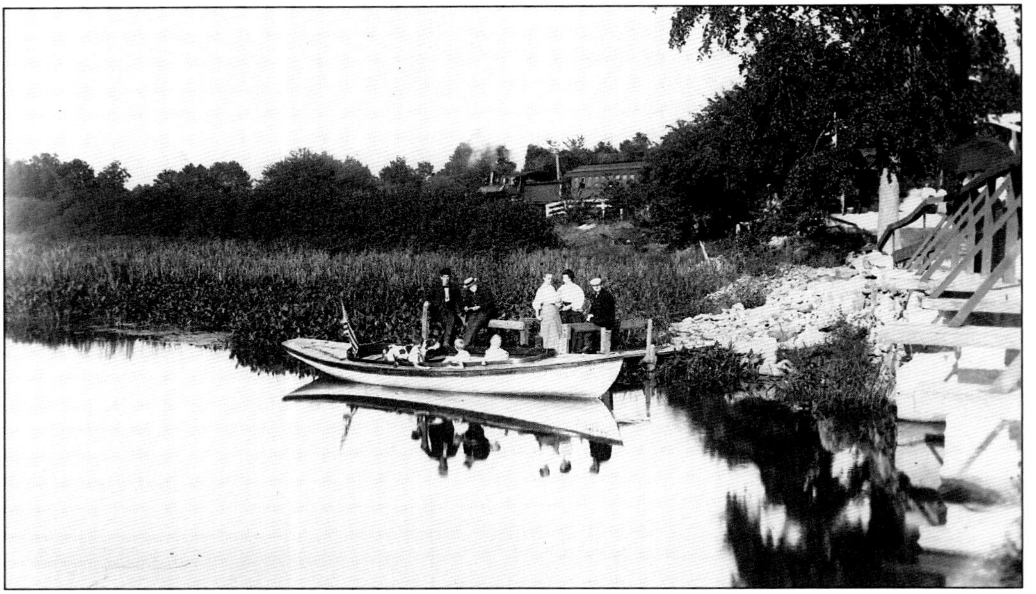

THE *QUEEN*—A RIVER LAUNCH. The *Queen* was the launch used by the boat line that ran between the Ben Smith Dam in Maynard to Whitman's Crossing near Lake Boon. It was established by Peter Wilcox and Fred Chandler of Maynard, and it was discontinued in 1914. Note the Boston and Maine Railroad train at its Whitman Crossing stop in the background. Both the launch landing and the railroad station were at the Sudbury Road river bridge, a five-minute walk from the Lake Boon boat dock. (Berry.)

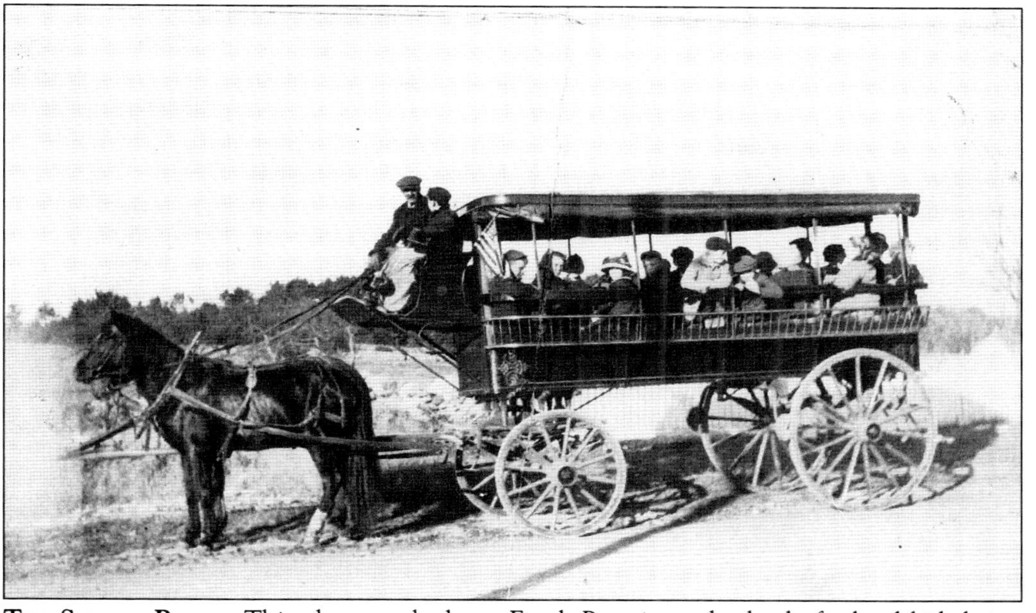

THE SCHOOL BARGE. This photograph shows Frank Prentiss and a load of school kids being picked up from around the lake and White Pond Road by his school barge to be taken to school (about 1910–1915). The barge had curtains that could be lowered in case of bad weather. Two horses were needed to draw this heavy wagon and all those children. (Stow.)

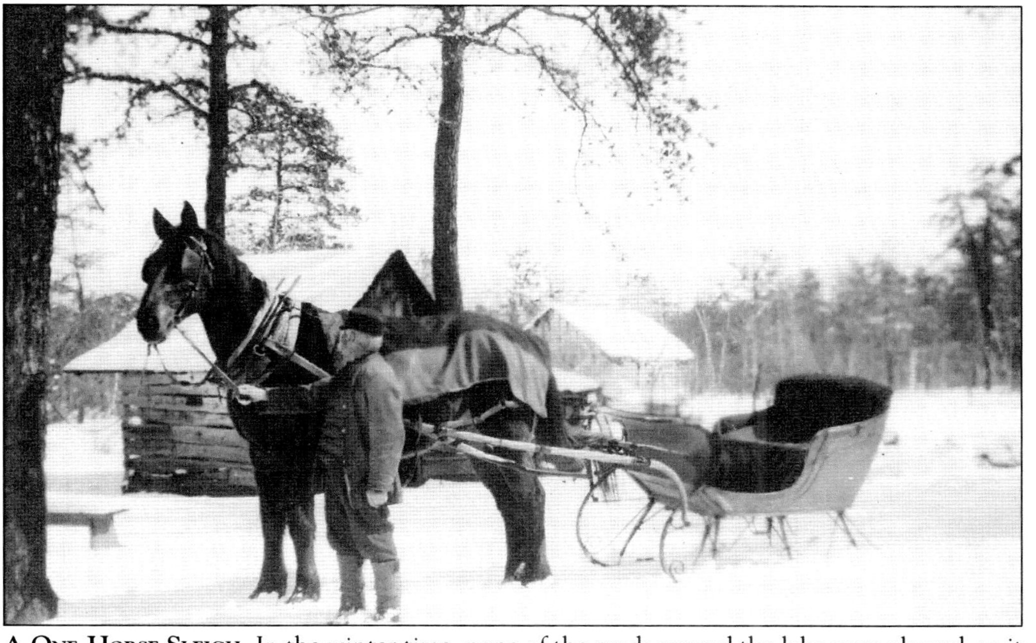

A ONE-HORSE SLEIGH. In the winter time, none of the roads around the lake were cleared, so it was necessary to have a horse and sleigh to get around when the snow was deep. Here, Mr. May tries to convince his horse that it is a good day to take a ride. When the Kettelle family bought Mr. May's farm in 1920, the horse went with the sale, but was soon disposed of because "he cost too much to feed." (The Kattelle family.)

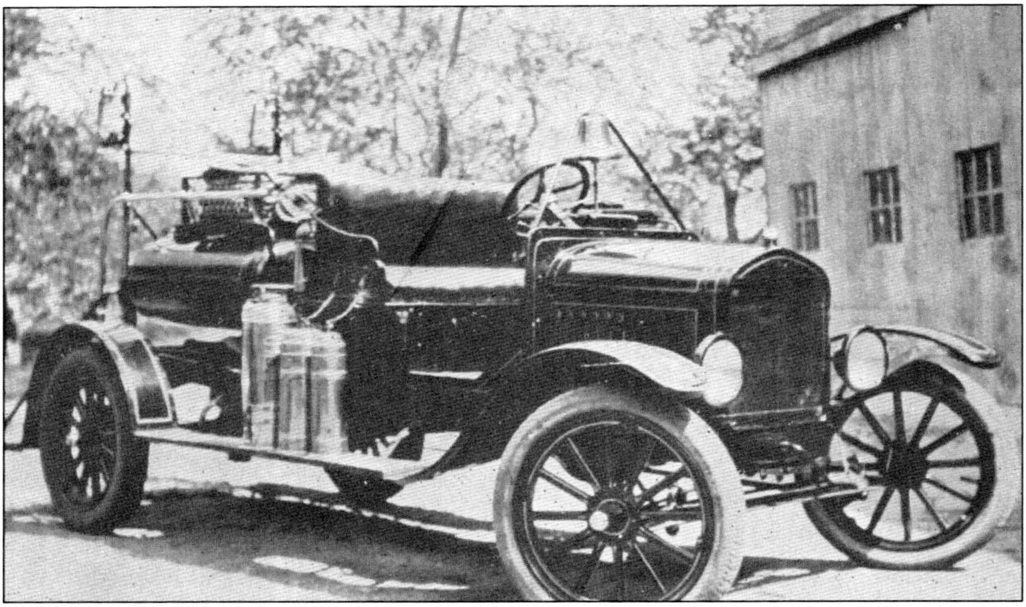

The Chemical Fire Truck. When a fire occurred at the lake, this fire truck would make its way from downtown Stow, or similar equipment from downtown Hudson, to spray the fire with water and chemicals. By the time the equipment got to fires by the lake, cabins were usually in full blaze and could not be saved by such meager equipment. (Stow.)

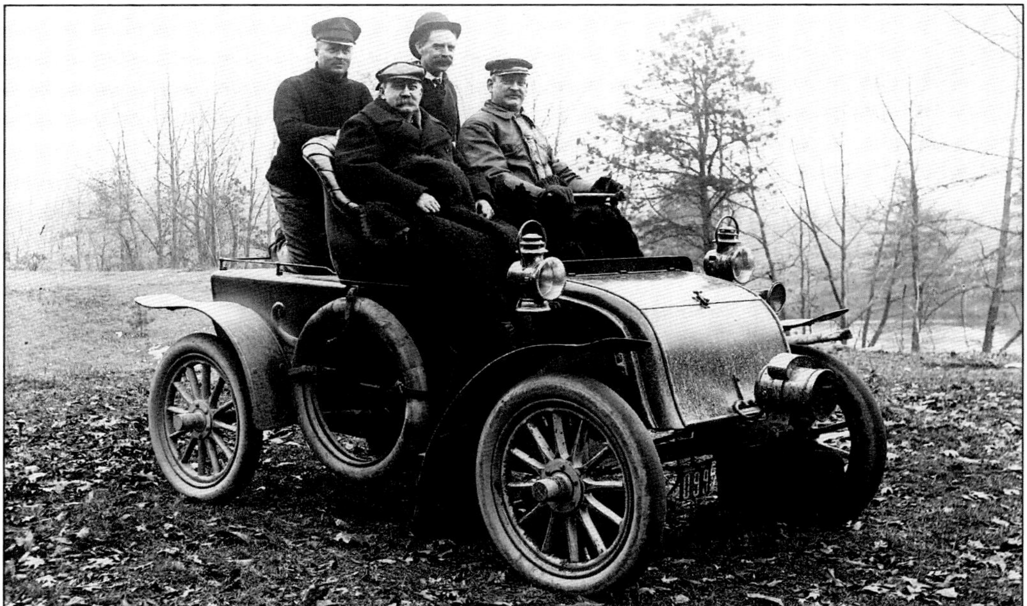

Full House. The four gentlemen are seated in what is believed to be a "curved dash" Oldsmobile. Although the roads around Lake Boon were unpaved, suitable mostly for horses, that did not stop the truly adventurous from using the new automobile machine as a means to transport themselves around the lake and to the nearby towns. (Berry.)

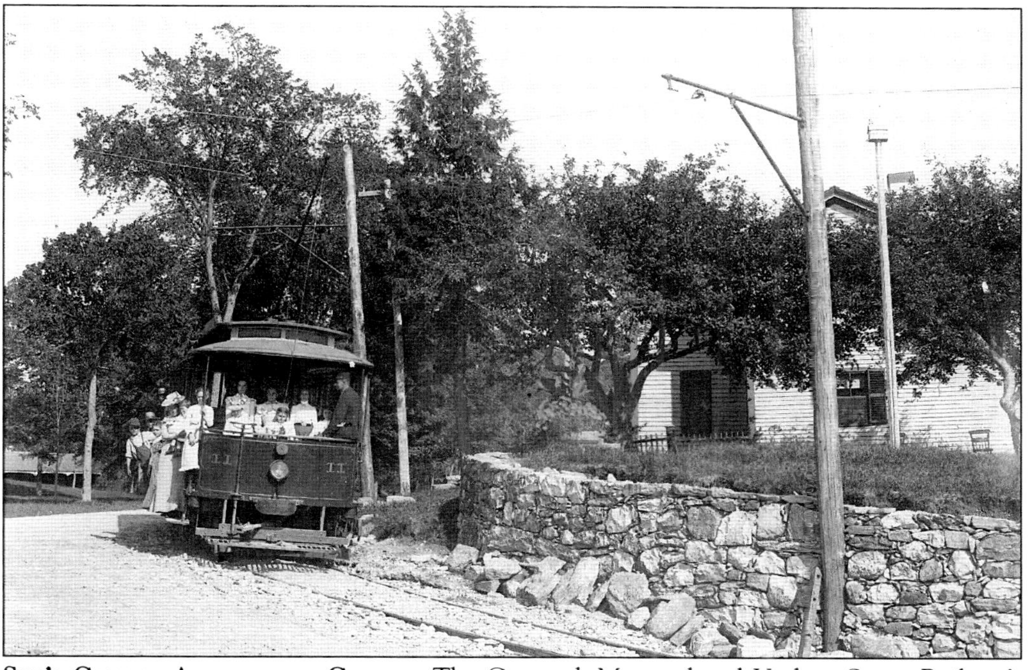

SHE'S COMING AROUND THE CORNER. The Concord, Maynard and Hudson Street Railway's open car makes the turn at Clark's Corner, about 1905. This stone wall still stands, where Rt. 62 meets Rt. 117 by the Randall Library. The streetcar passed close enough to the lake when going between Hudson and Stow that many people used this means of transportation to reach the lake for an exciting day trip. (Stow.)

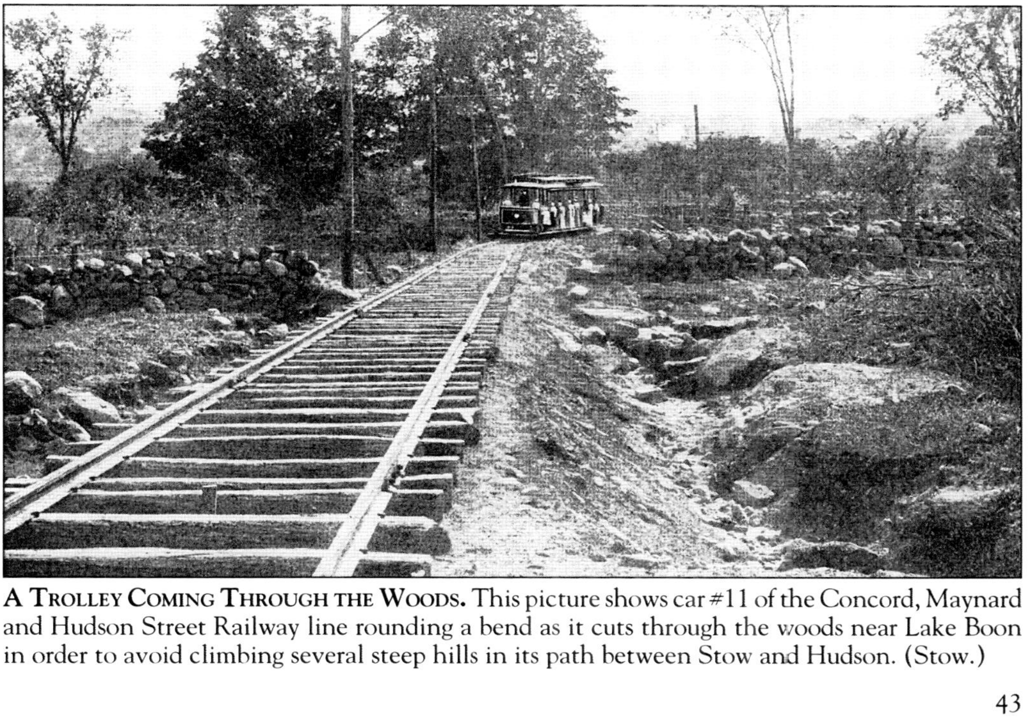

A TROLLEY COMING THROUGH THE WOODS. This picture shows car #11 of the Concord, Maynard and Hudson Street Railway line rounding a bend as it cuts through the woods near Lake Boon in order to avoid climbing several steep hills in its path between Stow and Hudson. (Stow.)

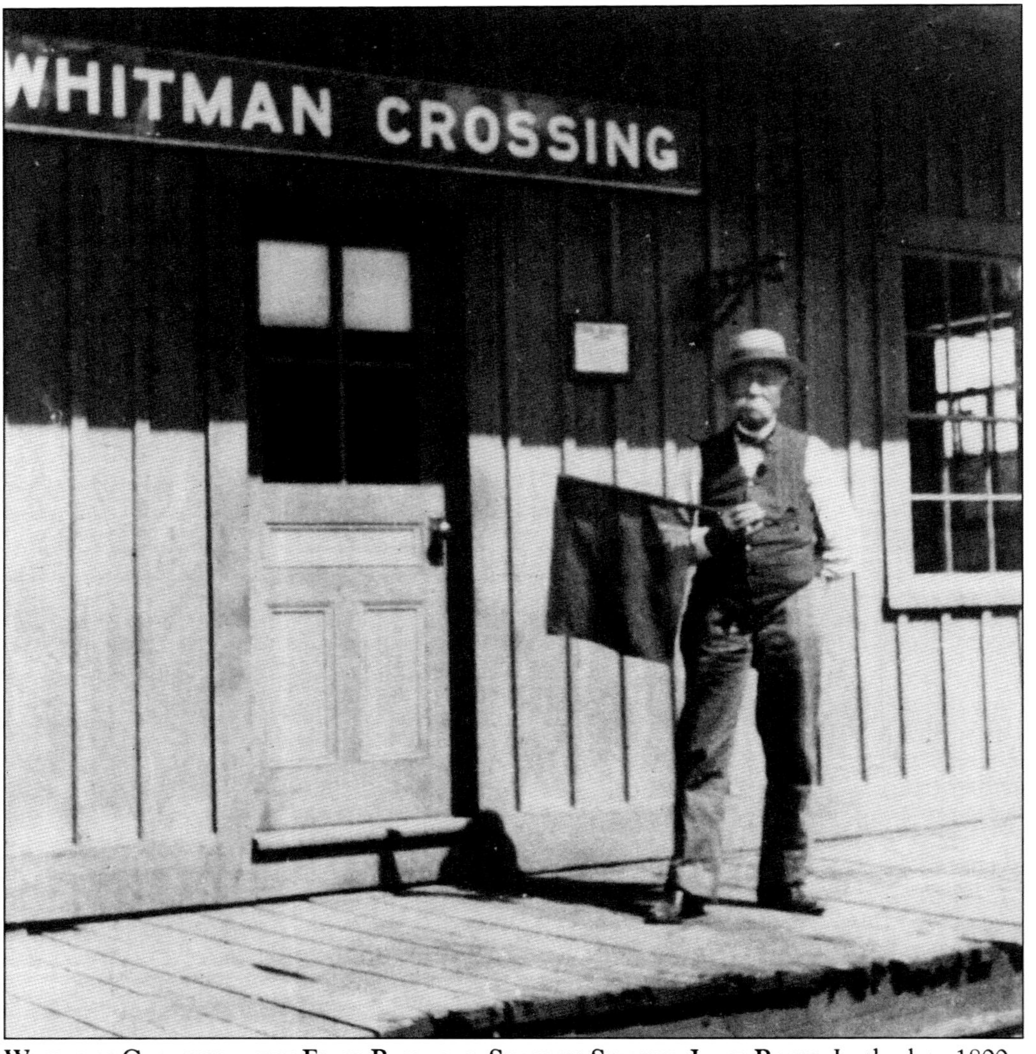

WHITMAN CROSSING—THE FIRST RAILROAD STATION SERVING LAKE BOON. In the late 1800s, the Boston and Maine Railroad wanted to build a Marlborough branch connecting their main line, which went through Marlborough, to the one that went through Acton serving Hudson, Gleasondale, and Maynard. This new road would follow the Assabet River for much of its route. The Boston and Maine wanted to purchase some of the river land owned by Capt. Whitman for constructing the line. The requested land was given to the railroad on the condition that a station be built at the Sudbury Bridge crossing. This was done and the station was called Whitman Crossing. This picture shows Mr. Potter, the crossing guard at Whitman Crossing (about 1900). He reportedly received $1 per diem for his duties. It was said that as many as 30 trains a day passed this crossing, so Mr. Potter was kept very busy for that dollar.

Although this was a small station, its importance to the area was great. It provided a very efficient way for the local farms to send produce to Boston. It also provided a way for people in the area to commute into Boston daily for work and return to their country home at night. After the dam was built that caused Lake Boon to grow to its present size, much of the credit of it becoming a popular recreation area has to be given to the existence of the Whitman Crossing railroad station. (Kattelle.)

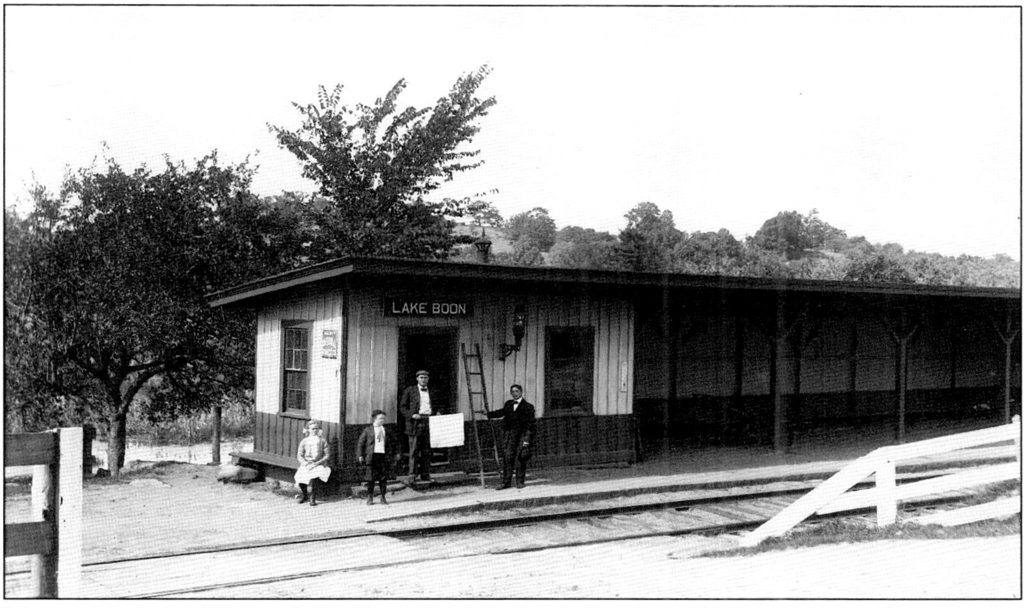

Waiting for the Train. A family patiently waits to flag down the next train so they can start their journey. Note that the name of the station was changed from Whitman Crossing to Lake Boon because there was confusion with a "Whitman" station elsewhere on the railroad. The majority of the people using this station were also heading for Lake Boon. (Berry.)

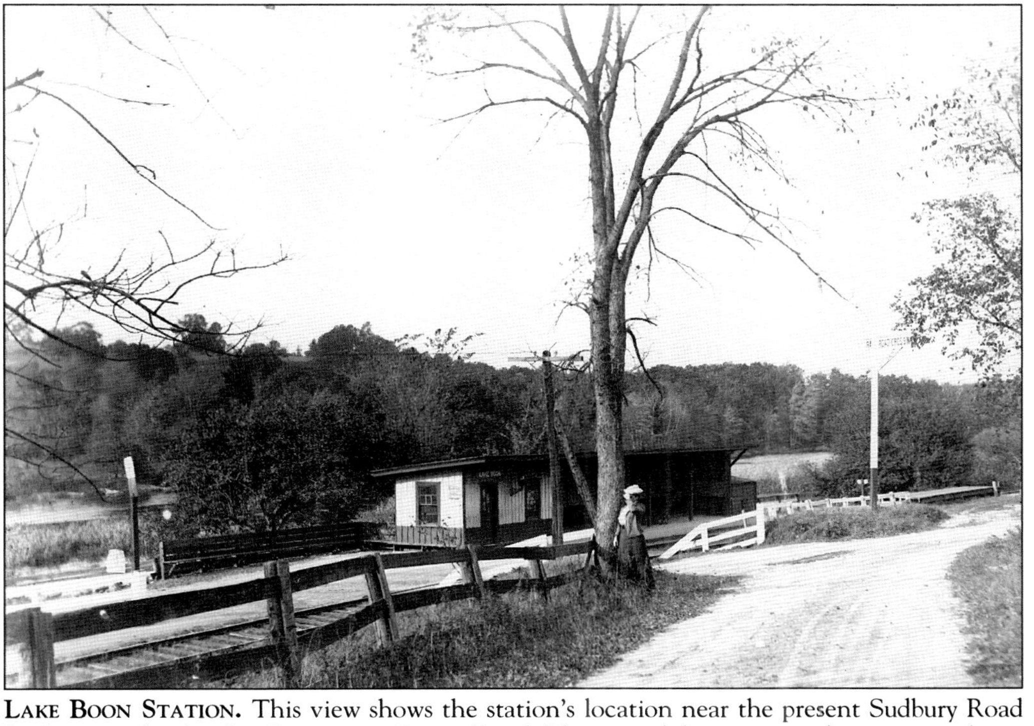

Lake Boon Station. This view shows the station's location near the present Sudbury Road Bridge over the Assabet River, near Barton Road. The train did not stop at the station unless a passenger wanted to get off, or unless someone at the station flagged down the train. (Berry.)

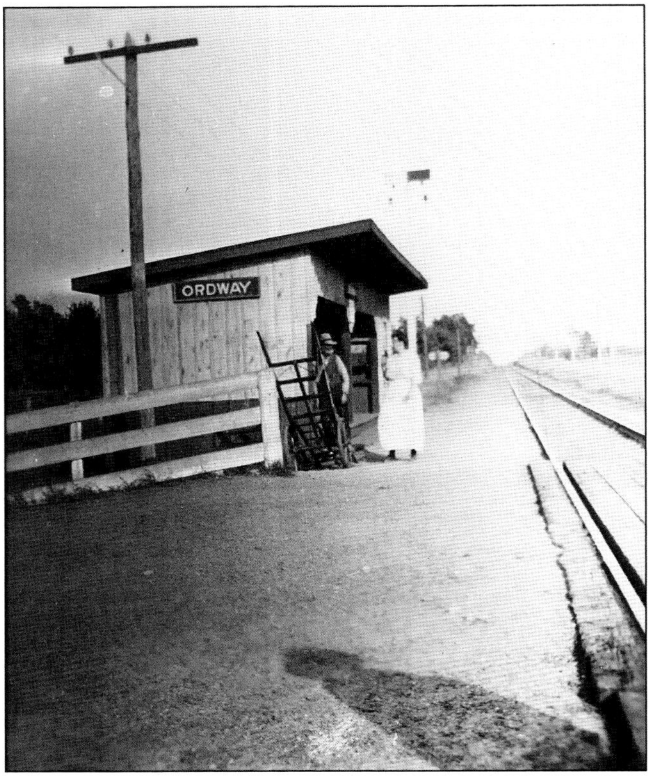

Station Masters. The Ordways were the station masters for the "Ordway Crossing" railroad station, located at Ordway's farm where the Central Mass branch of the Boston and Maine Railroad crosses Parmenter Road. It was just a little flag stop station that serviced the Lake Boon population residing on the second and third basins. (Kattelle.)

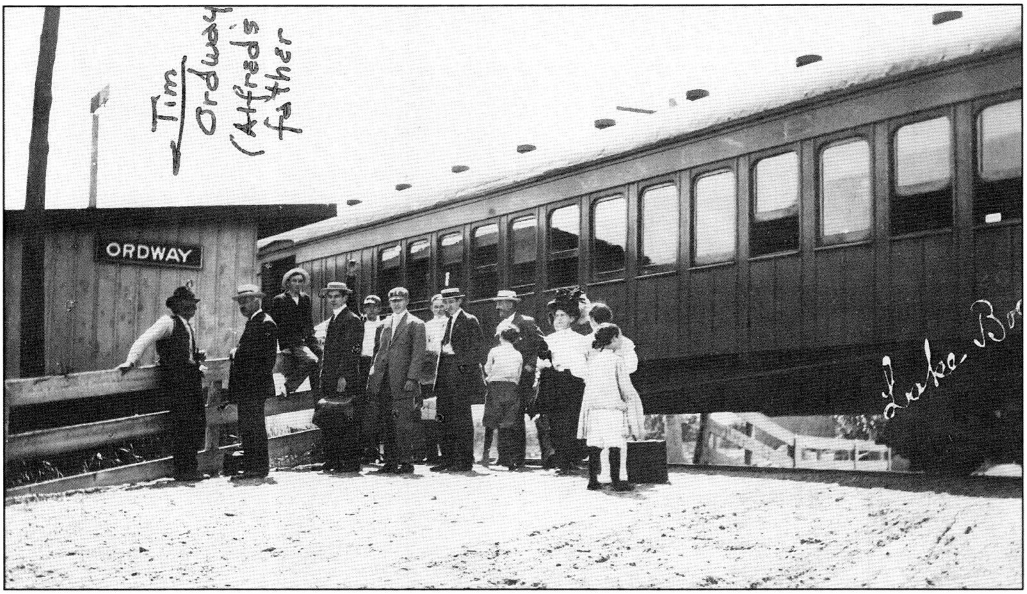

Ordway's Crossing. A passenger train on the Boston and Maine Central Mass Branch unloads a bunch of people destined for relaxing at nearby Lake Boon, who are wishing there was a taxi to take them to their cabins or cottages. Tim Ordway is the station manager. (Halprin.)

Four

Fun Came in Many Ways

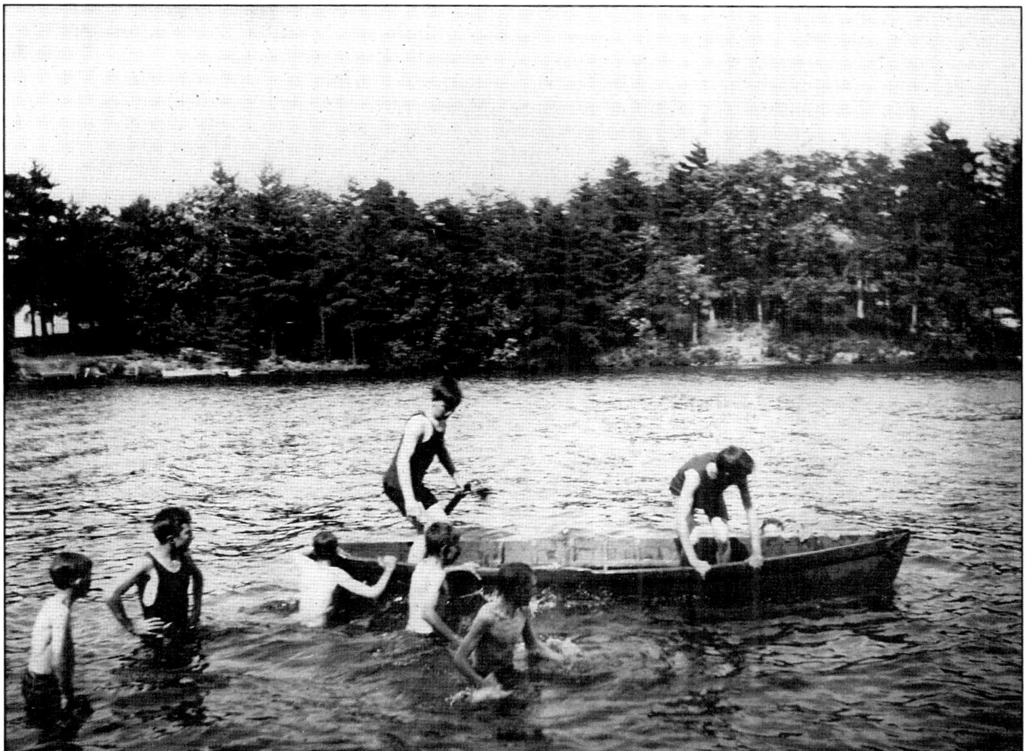

Canoe Mischief. Canoes always seem to tip over when occupied by young boys, but that doesn't stop them from having lots of fun.

WATER CARNIVAL AND BAND CONCERT

Monday Night, 7.15 to 10.00 p. m.

In order to assist committee in arranging the formation, all persons are requested to send in entries as soon as possible.

Everyone is urged to enter and decorate boat or canoe at least with one or more lights, and to illuminate cottages and shore in similar manner to the band concert nights last season.

Japanese lanterns may be procured of the committee at 6 cents each. Red are at 15 cents.

No prizes are offered in this carnival, but souvenir banners will be supplied by the committee to every boat and canoe.

The band will move to the middle of the Lake at 7.15, which is the signal for the canoes to form around the band; after which the band will circle the First Basin. Motor boats falling in line. After one complete circuit of the First Basin the band and motor boats will circle the Second Basin. As soon as the motor boats have passed into the Second Basin the canoes will follow into the Second Basin, forming around the band for a concert.

On the completion of the concert in Second Basin the band and motor boats will move to First Basin, circling the First Basin while the canoes move straight to the middle forming around the band. On the completion of the concert, the band will circle the Lake, motor boats returning to their own wharves and canoes will disband.

The following rules will greatly aid to make the Carnival success.

1. All entrants must be ready at 7.00 p. m.

2. Every boat, canoe or motor boat, whether entered or not, must for safety sake carry a light at either end.

3. To be entitled to a pennant at least 2 fancy lanterns must be shown.

4. During the Concerts in either basin, motor boats will please stop their engines and canoes will remain as near stationary as possible.

COME ONE, COME ALL. The water carnival and band concert was the big lake event that was held every year and had something for everyone who wanted to participate, even if it was just listening to the band play from the middle of the lake.

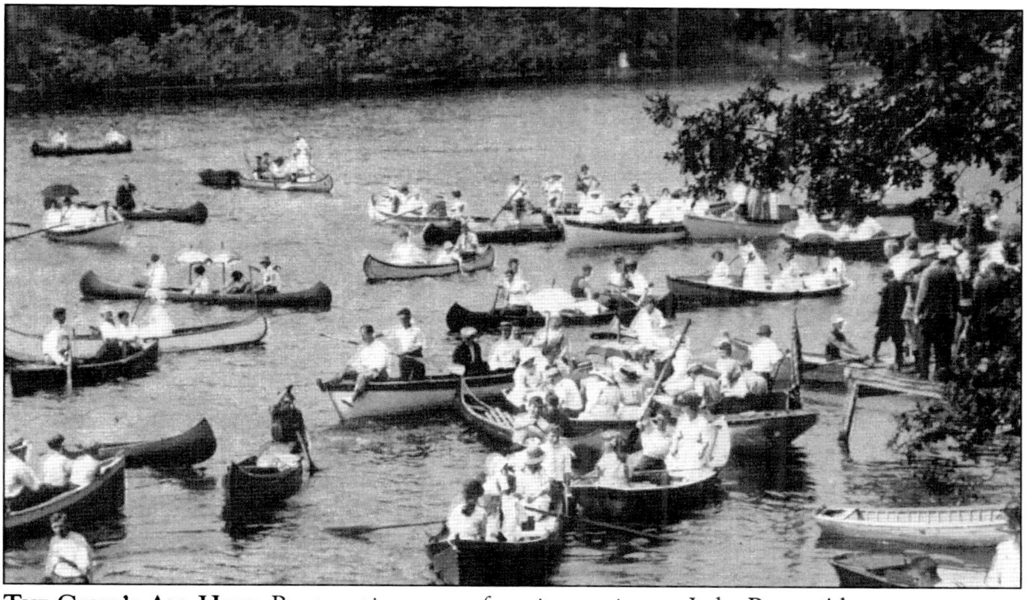

The Gang's All Here. Boat parties were a favorite pastime at Lake Boon. Almost any excuse could be used for such a party. This one was probably Independence Day. It appears that a speaker may be at the focus point on the dock (far right) addressing the gathered "Booners" dressed in their finest on a calm sunny day. (Halprin.)

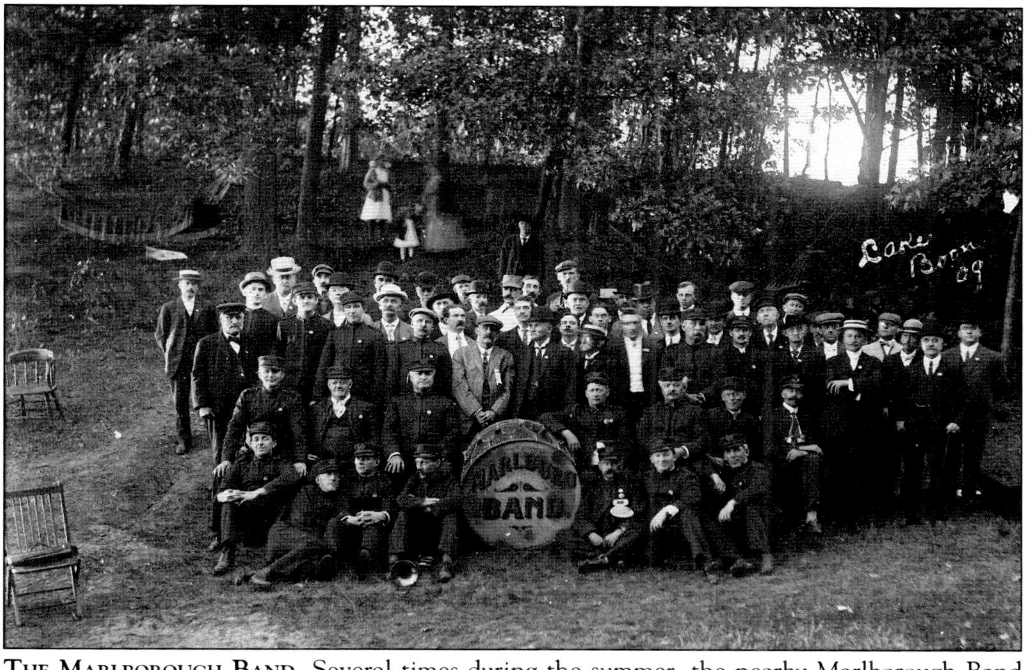

The Marlborough Band. Several times during the summer, the nearby Marlborough Band would come and play concerts along the lake. The lake would be full of canoes and boats listening to the band. In the front row on the far left is Henry Werner, and in the front row on the far right is Bob Bird. Back in 1909, the band was much more formal looking, but the music was just as good. (Berry.)

1913 Labor Day Sports

LAKE BOON

==

SWIMMING AND DIVING

1. - 25 yard straight away for boys up to thirteen years of age. Diving start from float. Preliminary heats.
2. - 25 yard straight away for girls up to fourteen years of age. Start at discretion of contestants.
3. - 25 yard straight away for boys up to sixteen years of age. Diving start from float. Preliminary heats.
4. - 25 yard free for all straight away for women and girls. Preliminary heats. Diving start from float.
5. - 25 yard straight away for men over forty years of age. Start at discretion of contestants.
6. - 50 yard straight away for all comers. Preliminary heats and semi final if necessary. Diving start from float.
7. - Children under eight years. 20 feet swim.
8. - Diving from spring board for form. Program for men, women and boys.
9. - Plunge for distance from stationary point. Sixty seconds float allowed.
10. - Under water swim for distance from stationary float.
11. - Walking greased pole for flag. All comers, men and women.
12. - 100 yard relay race. Four contestants to a team. swimming 25 yards each. Dive from and finish at float.
13. - Canoe stunt. Jump out and enter canoe from water.
14. - Egg race. Swim ten yards, take egg in spoon and return to float.

TUB RACES

15. - 25 yards, boys under 15 years.
16. - 25 yards, girls under 15 years.

Tubs of a size will be supplied by the Committee.

TILTING

17. - Log Rolling.
18. - Tilting. Free for all.
19. - Cask Joust

DINNER 12.30-2.00

MOTOR BOAT RACES

2.00 to 3.00 p. m.

20. - Innovation. Details to be given at start of race.
21. - Free for all.

BAND CONCERT

Highland City Band of 20 pieces and Singer

WATER BASE BALL

22. - Water Baseball. First Basin vs. Second Basin for Championship Banner.

SPORTING EVENTS. The Lake Boon Association was a very active organization during the 1910s and 1920s. This list of sporting activities was scheduled for the last day of the summer season. (Kattelle.)

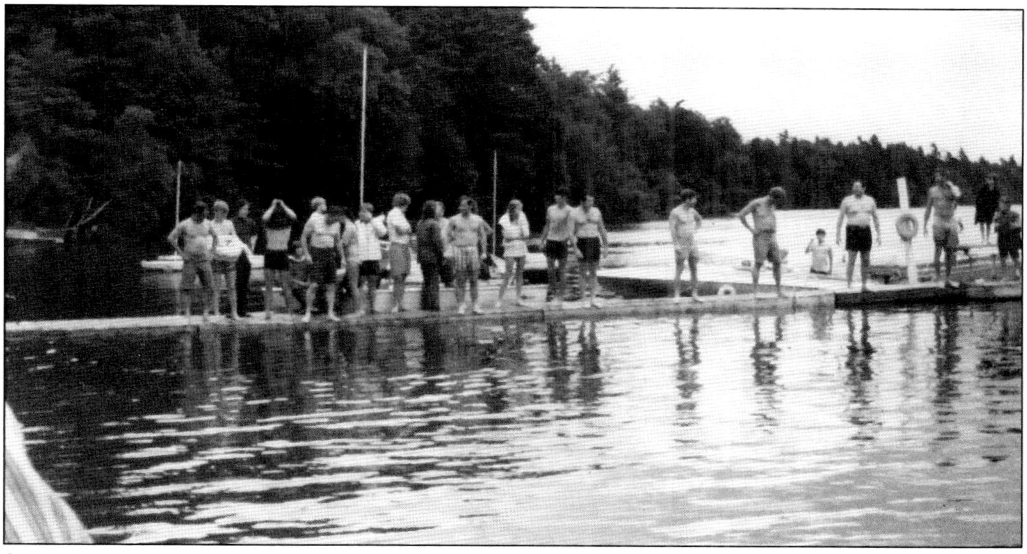

Swimming Race. Every Labor Day there was a swimming race, starting from Hanson's Beach. Sometimes the swimming race was combined with portions of the race that had to be run or completed by canoe.

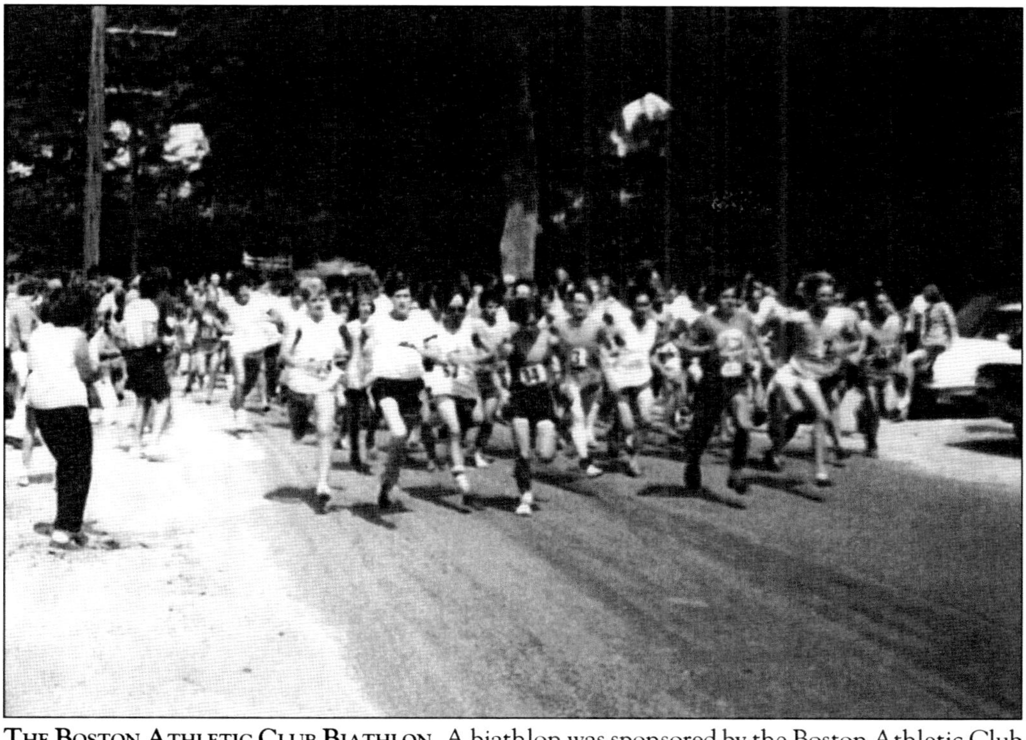

The Boston Athletic Club Biathlon. A biathlon was sponsored by the Boston Athletic Club and was run for five years, probably in the mid-1940s. The entrants would first run on Sudbury Road from Hanson's Beach down to the end of Sudbury Road (to State Road), then back again to the beach. They would then have to swim from the beach to Pine Point and return.

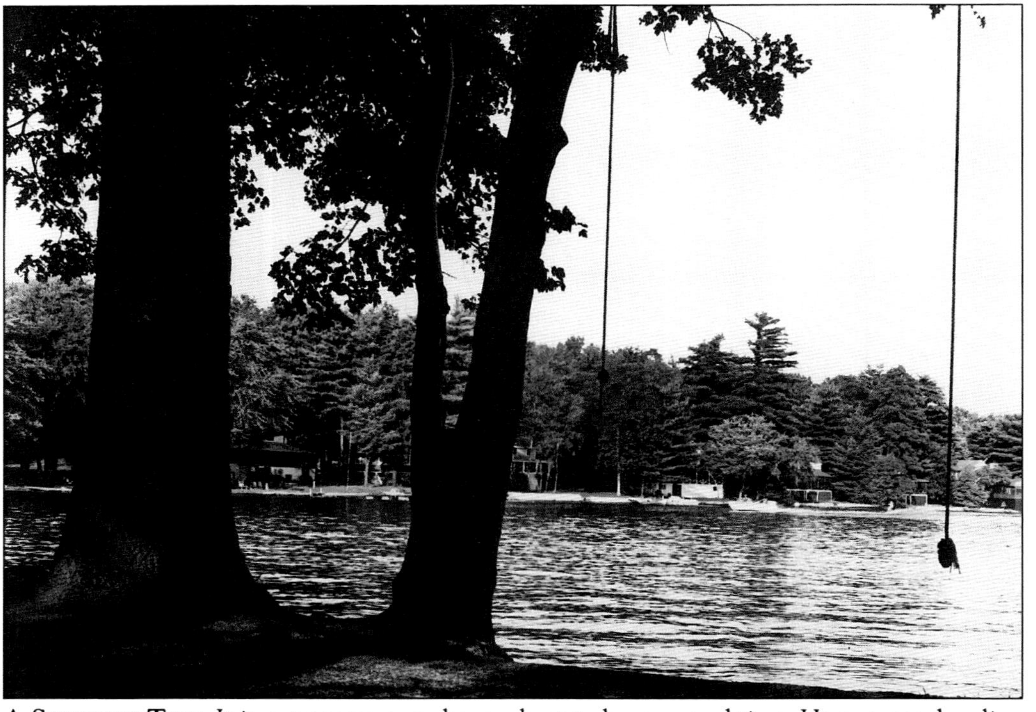

A Swinging Time. It is not necessary to have a boat to have a good time. Here, ropes dangling from trees near the lake's dam tempt the younger generation to grab hold, take a short run, a long swing, and splash into the refreshing waters of the lake. (Stow.)

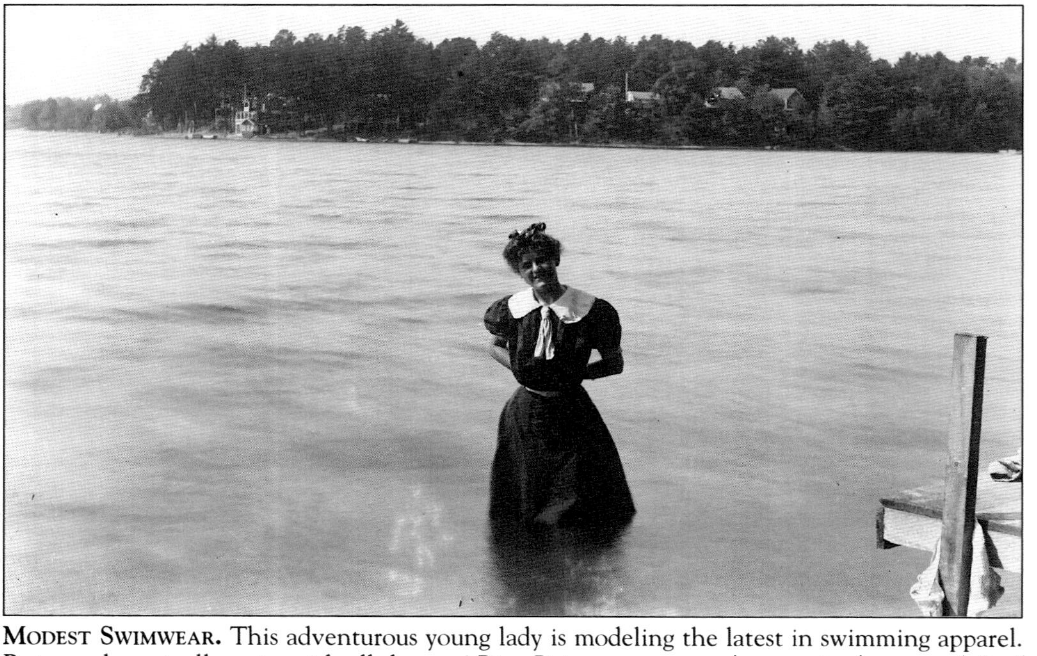

Modest Swimwear. This adventurous young lady is modeling the latest in swimming apparel. But can she actually swim with all that on? Pine Point cottage can be seen in the upper left of the picture. (Berry.)

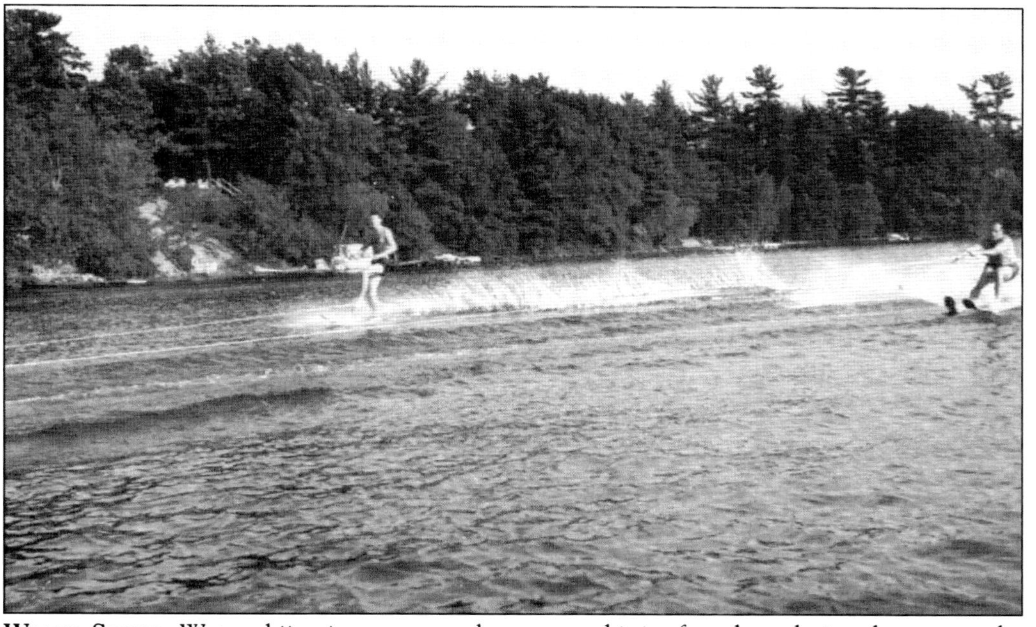

Water-Skiing. Water-skiing is a very popular sport and it is often done during the summer by the athletically talented, usually in the larger first basin of the lake. (Phalan.)

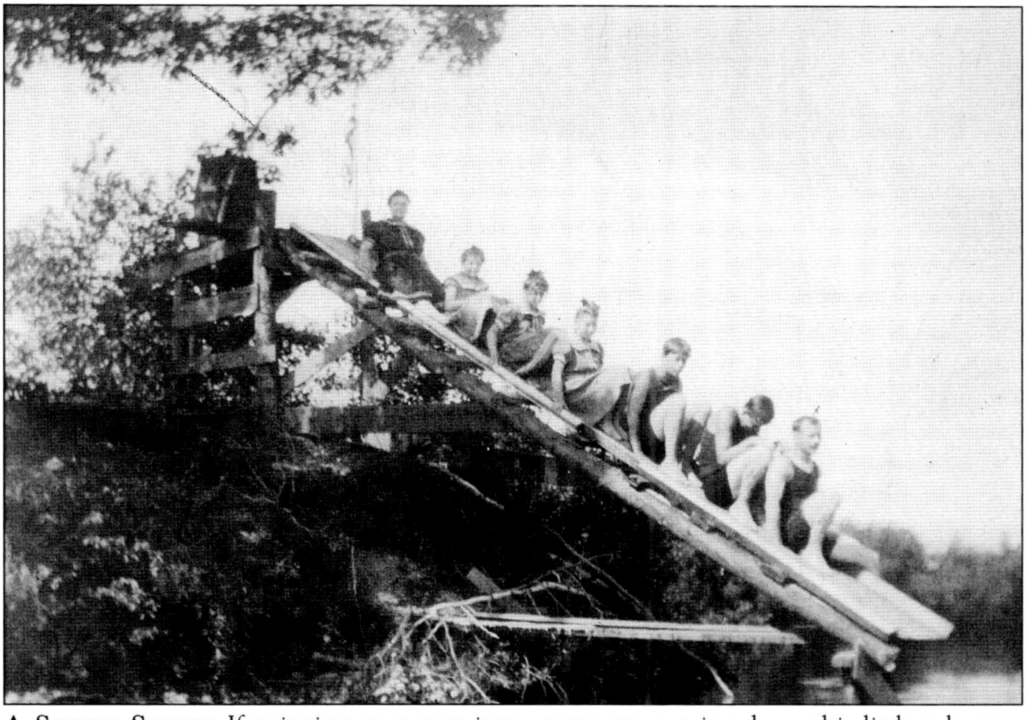

A Sliding Splash. If swinging on a rope is too tame, try coming down this little toboggan slide built in front of the Jackson family's "West Point" cottage a few houses away from the lake's dam. Another larger toboggan was located near the second basin at Matthew Boon Gardens. (Jackson.)

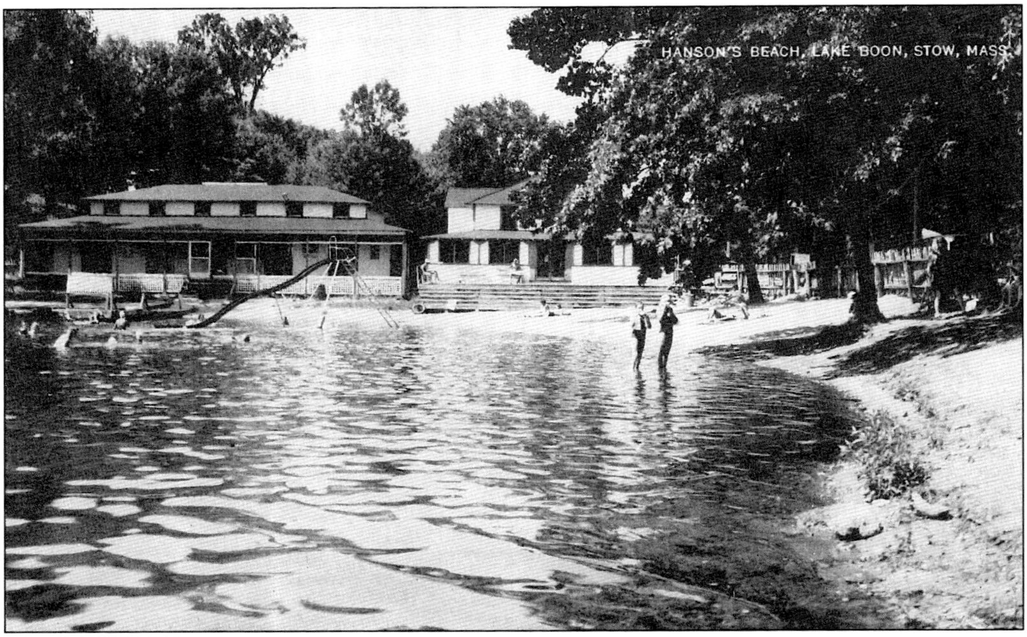

HANSON'S BEACH. At the northern tip of Lake Boon, a natural beach was formed and a formal beach facility was developed. In its heyday, it was known as Hanson's Beach, after its owner, and consisted of a well-cared-for beach with lifeguard, and a large building used for changing, featuring lockers and showers. (Phalan.)

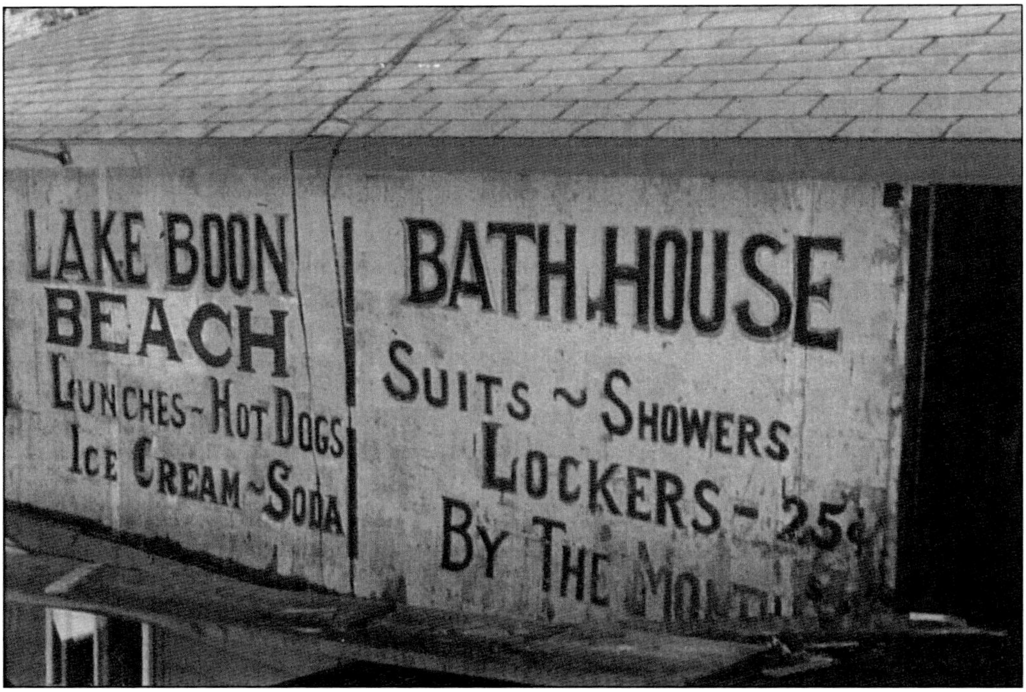

HANSON'S SIGN. This sign was on the side of the cottage at Hanson's Beach showing that they provided everything that was needed to enjoy a sunny day at their beach.

WINGING IT WITH WATER. Here swimmers try out new bathing suits and water wings fill with air to keep them afloat. In the background is Bolam's store near Hanson's Beach. (Berry.)

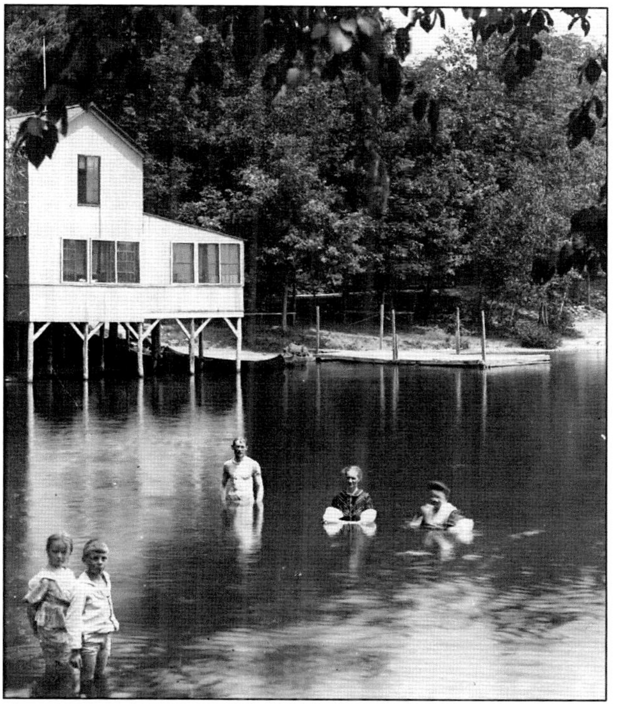

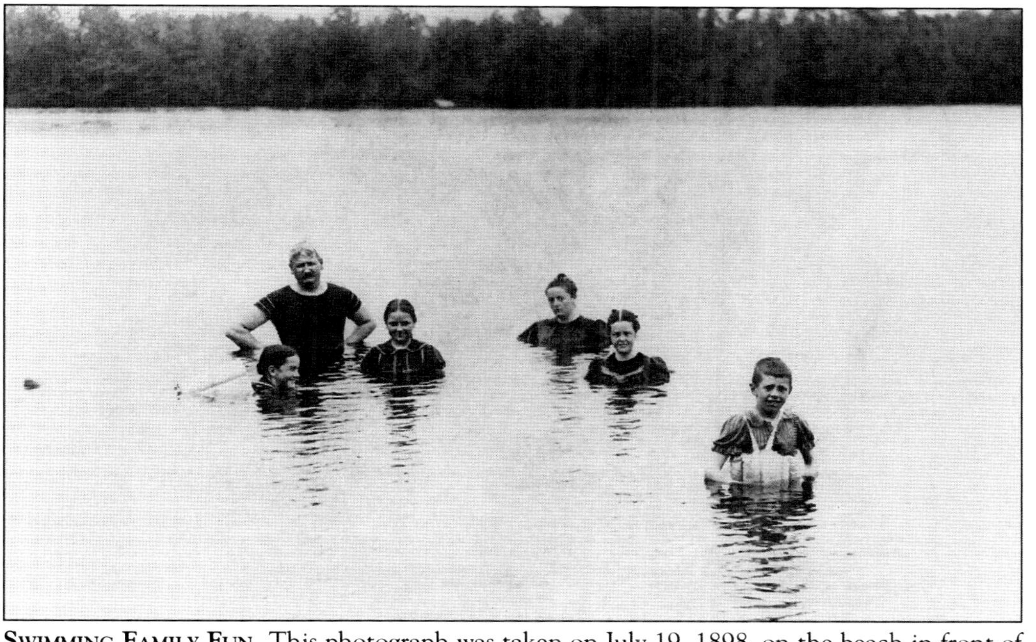

SWIMMING FAMILY FUN. This photograph was taken on July 19, 1898, on the beach in front of "Satawisa" cottage on Lake Boon. The girl on the left and the boy on the right are wearing a type of flotation device that kept them above the water while they were "swimming." The gentleman on the left is Charles Onthank of Marlborough with his daughter Charlotte and a friend. At the right are Elsie, Fannie, and Laurence Kattelle (Alan Kattelle's father). (Kattelle.)

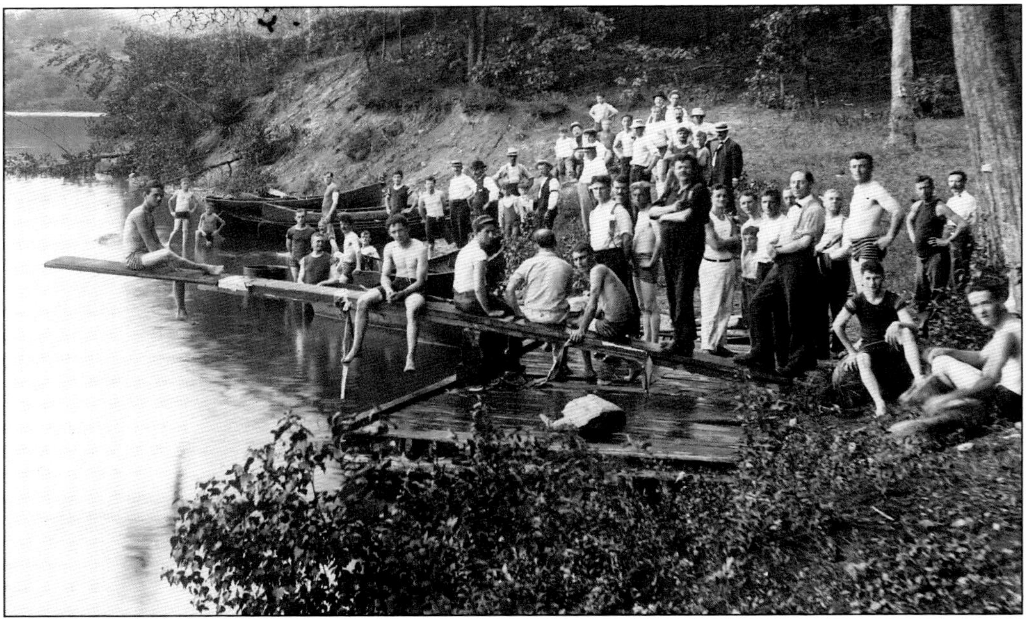

Who Wants to Jump in First? A large group of young men have congregated at a swimming hole by the lake, but no one seems inclined to actually get in the water. (Berry.)

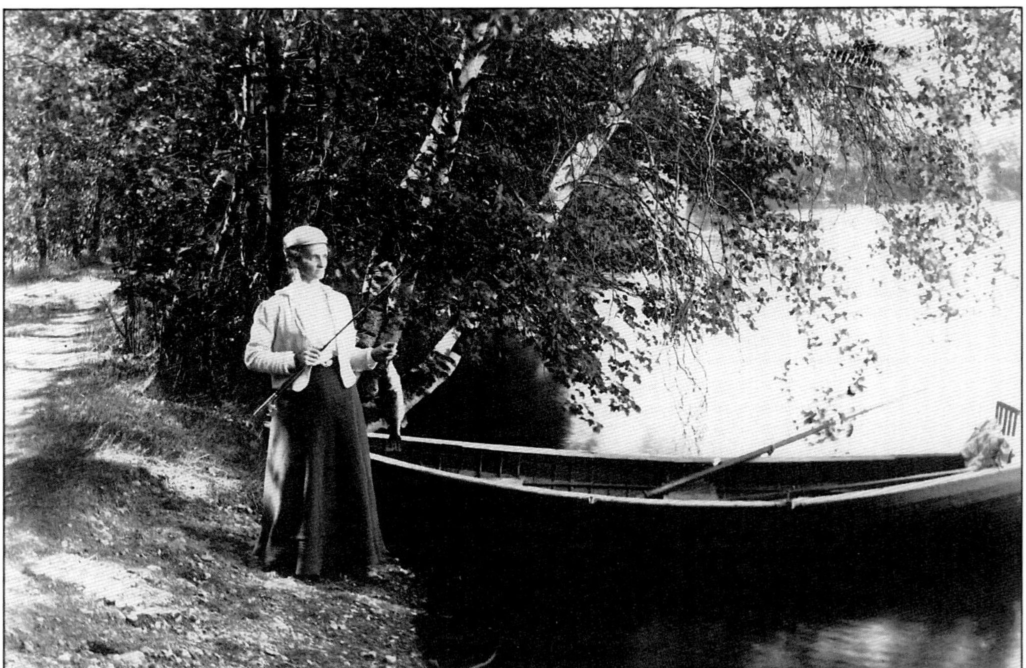

A Line Fisher Woman. You didn't have to be a man to enjoy sports around the lake. Here a sporting woman returns to the shore with a respectable catch of fish hauled out of the lake with her trusty fishing pole. (Berry.)

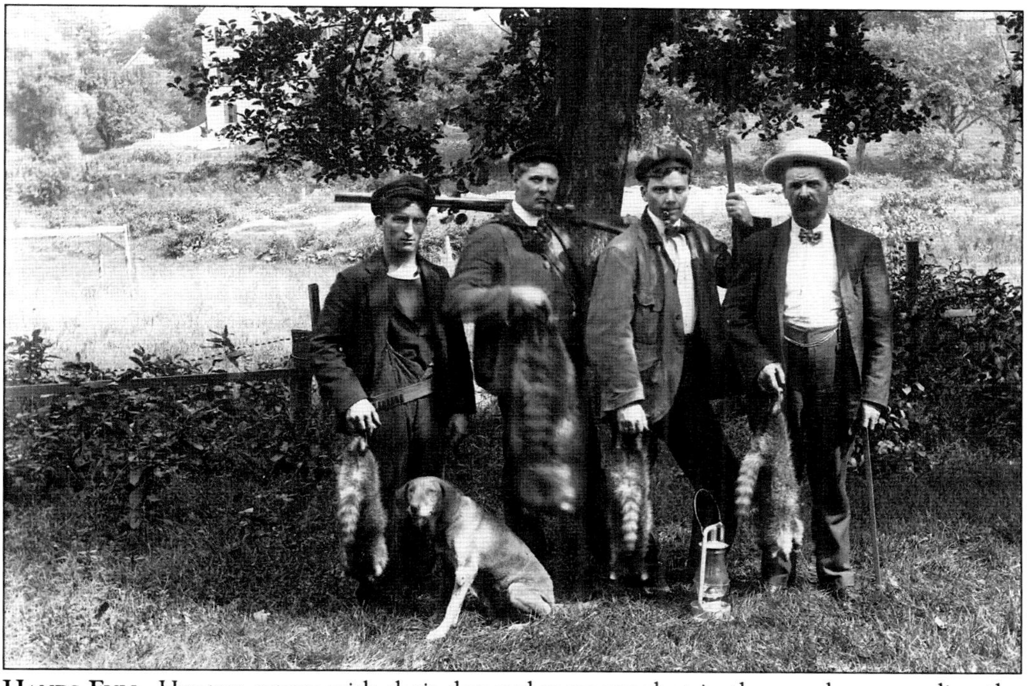

Hands Full. Hunters return with their dog and raccoons shot in the woods surrounding the lake. (Berry.)

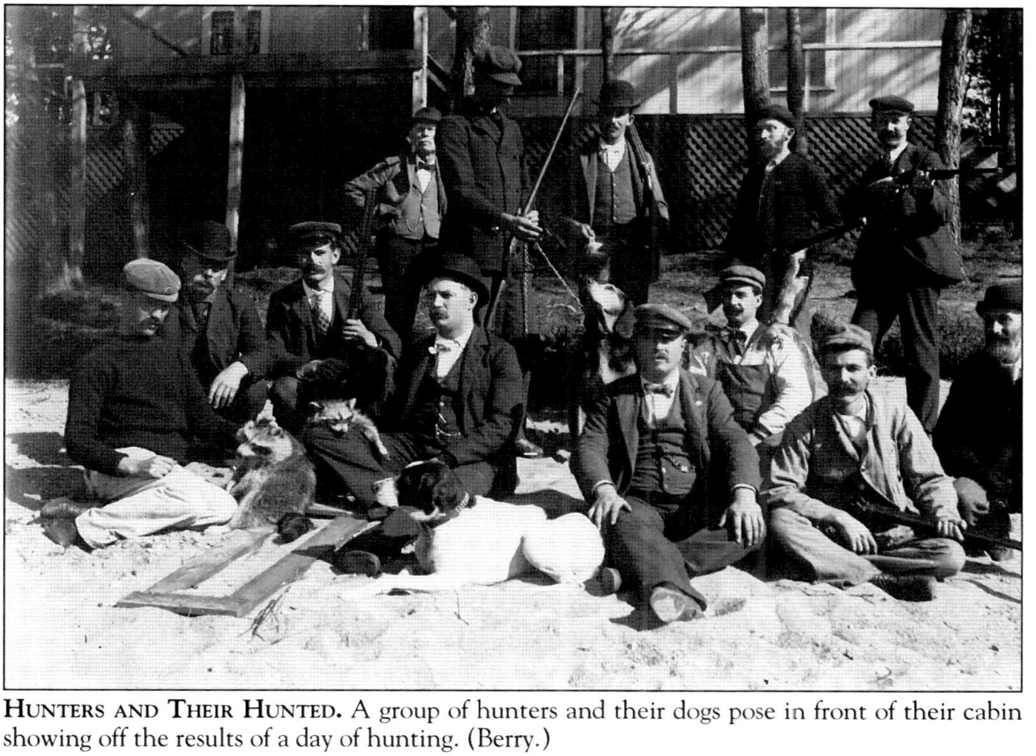

Hunters and Their Hunted. A group of hunters and their dogs pose in front of their cabin showing off the results of a day of hunting. (Berry.)

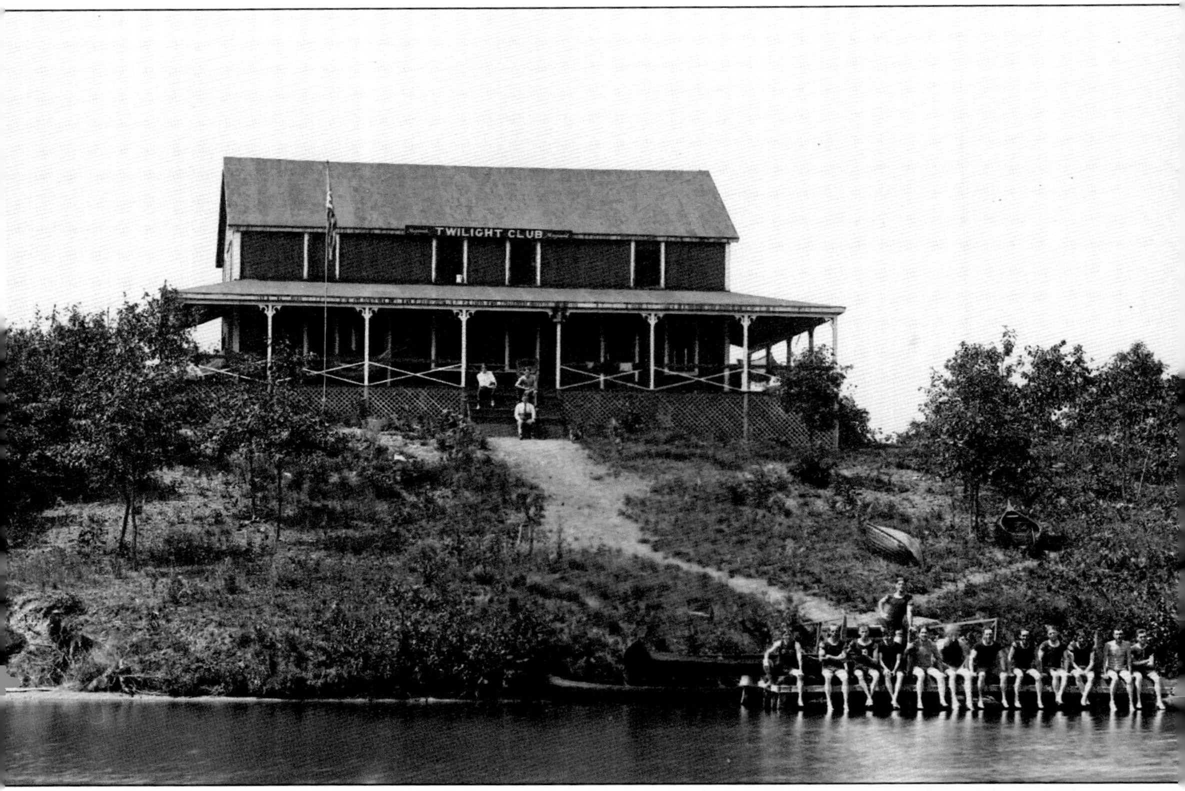

THE TWILIGHT CLUB. This club was organized in 1904, dedicated on August 5, 1905, and closed in 1964. The building is no longer standing. The following is an article from the 1905 Hudson Daily Sun:

The Twilight club has nearly completed its cottage at Lake Boon and the members have the finest place at this popular resort. The cottage is situated on a high bluff at the right of the narrows and a fine view in both directions can be had. Aside from being one of the roomiest cottages at the pond, it is also the best constructed. Everything is of the best material and workmanship, the whole being a credit both to the builder and owners. The first floor is divided into two large rooms, which by folding doors can be transformed into a large room, sufficient in size to accommodate a large dancing party. In the second story are five bedrooms, each large enough to easily hold four beds, with plenty of spare room left. A fifth room will contain lockers for members of the club. The cottage is to be furnished with the best of everything, including a piano. At present, each bedroom contains two iron couch beds, with other necessary furniture. One of the lower rooms has an open fireplace. The floors are of hard pine and the walls are all sheathed with narrow matched boards. A broad piazza extends around three sides of the building. The boat landing is also more substantial than other landings at the pond. In fact, the Twilight club seems to have gone all other cottage owners "one better." (Berry.)

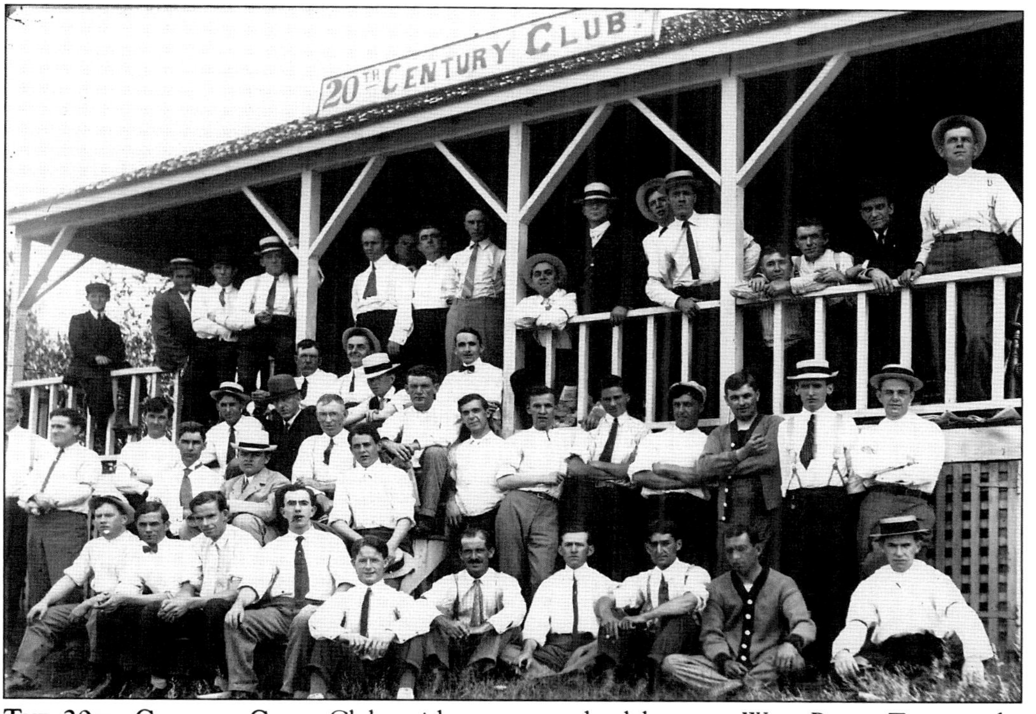

THE 20TH CENTURY CLUB. Clubs with camps at the lake were West Point, Tonawanda, Wisteria, Parks, Lone Pine, Sea Gull, Lincoln, Fairview, and Twilight. They were mostly for single men only, though there were many activities in which single women could be invited as guests. (Berry.)

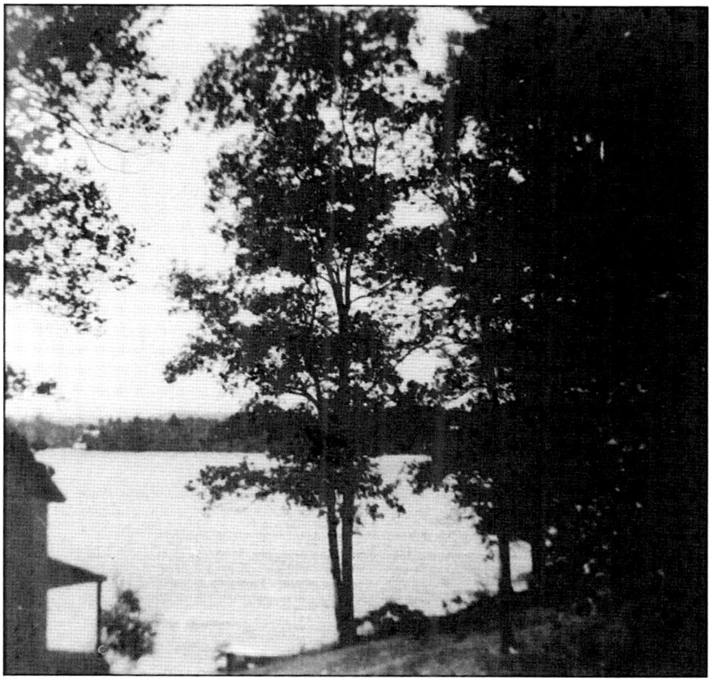

LINCOLN'S VIEW. The Lincoln Club, located in what was called Lincoln Club Cove, is said to be the oldest cottage on the lake (no longer standing). It was located at the spot currently occupied by the Stow Town Beach, and was right on the water's edge.

CANNING'S PICNIC GROVE

NEW MANAGEMENT

Special Rates for Sunday Schools and Lodges. Bring your picnic here.

DANCING EVERY SATURDAY EVENING

Pavilion To Rent. Positively no intoxicants allowed on the grounds.

ADDRESS, BENJ. B. LOVETT, HUDSON, MASS.

CANNING'S A.D. Canning's grove (now called Indian Point) was a popular location for picnics and dances. Mr. Canning started the boat line, first with the steamship *Cleo*, then the gasoline-powered *Princess*, in order to get people from the train to his picnic grove. (Hudson.)

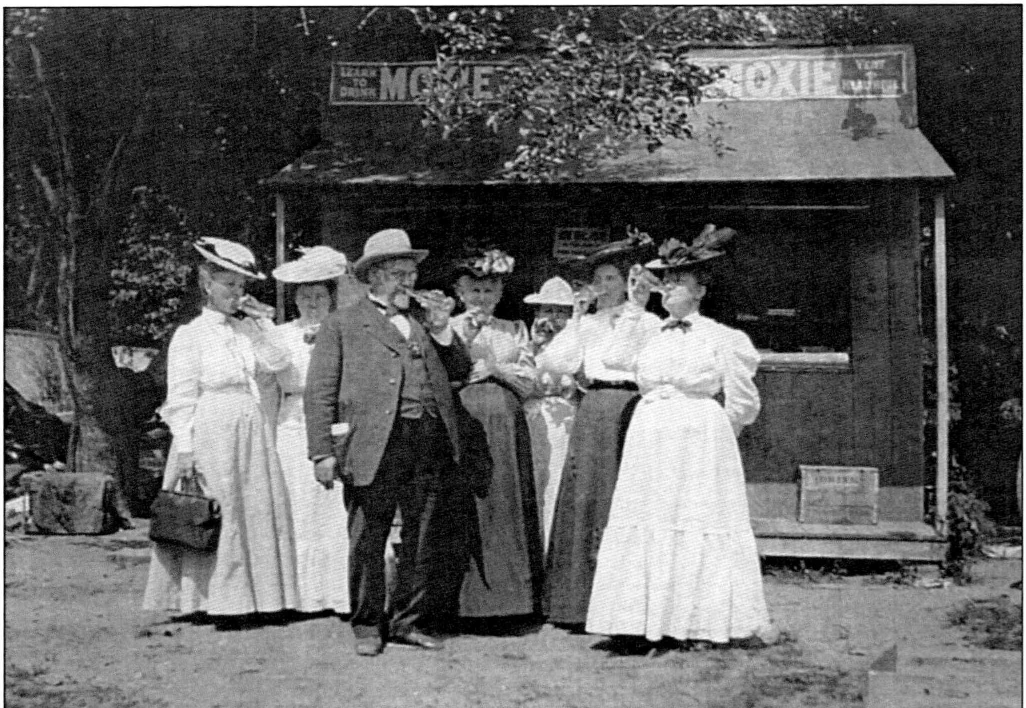

MOXIE ANYONE? There were many refreshment stands around the lake featuring the then-very-popular soft drink Moxie. The location of this one is unknown—possibly it was at the picnic grounds at Cannings (Indian Point). The sign above the store says "Learn To Drink Moxie" and "Moxie, Very Refreshing." On the lawn are a group of people all "learning" to drink Moxie. (Parker.)

Five

Selling to the Summer People

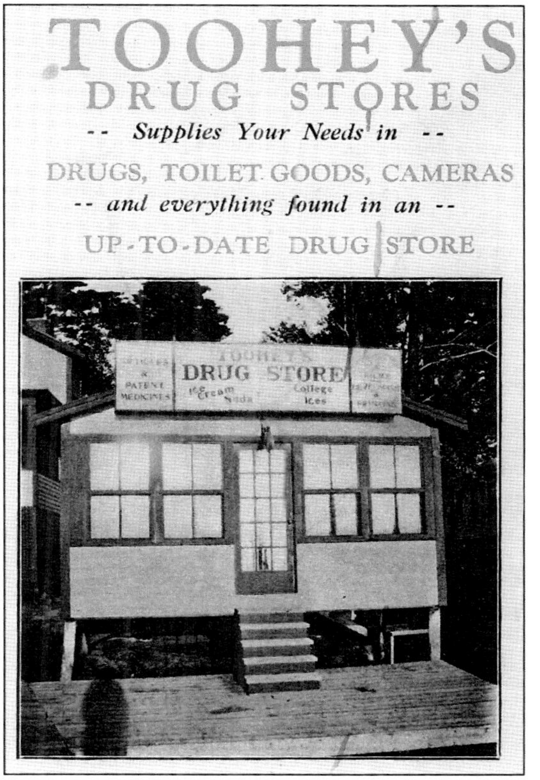

A Very Popular Lake Store. Most of the people who stayed at the lake during the summers between 1910 and 1935 did not have any personal transportation. They used the lake boat, or the nearby trains or streetcars to get around, or they walked. This type of transportation was not suitable for buying groceries, or getting ice, or any of the kind of shopping we normally take for granted today. So the merchants came to the lake instead. Some toured the lake with horse and wagon selling their wares, others established small stores, often an extension of their main store. Such was the case for the Lake Boon branch of Hudson's Toohey's Drug Store. (Hudson.)

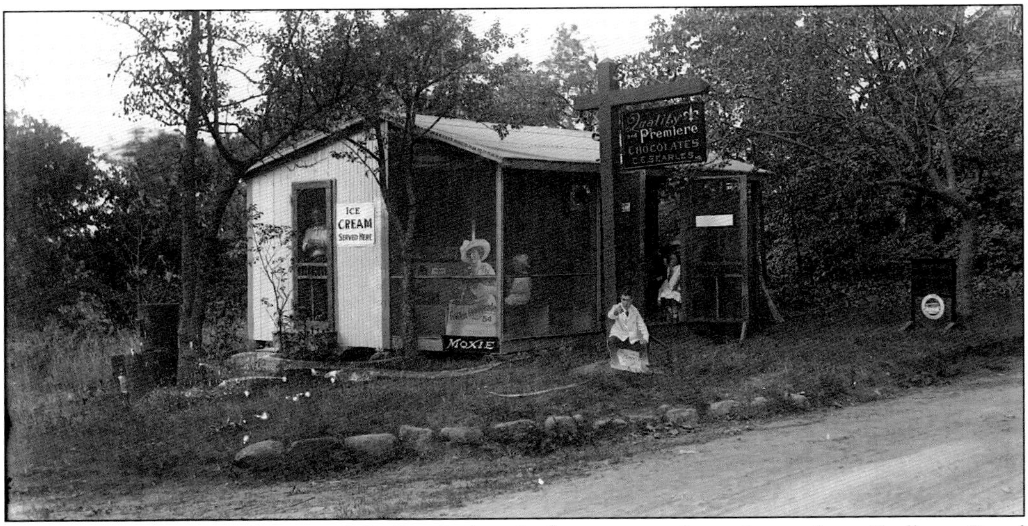

Let's Get Some Ice Cream. C.E. Searles's refreshment stand was located on Sudbury Road halfway between the Whitman (Lake Boon) Railroad Station and the *Princess* dock. As such, it was frequented by lake-goers as they passed it on the way to the boat and their cottages. Some of the signs read "Ice Cream Sold Here" (by the door), "Golden Orangeade 5 cents" and "Moxie" (inside the porch), "Quality Premiere Chocolates" (on the front lawn, with a cutout of a boy sitting on a case of Moxie at the base of that sign), and "TAIT Bros Ice Cream" (by the road). (Berry.)

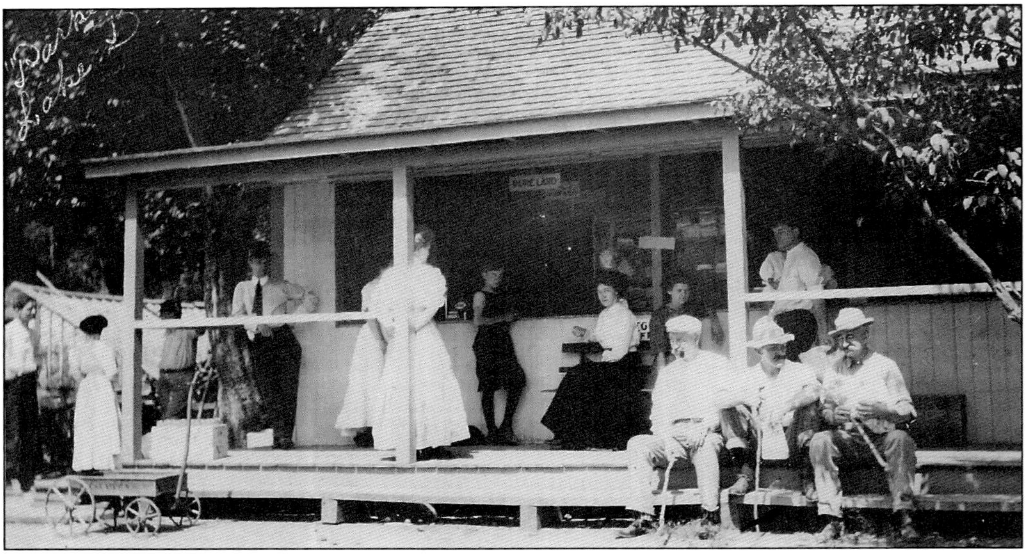

Lake Folk Gather for Food and Gossip. The Parker family owned a large farm next to the original Lake Boon (first basin). As the lake began to be used for recreational purposes, they built a string of cottages by the lake that were rented for summer use. They also built this delightful store on Sudbury Road where they would sell the farm produce, the ever-present Moxie, and other refreshments. The large porch was a favorite gathering place for the nearby lake folk to sit and gossip about the latest goings-on. (Jackson.)

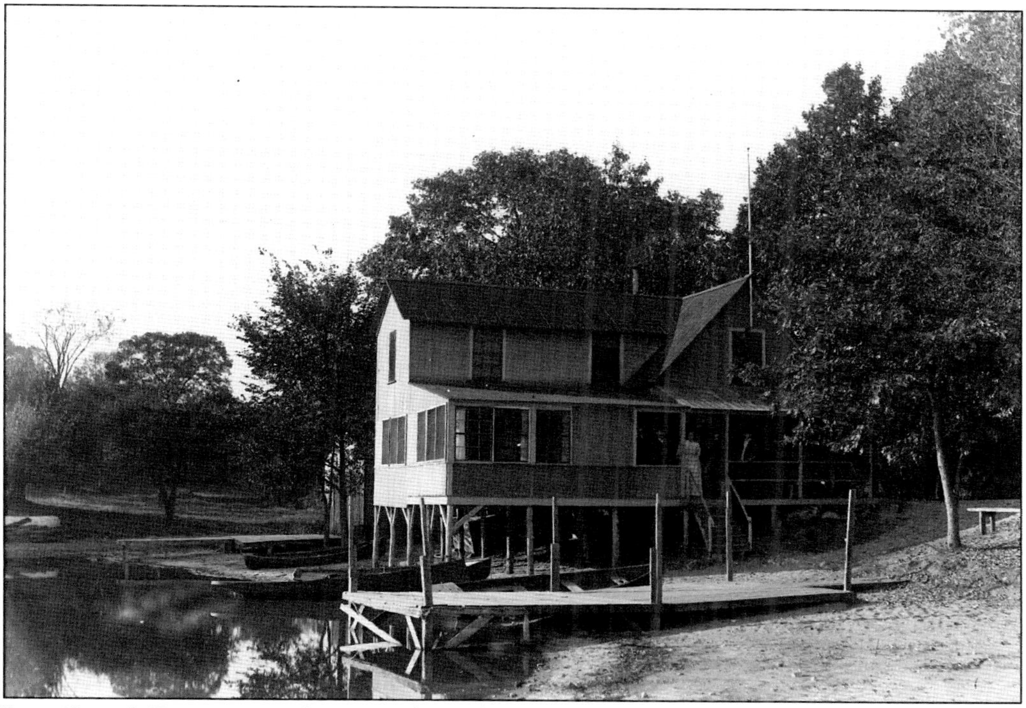

Lake Boon's Department Store. Bolam's department store (or Bolam's Home Cafe) was built in 1897 and was located on the water near what later became known as Hanson's Beach. It was said to have a small cafe, and each of the other rooms in the house was used to sell different kinds of merchandise. (Berry.)

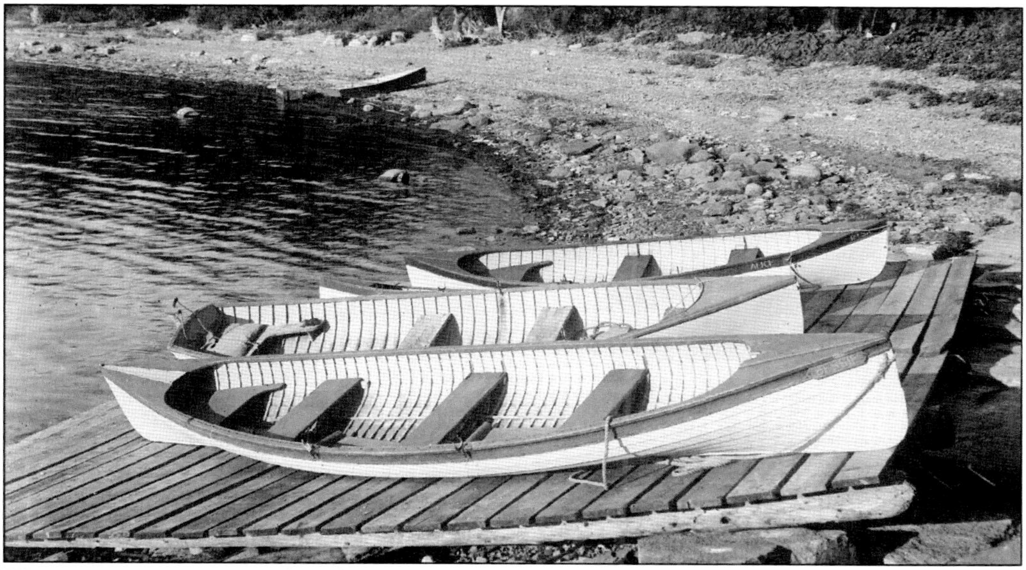

Waiting on the Dock. These boats are waiting patiently on their dock for some lake people to come around and rent them. (Jackson.)

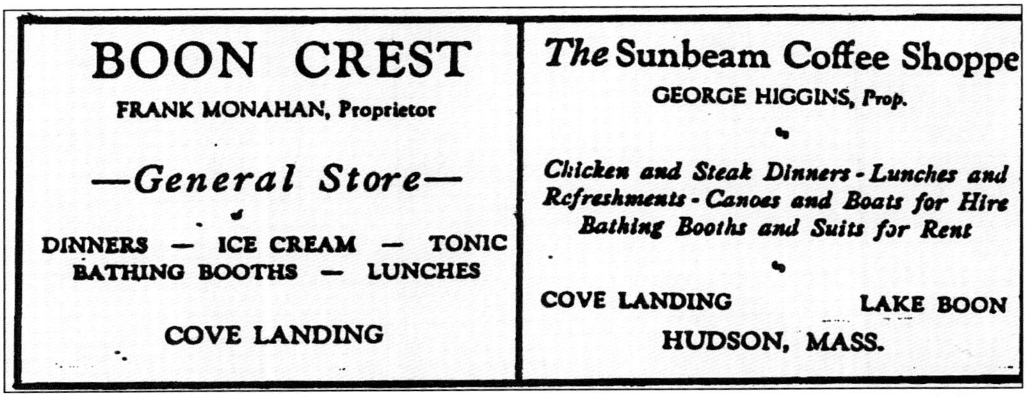

LET'S EAT OUT. Not all meals were prepared by the women at the cottage. On special days, a short walk would get you to one of the little coffee shops or restaurants dotting the lake where someone else would prepare and serve the food and even clean up afterwards. (Hudson.)

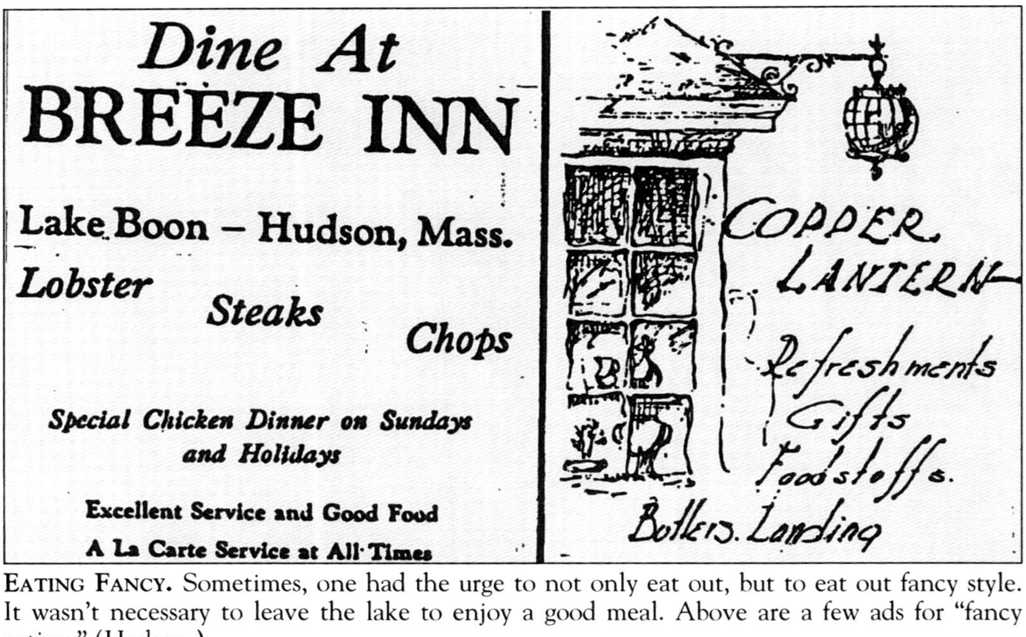

EATING FANCY. Sometimes, one had the urge to not only eat out, but to eat out fancy style. It wasn't necessary to leave the lake to enjoy a good meal. Above are a few ads for "fancy eating." (Hudson.)

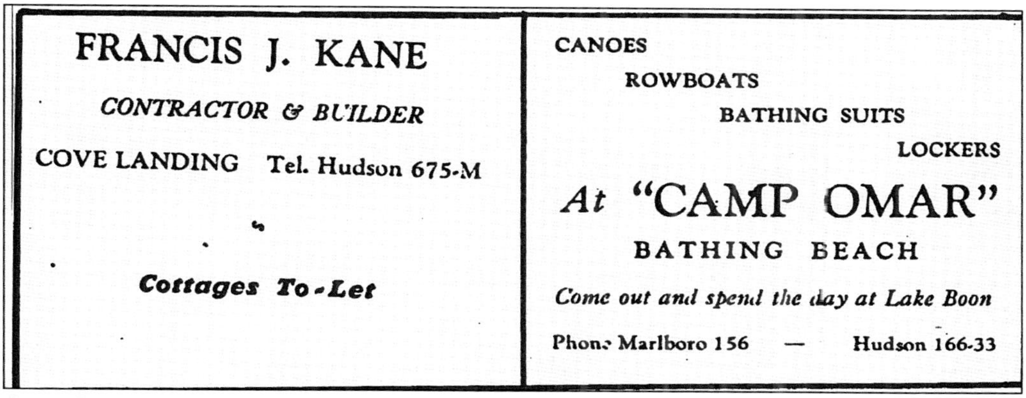

COZY COTTAGES FOR RENT. There were several areas around the lake where farm owners of adjacent lake-front land built cabins and rented them during the summer. The Parker and Kane family did a big business in cottage rentals, and the Barton family leased their land for others to build their own cottages. (Hudson.)

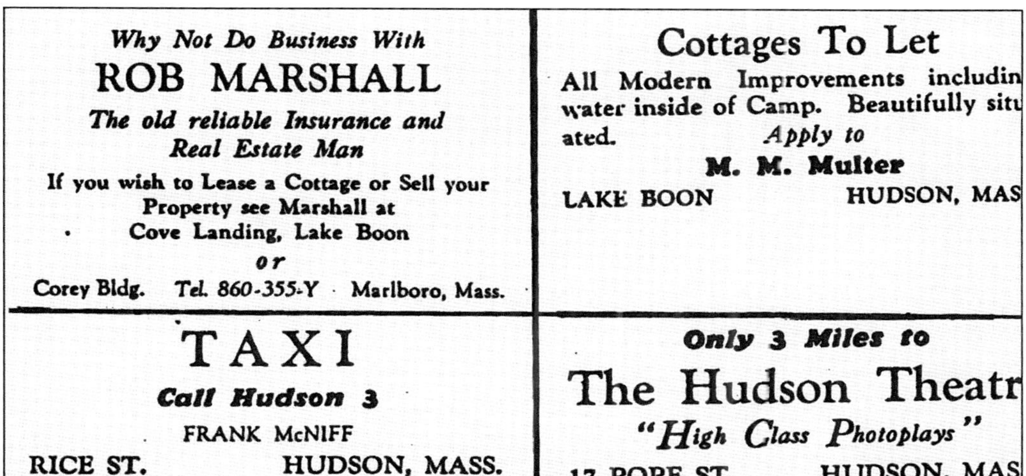

OTHER SERVICES. Vendors of services in nearby Hudson and Marlborough also advertised their businesses to the summer lake people. (Hudson.)

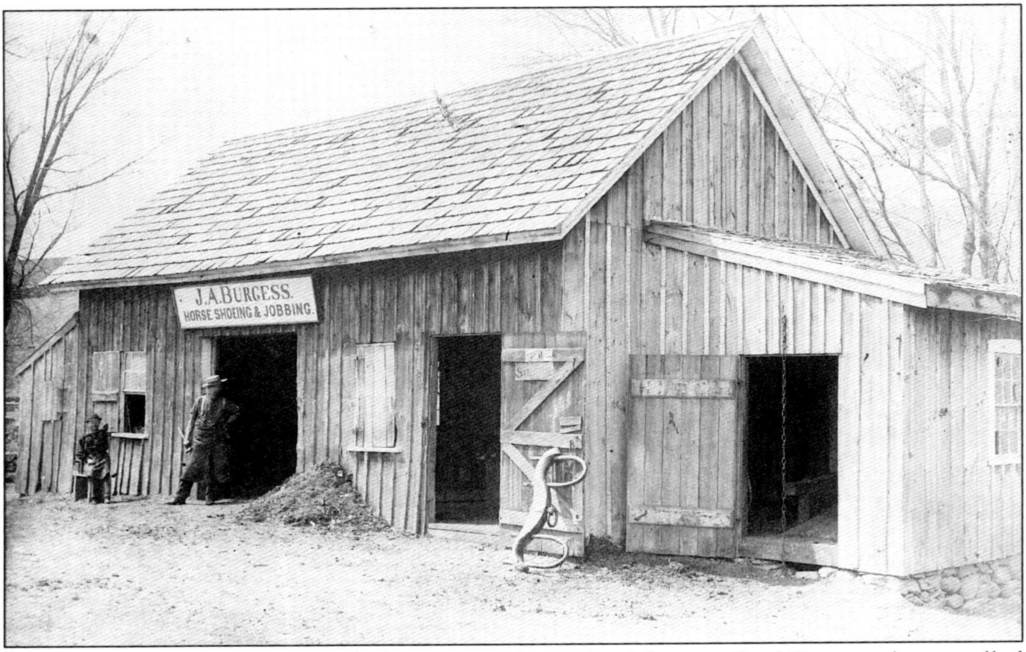

Blacksmith Burgess. Around the corner from the lake, in RockBottom (now called Gleasondale, a village within Stow), stood a substantial blacksmith's shop where one could have iron work done or horseshoes serviced. (Stow.)

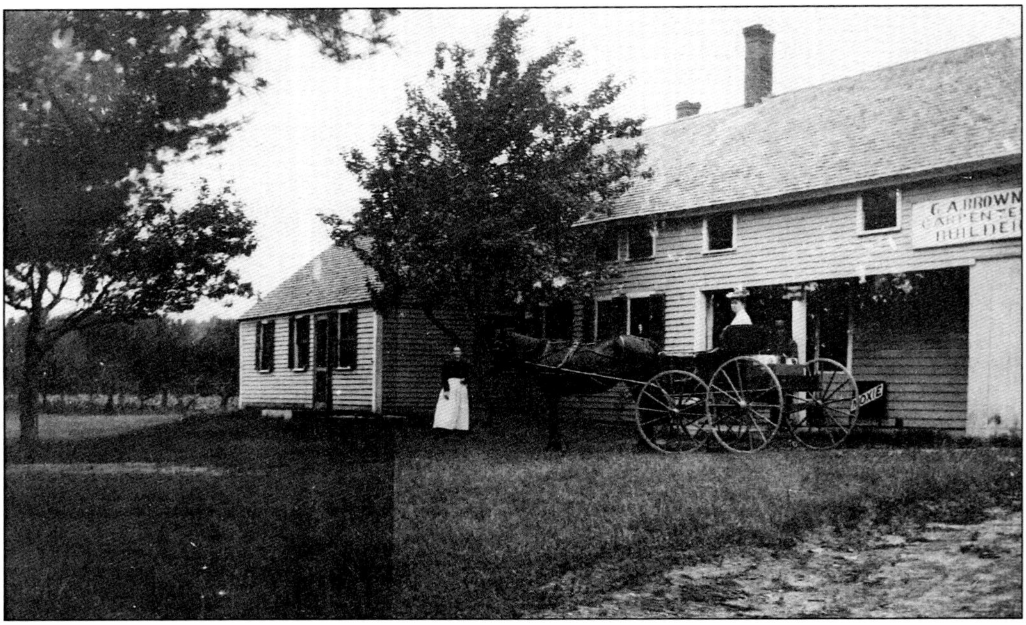

Builder and Carpenter. Also near the lake was the home, store, and barn of G.A. Brown, a carpenter and builder. He provided anything in wood from a simple bookcase to a complete cottage, and was kept busy during the summer by tasks from the lake folk. This is the site of the present Lake Boon Convenience Food Store. (Kattelle.)

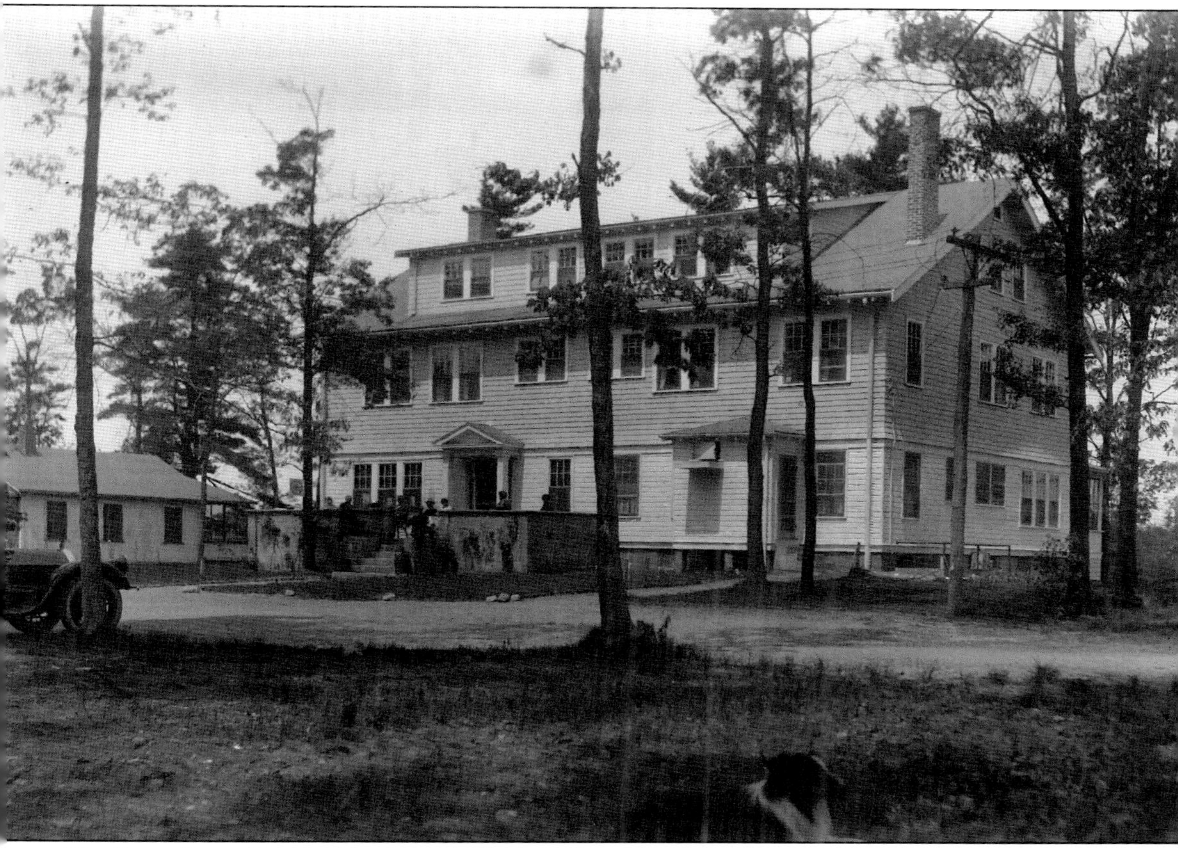

THE LAKE BOON LODGE. The lake also had a full-size hotel on the southern shore of the second basin. The Lake Boon Lodge was located on Lakeside Avenue in Hudson. It was very popular and was almost always full during the summer. Unfortunately, it burned down in January 1927 after only four short years of operation, and was not rebuilt. The following are articles taken from issues of the Hudson Daily Sun:

May, 1923. Bert Dooley was manager of the newly opened Lake Boon Lodge motel.
May, 1923. Boston college freshman class held their banquet and dance at Lake Boon Lodge. The day was spent playing baseball and foot racing, after which the boys enjoyed a swim in the lake.
July, 1923. The Twentieth Century club of Boston held their annual dinner at Lake Boon Lodge, Sunday.
Aug., 1923. The Ace of Clubs of Marlborough held a banquet and dance at Lake Boon Lodge. Sixty members were present.
Feb., 1926. Many winter merrymakers enjoyed the weekend at Lake Boon Lodge, including a toboggan slide that carried coasters clear across the lake.
Jan. 28, 1927. Lake Boon Lodge and the Alhambra cottage adjoining were totally destroyed by fire, and another owned by the Hurley estate of Marlborough was partially destroyed. The fire was of unknown origin, and the lodge was unoccupied at the time. The blaze was discovered soon after six o'clock and Mrs. Frank Wilson telephoned to Hudson for assistance. Engine 1 and the squad wagon responded. The flames had gained such headway that the lodge was doomed before the apparatus could reach there. The lodge had done a good business, being very popular with Boston people. The total loss will be upwards of $40,000. (Berry.)

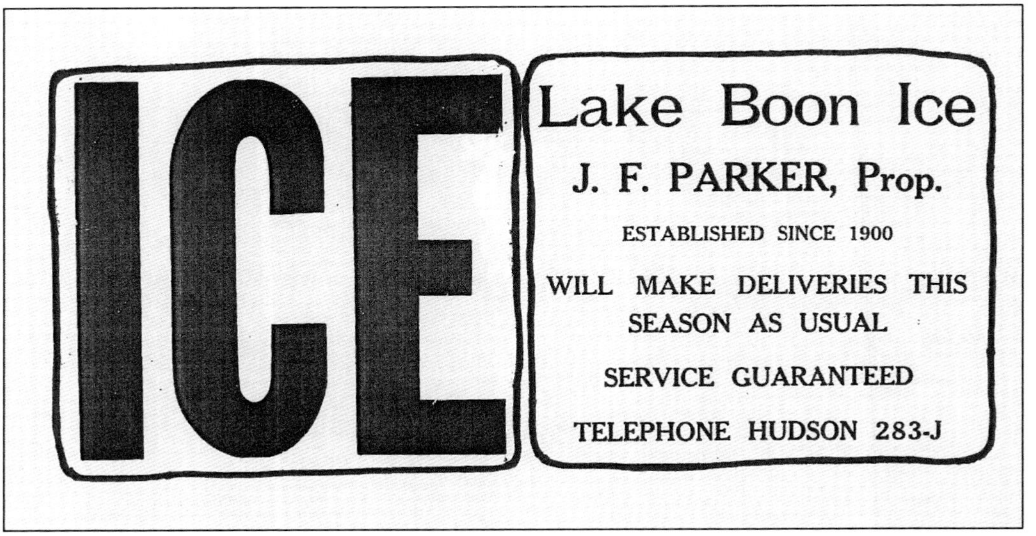

WE NEED ICE. Since the early lake residences were without electricity, the only means they had to keep food from spoiling was to put it into an ice box, which needed a fresh block of ice to be delivered every day or so. The ice trucks would circle the lake roads, and the cottages would display a 10-inch-square "ICE" sign in their front window if ice was needed. The Parkers had an icehouse on their property to store ice harvested from the lake in the winter and sell it to the lake people during the summer. (Halprin.)

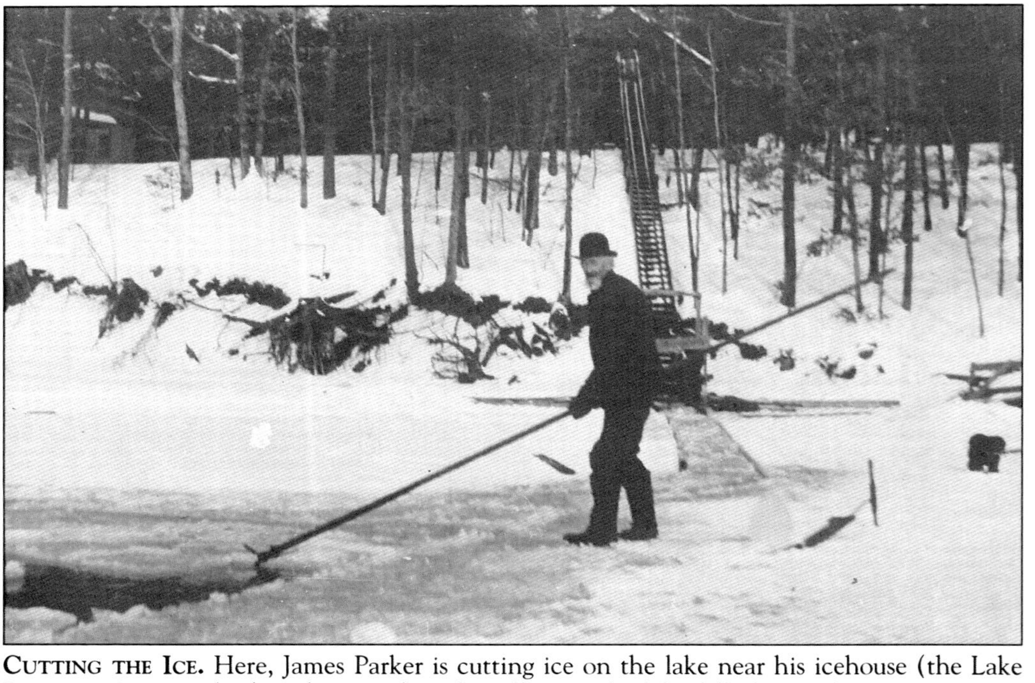

CUTTING THE ICE. Here, James Parker is cutting ice on the lake near his icehouse (the Lake Boon Ice Company) where he stored ice for selling to the lake folk during the summer. After the ice was cut away from the pack, it was dragged by a long pole over to the side of the lake and then to the conveyor (visible behind Mr. Parker) that carried it up to the icehouse on top of the bluff. (Kattelle.)

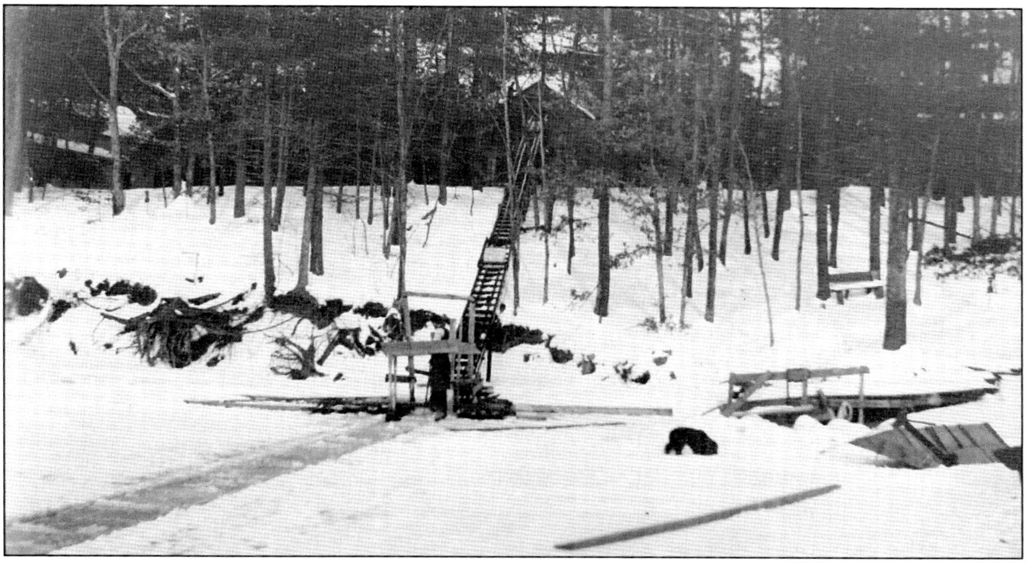

UP THE HILL YOU GO. Since the Parker Icehouse was at the top of a steep bank by the side of the lake, a conveyer was built that would haul the ice from the lake, up the side of the hill, to the second floor of the icehouse. This picture shows a block of ice on its way up the slope to the barn. (Kattelle.)

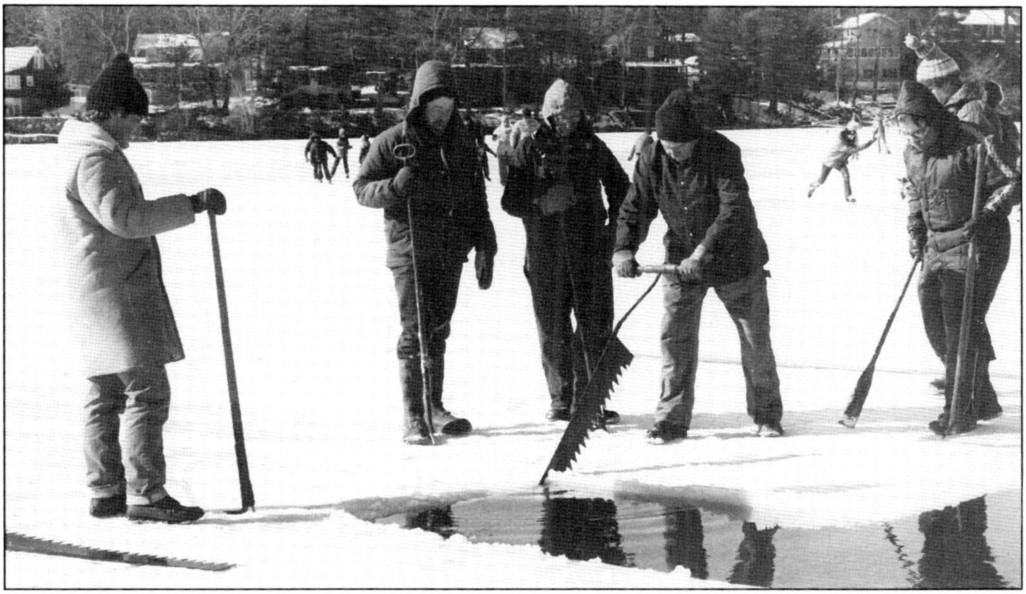

WHERE THE ICE CAME FROM. Lake Boon was a major producer of ice for use by nearby towns during the summer. During the winter, ice from the lake would be "harvested" by the local farmers, not unlike their fields would be harvested during the summer. The ice field would be divided into squares, carefully sawed away from the pack, then the blocks dragged to the shoreline for removal to the storage barn. This 1979 photograph shows a demonstration of the ice-cutting process and was sponsored by the Collings Foundation. The men, from left to right, are as follows: Bob Collings, Don Rising, Frannie Warren, Herb Potter, and Eric Sonnichsen. Note the kids ice skating in the background. (Stow.)

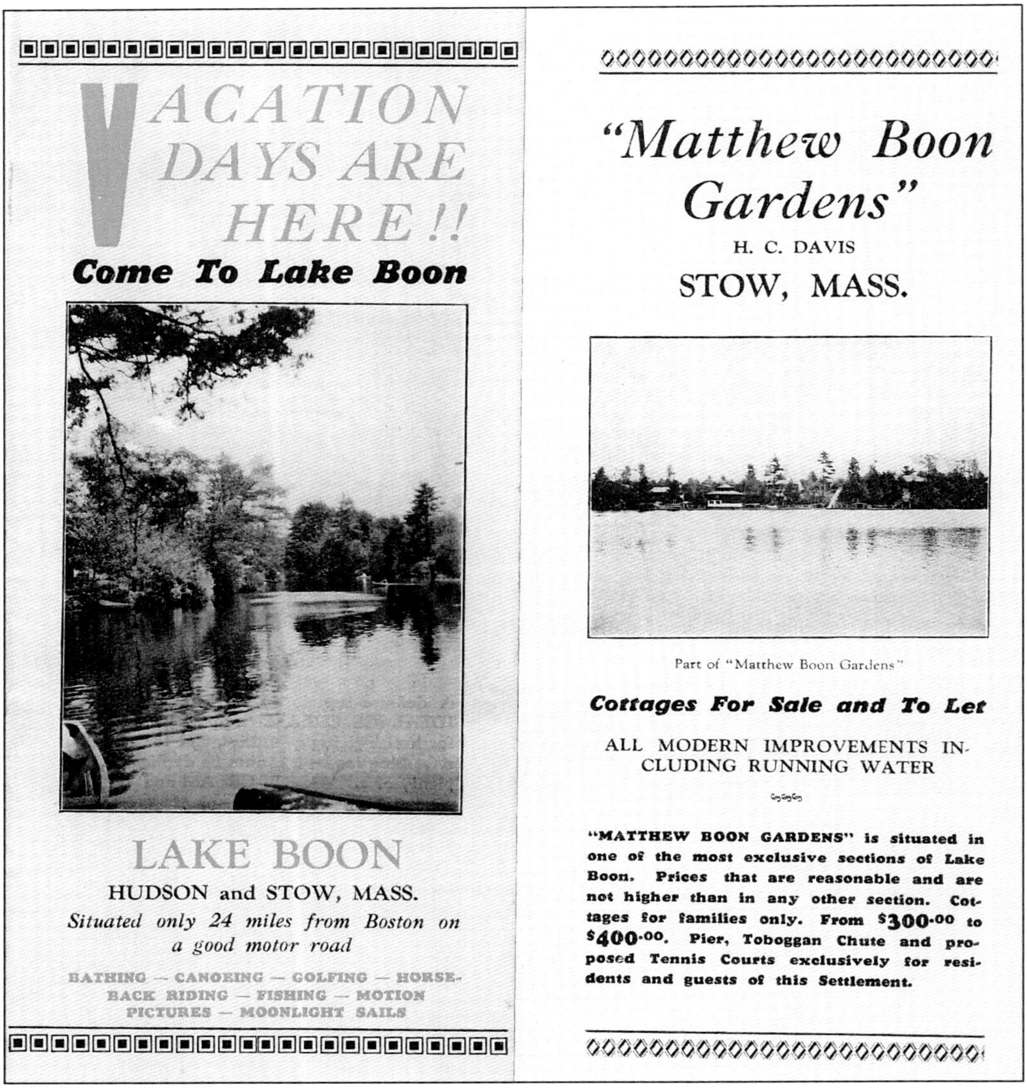

Some Lake Areas Were Said to Be Better Than Others. This advertisement implies that Lake Boon was a better place to spend the summer then other lakes, and that some parts of the lake were better then other parts. Ads such as this one appeared in a booklet published by the Metropolitan Advertising Service of Marlborough, Massachusetts, probably sometime in the 1920s. Matthew Boon Gardens was built and operated by Harry C. Davis, who came to the lake in 1904 and gave his name to Davis Road. (Hudson.)

Six

LAZY DAYS AT THE LAKE

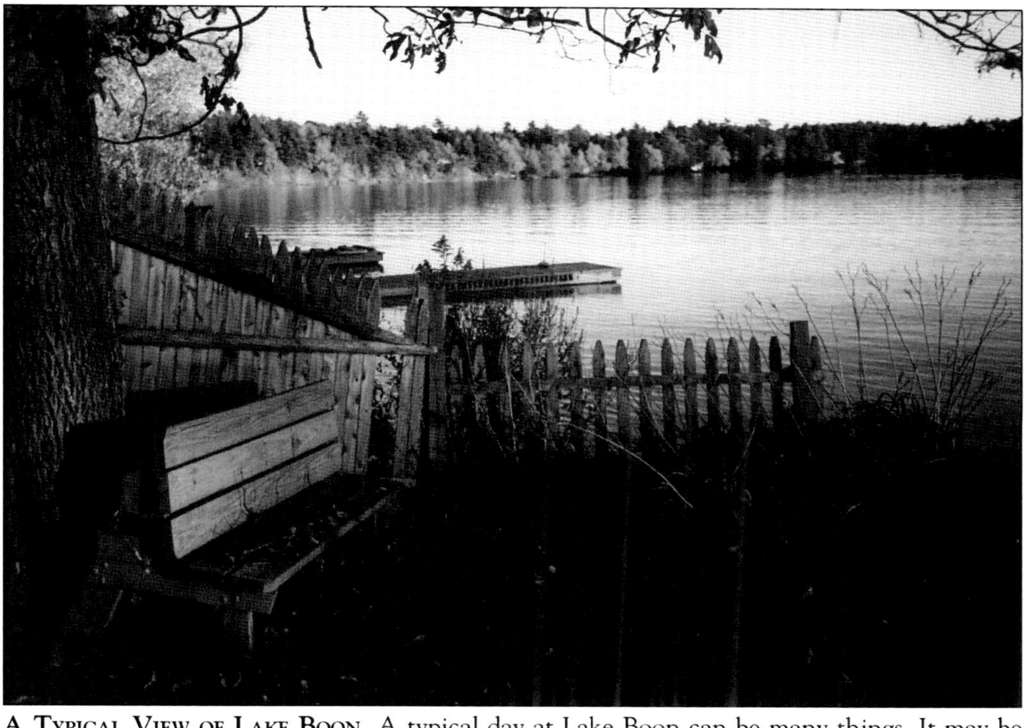

A TYPICAL VIEW OF LAKE BOON. A typical day at Lake Boon can be many things. It may be just a lazy day when the sun is warm, the wind is calm, and there is no place you would rather be doing nothing. Or there is the companionship of family or friends spending the summer just doing lake things. Or maybe it is a bit of sailing, strolling, hiking, fishing, canoeing, swimming, rowing, or just sitting by the dock watching the ducks go by. (Halprin.)

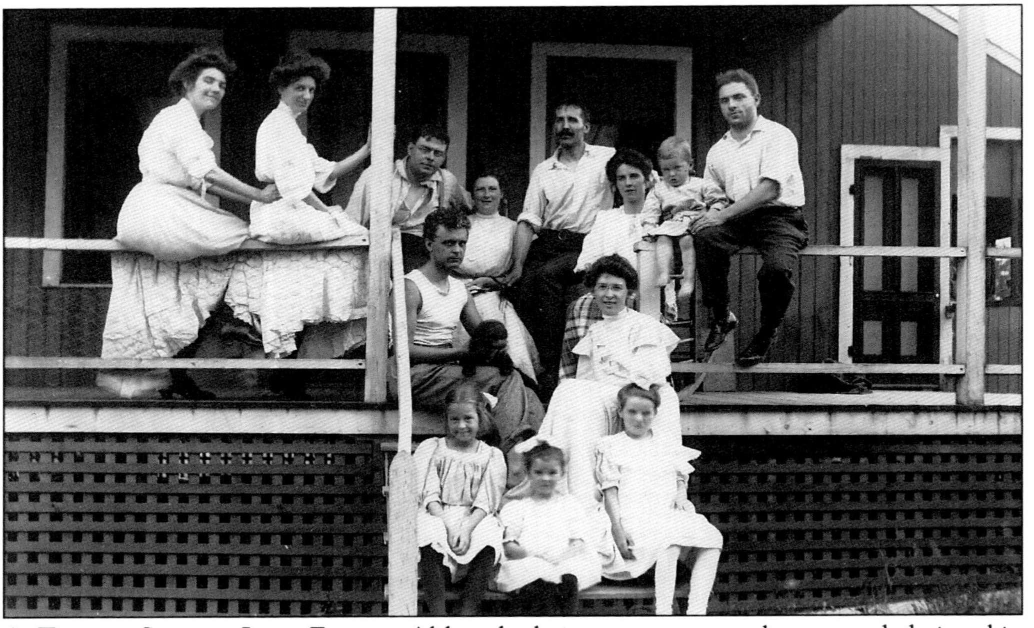

A Typical Summer Lake Family. Although their names are not known and their cabin location is a mystery, we know from the photograph that they are spending the summer at Lake Boon, and we can guess from the formal (almost) clothing they are wearing that it was prior to 1920. (Berry.)

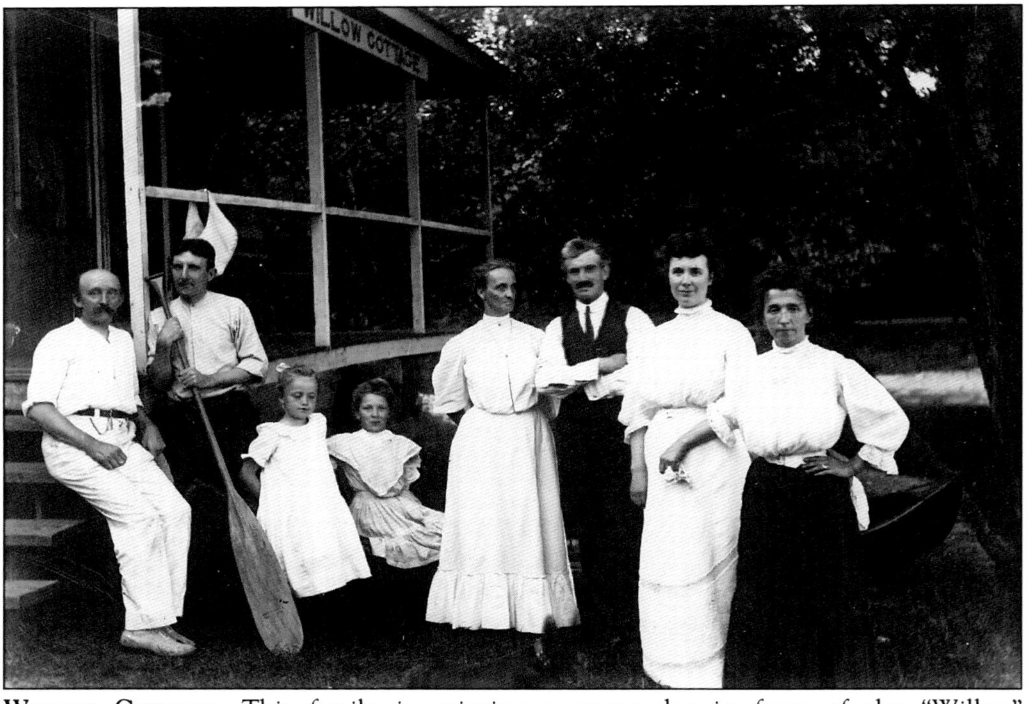

Willow Cottage. This family is enjoying a sunny day in front of the "Willow" cottage. (Berry.)

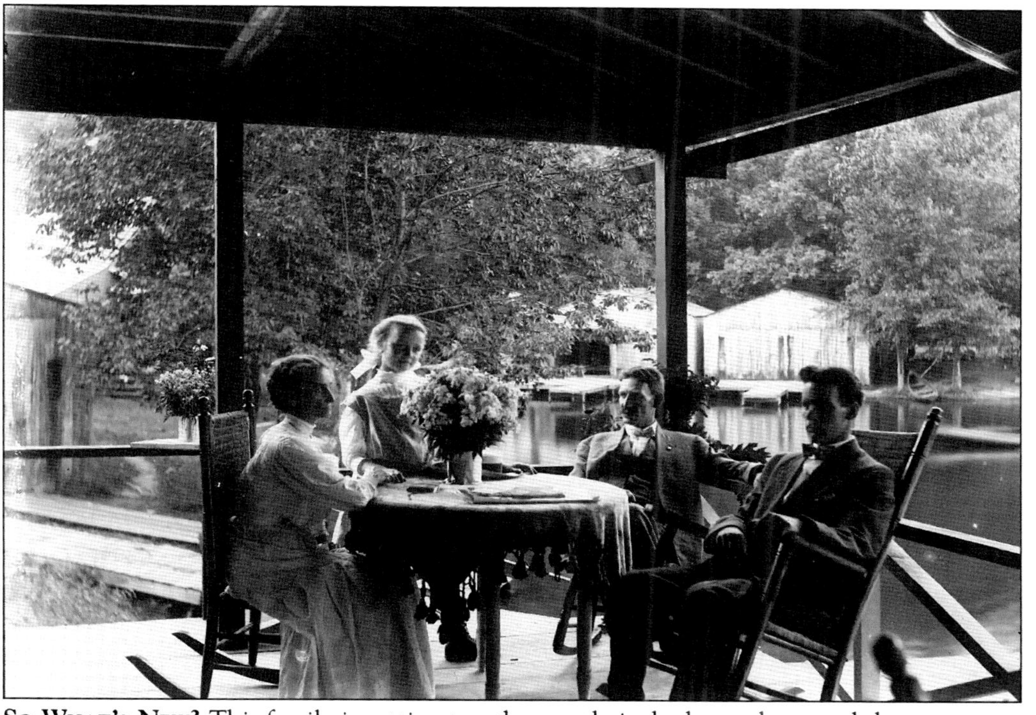

So What's New? This family is getting together on their shady porch to read the newspaper and play a few hands of cards. The location of the cottage might be in Boon Cove. (Berry.)

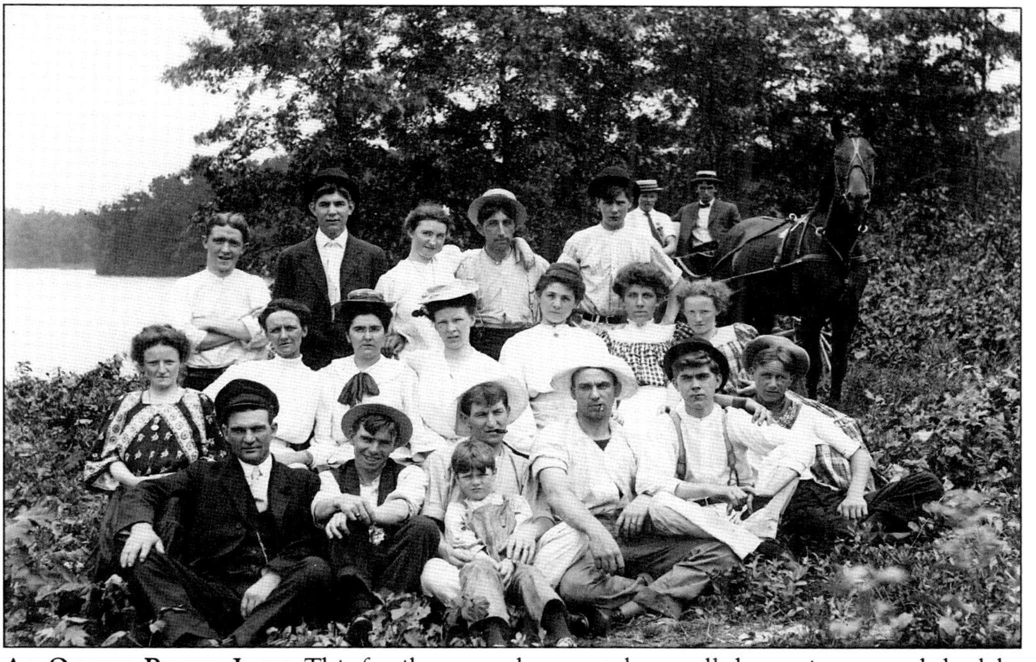

An Outing By the Lake. This family group chose to take an all-day outing around the lake assisted by their trusty horse and wagon. (Berry.)

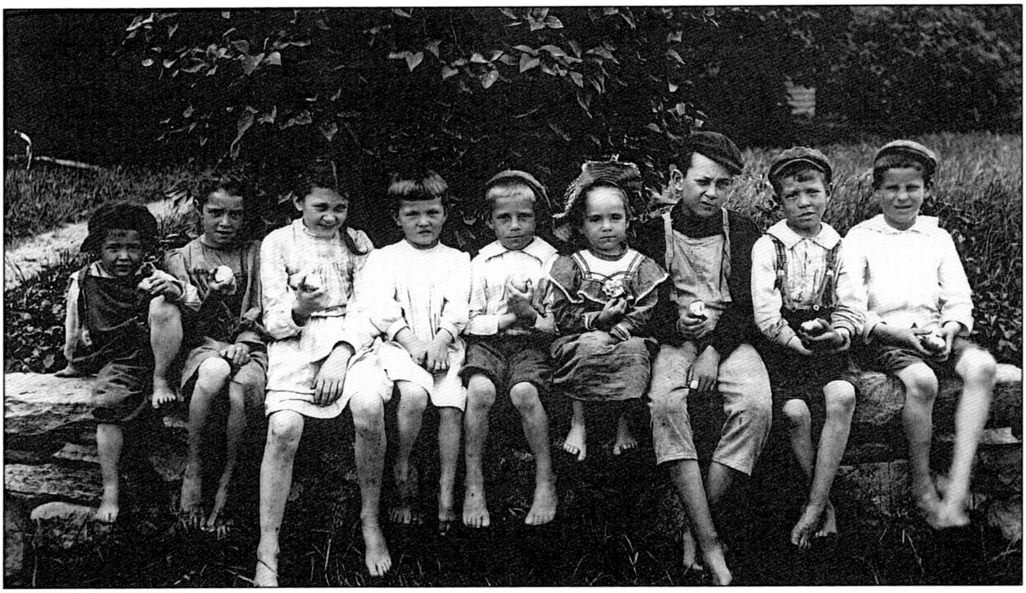

Our Gang. The neighborhood gang poses in front of the Beede farm (1902) near Lake Boon. From left to right are as follows: Art and Bertha Underwood, Helen Barton, Helen Parker, Donald and Emily Priest, Donald Barton, Walter Underwood, and Harold Priest. (Halprin.)

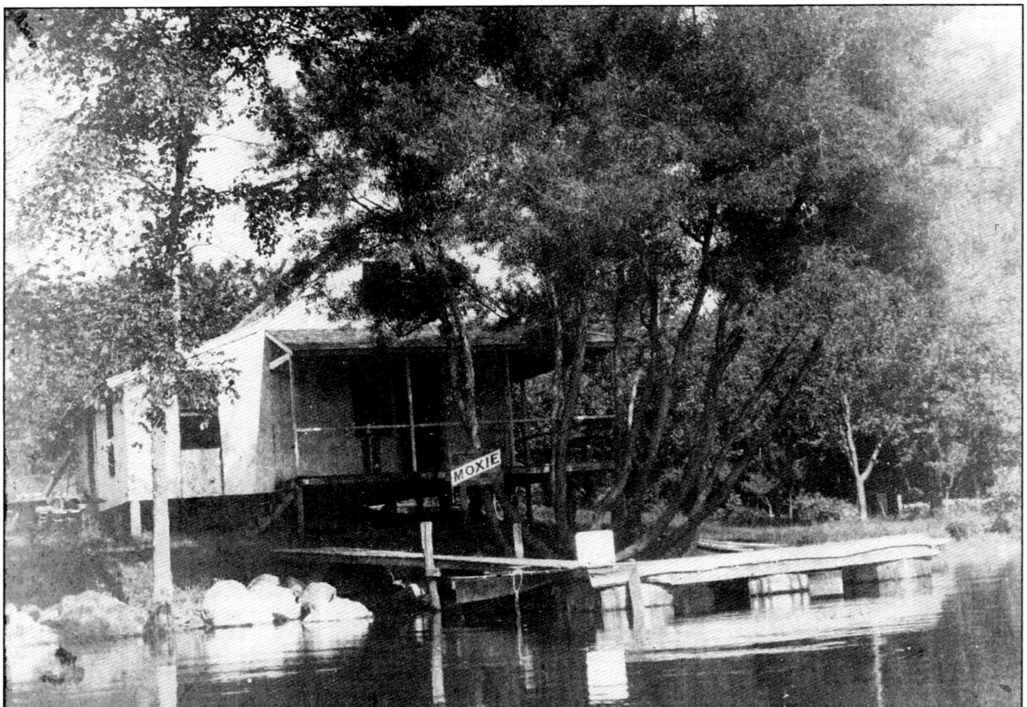

Steamer Landing. This lakeside store (1898) was the primary landing dock for the steamer, *Cleo*, and later for the gasoline-powered boat, the *Princess*. The sign on the tree says "MOXIE" (of course). (Kattelle.)

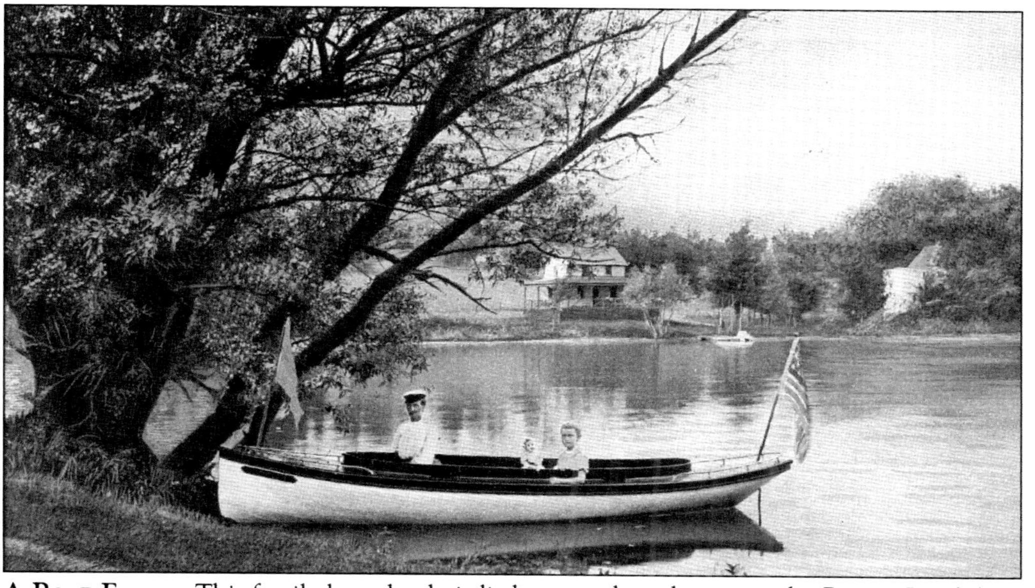

A Boat Family. This family brought their little motor launch over to the Barton Road dam. Boon Hill and Pine Point Road are showing in the distance. (Halprin.)

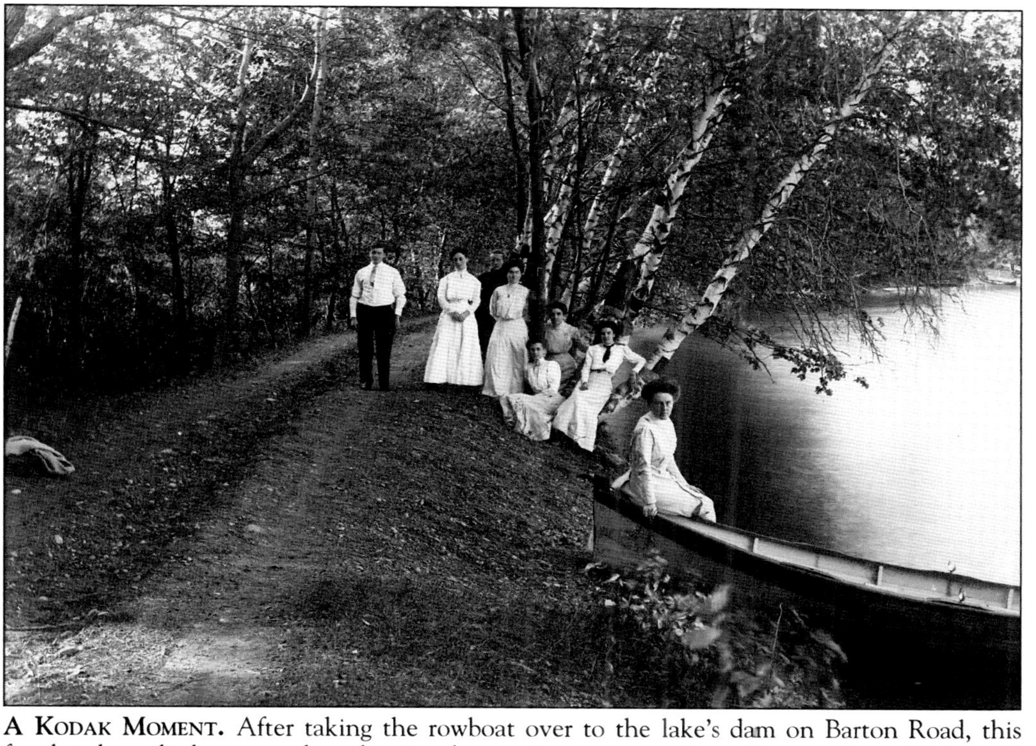

A Kodak Moment. After taking the rowboat over to the lake's dam on Barton Road, this family takes a little rest, perhaps hoping that an ice-cream vendor will come along. This small strand of birch trees is a favorite spot for photographers. (Berry.)

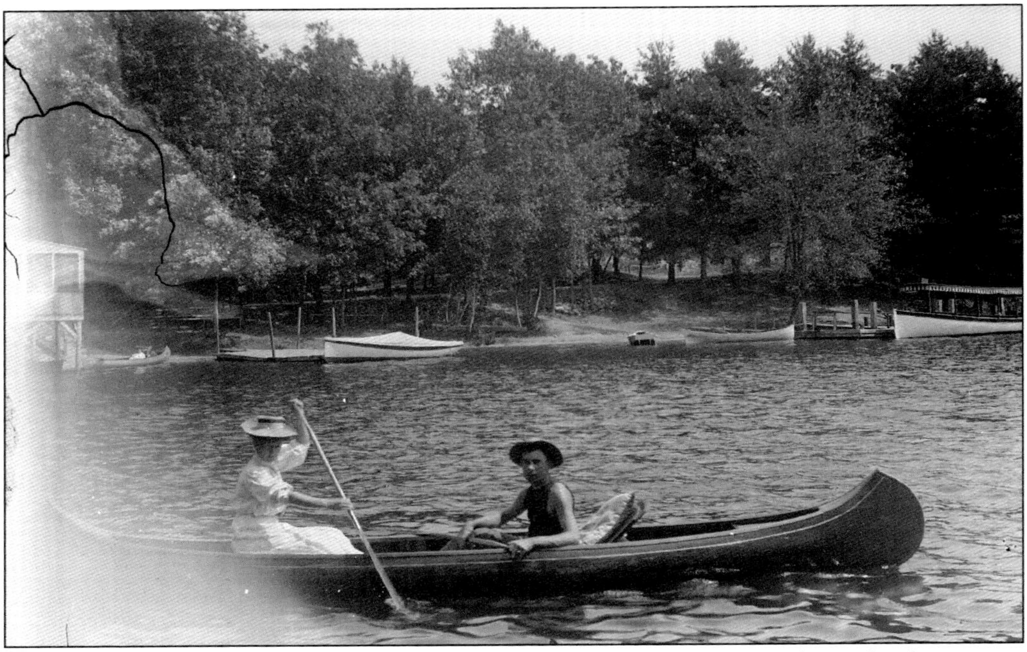

Row Harder. Paddlers take a lazy stroll down the lake in the canoe. Obviously, the woman doing all the paddle work is the man's wife. The *Princess* is in the background. (Berry.)

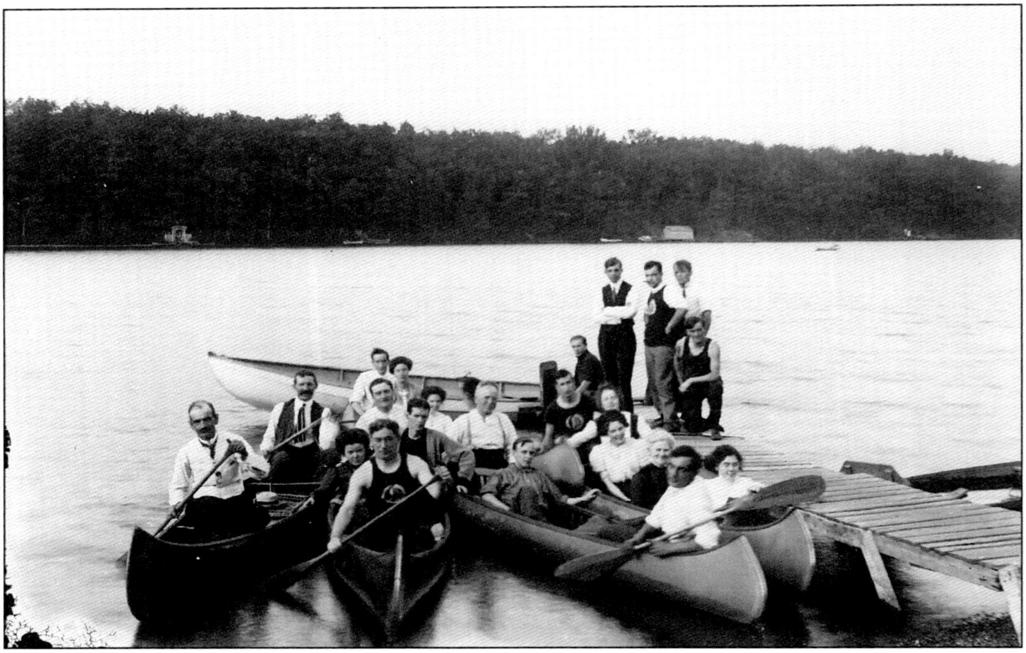

All Aboard. The canoes are loaded and all are ready to start a group canoe trip around the lake. The four men on the dock will keep up with the canoes in their rowboat, probably carrying the picnic baskets. (Berry.)

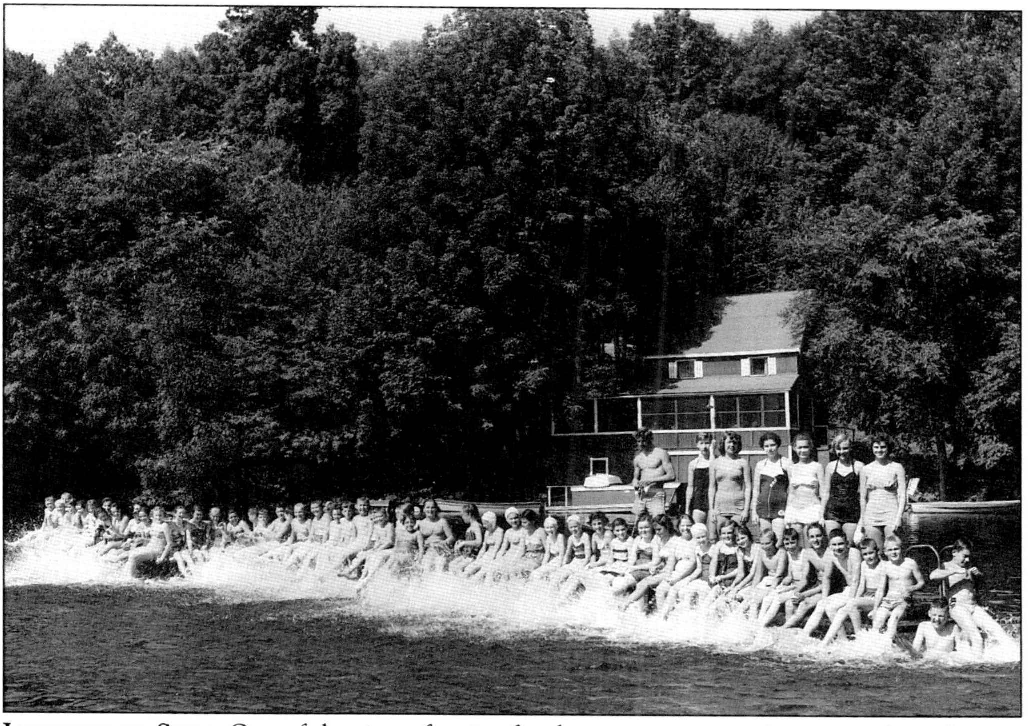

LEARNING TO SWIM. One of the rites of spring for the younger generation was to learn how to swim at Hanson's (Rooney's) Beach. Here is a typically large group of kids that made up the swim class kicking up a fuss in the lake water. Behind them are their teachers.

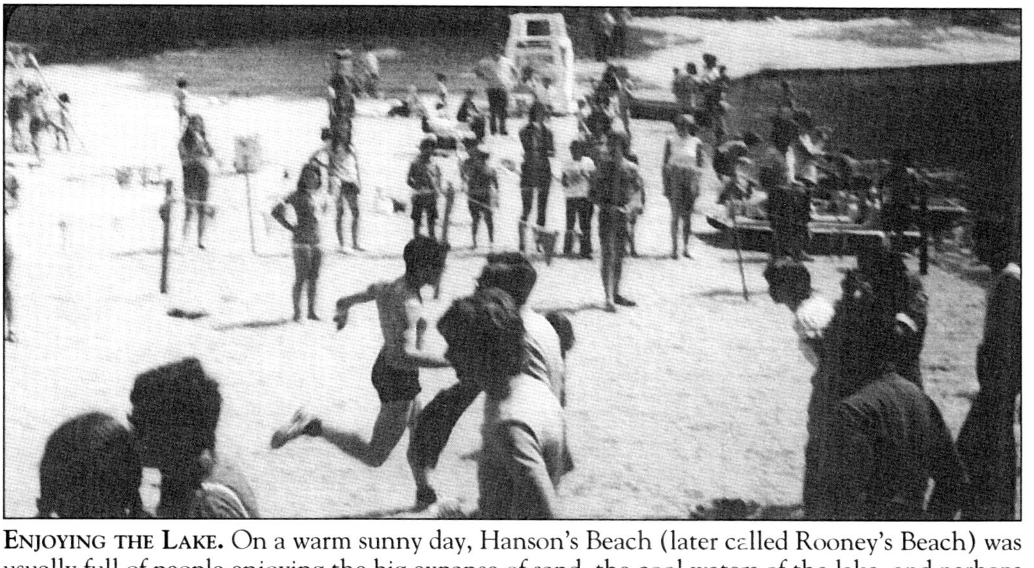

ENJOYING THE LAKE. On a warm sunny day, Hanson's Beach (later called Rooney's Beach) was usually full of people enjoying the big expanse of sand, the cool waters of the lake, and perhaps a leisurely canoe ride. Summer membership was required and the beach provided a great way for nearby people who did not live on the lake to still be able to enjoy all that it had to offer.

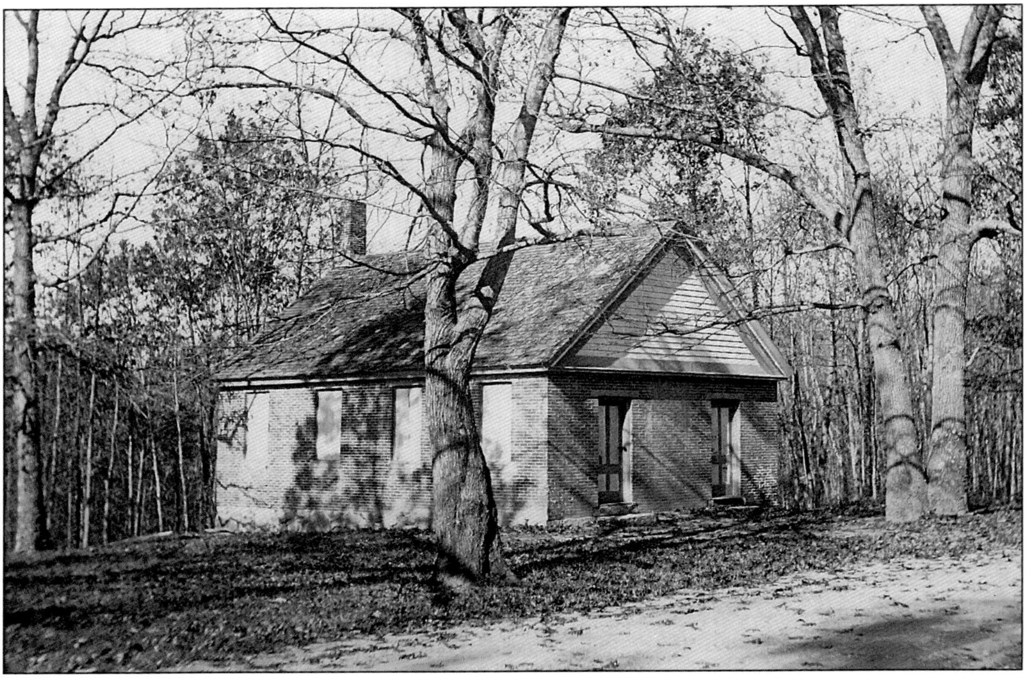

School Bells. This schoolhouse, the Grove School on the corner of Gleasondale Road and Boon Road, since torn down, provided education for the children that lived year-round near the lake, and was one of five schoolhouses located around the town of Stow. (Stow.)

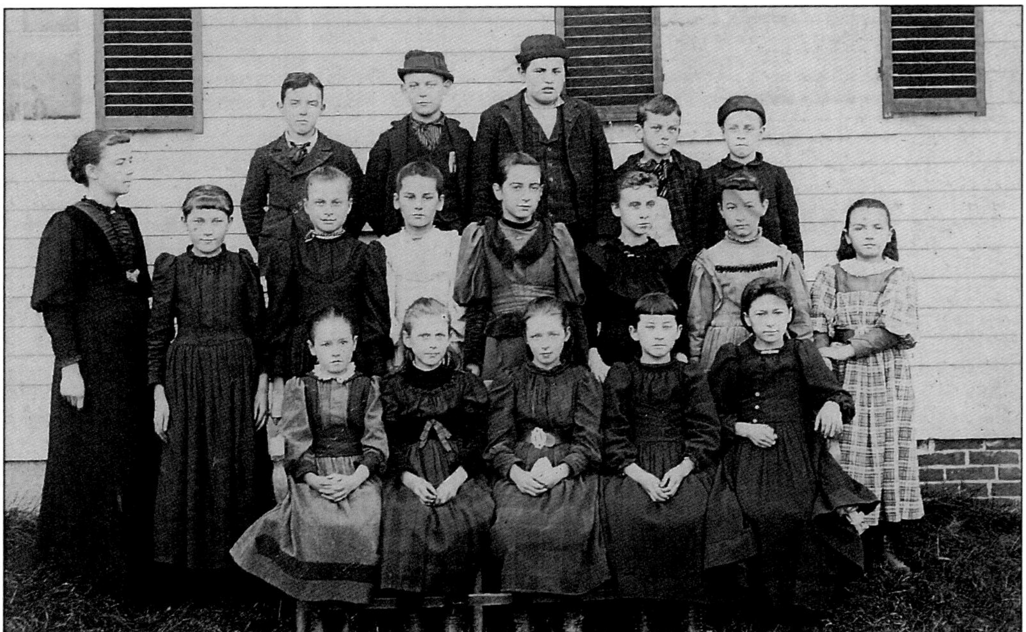

School Kids. The teacher and her students, all dressed in their finest, take a break from their studies by the side of their schoolhouse. (Stow.)

Seven

WINTER SHIVERS

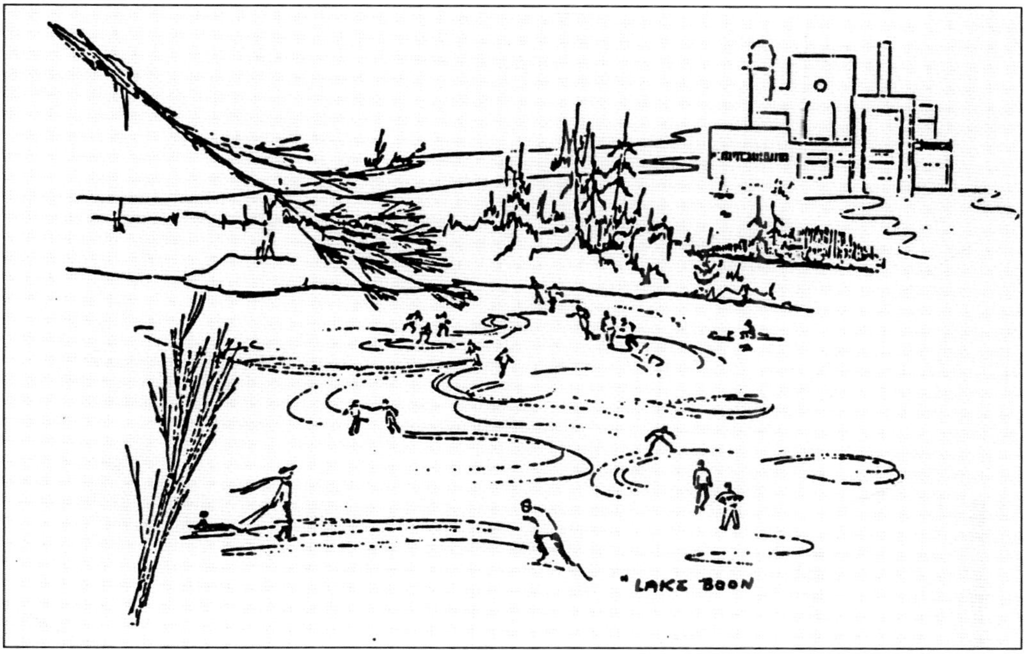

DRAWING ON WINTER. The lake doesn't stop when the summer people go home. Some of the more hardy people stay year-round, and even the summer people were known to make winter trips to their cottages on sunny winter weekends to experience a different life. This drawing, by lake resident Marika Barnett, captures some of the life that exists on the lake during the winter.

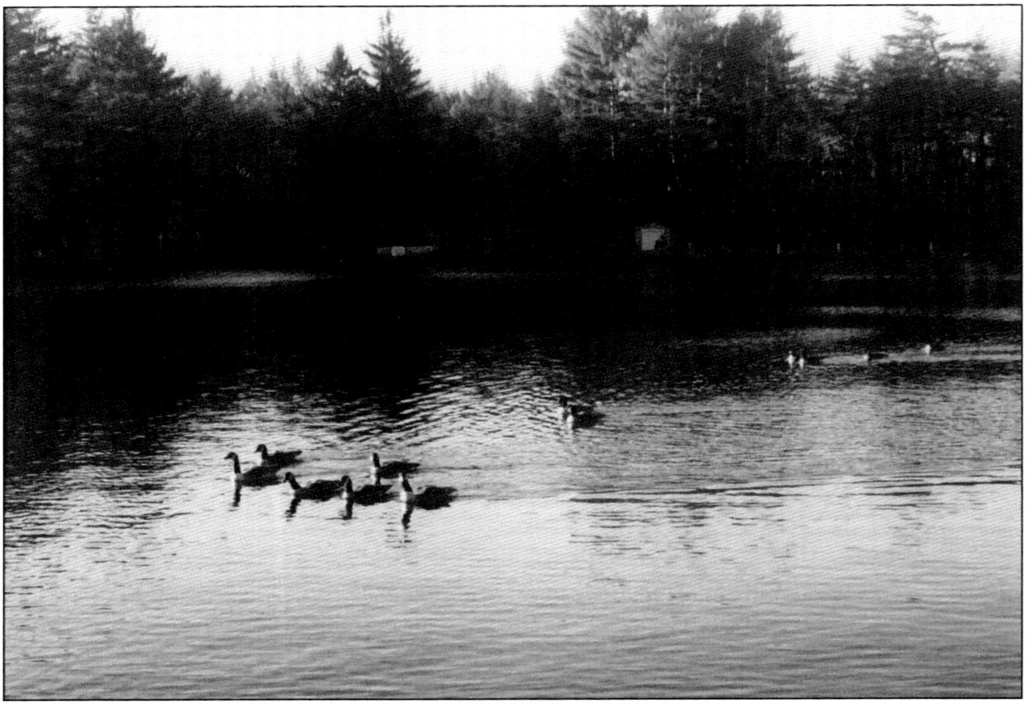

Geese Heading Home. In the fall, the Canadian Geese head to their winter homes in the south, but many make a stop on the safety of Lake Boon in order to rest for the night. (Halprin.)

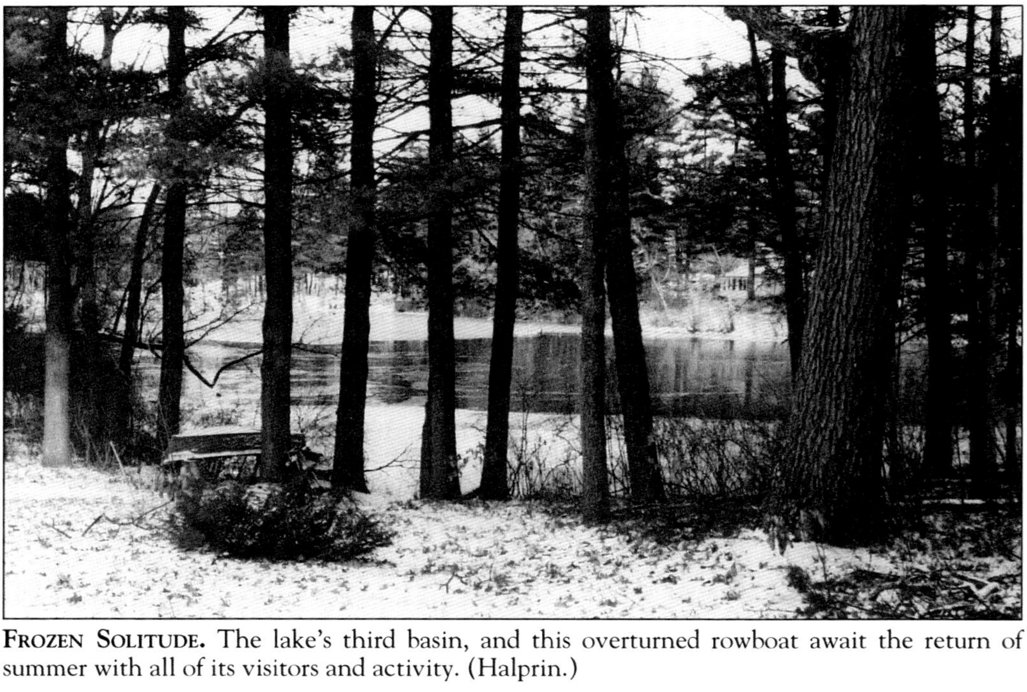

Frozen Solitude. The lake's third basin, and this overturned rowboat await the return of summer with all of its visitors and activity. (Halprin.)

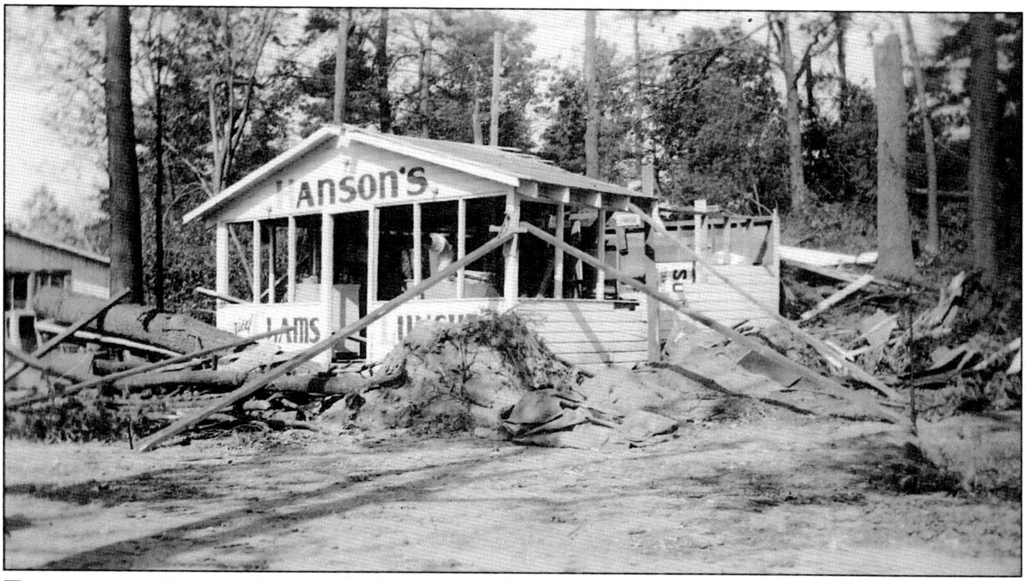

Temporarily Closed. During the hurricane of October 1938, a great deal of damage was done to the Lake Boon area, especially the trees. The snack cabin at Hanson's Beach was also a casualty of the hurricane. (Jackson.)

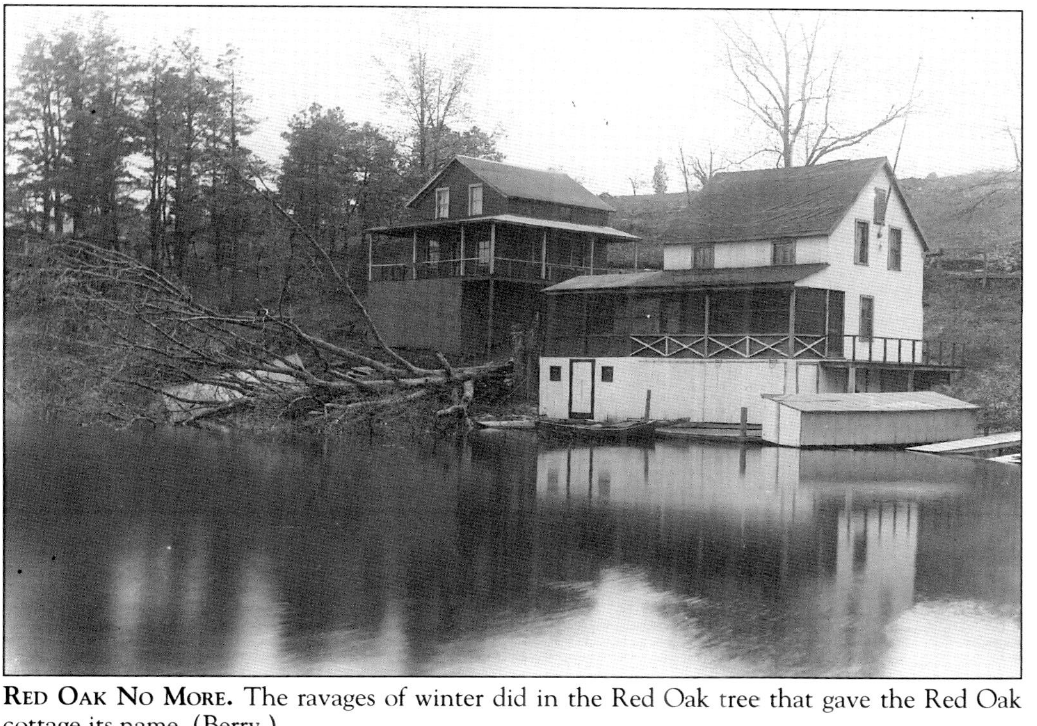

Red Oak No More. The ravages of winter did in the Red Oak tree that gave the Red Oak cottage its name. (Berry.)

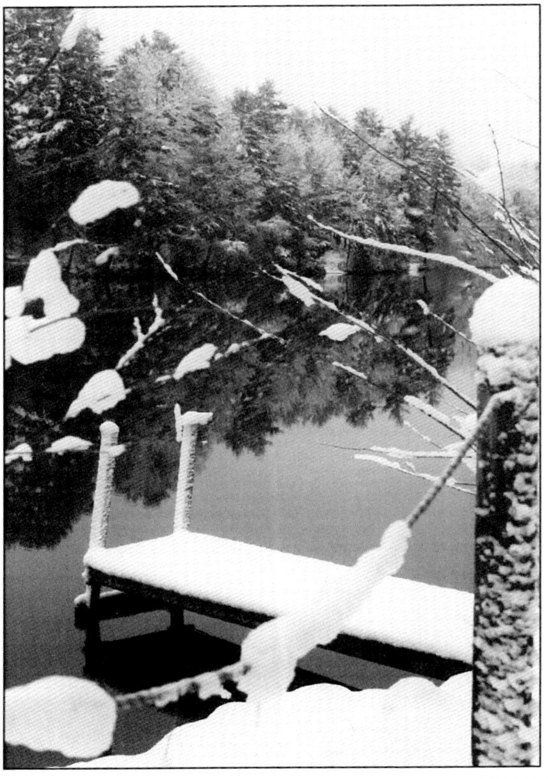

First Snow. This lake is not yet frozen, but the dock's cover of white snow indicates that winter is definitely here. (Halprin.)

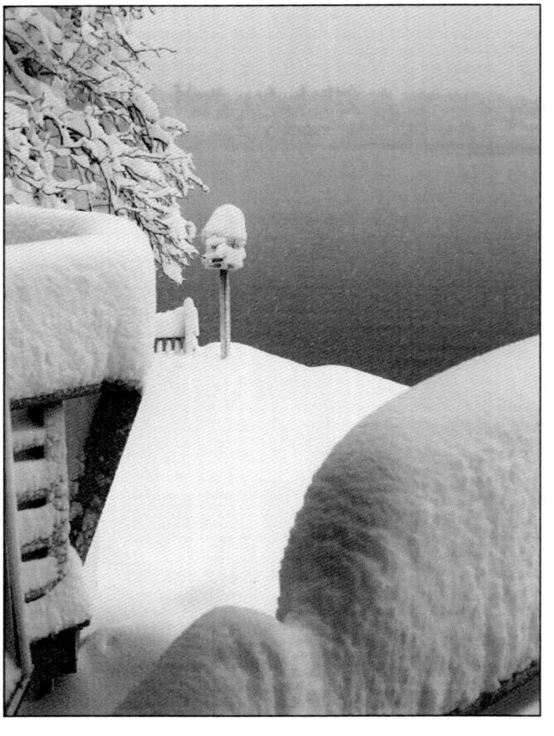

Deep Snow. Twenty-four inches of white crunchy snow around the lake stand in stark contrast to summer green. (Halprin.)

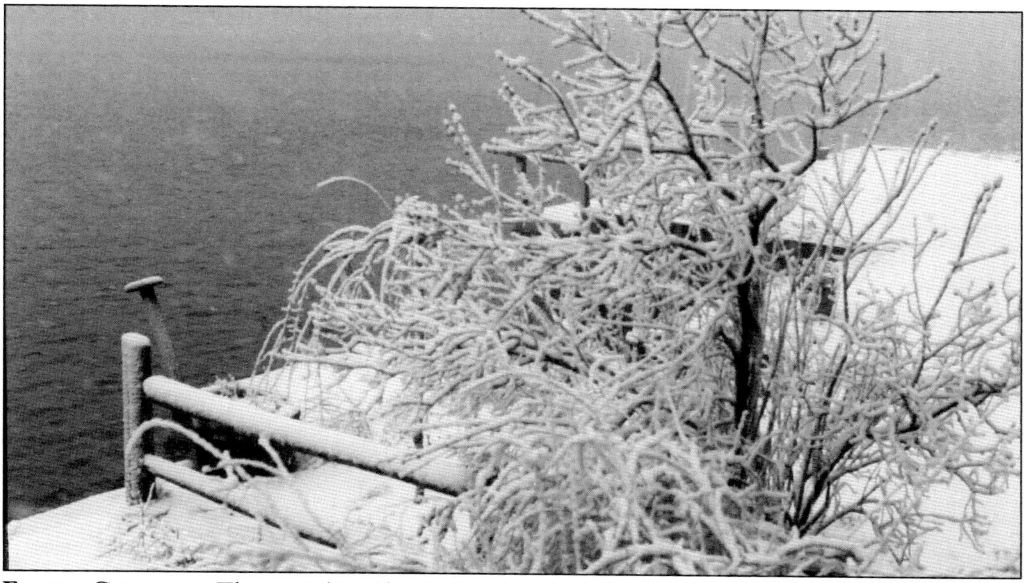

Frozen Greenery. The trees have long since lost their leaves and all traces of green, and they now show off a winter cover of snow glazed with clear ice. (Halprin.)

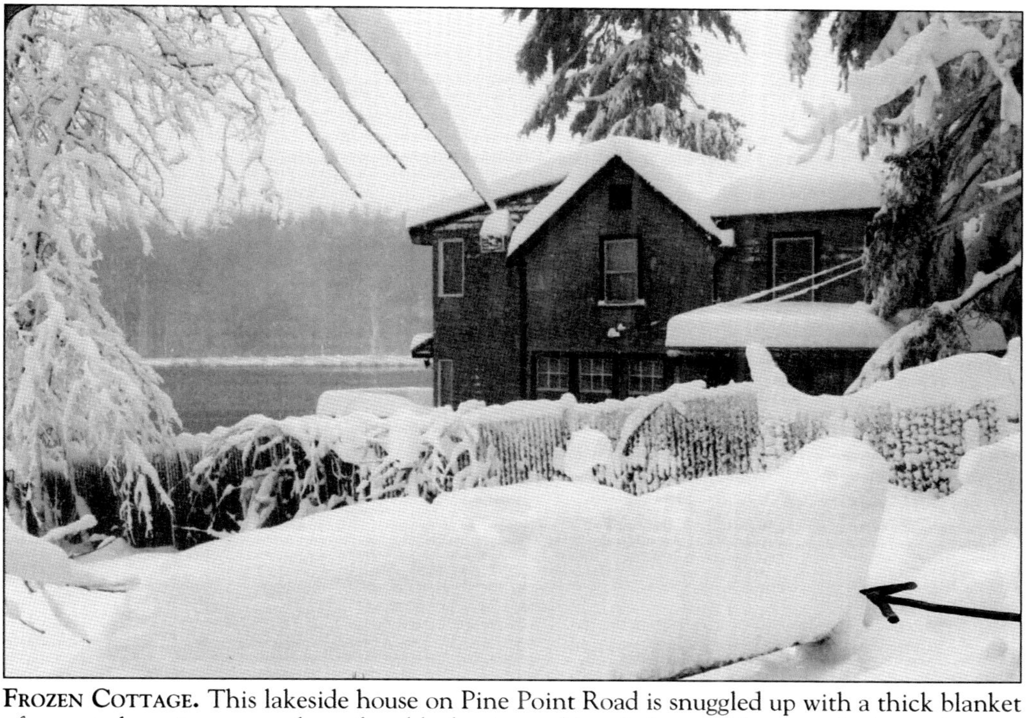

Frozen Cottage. This lakeside house on Pine Point Road is snuggled up with a thick blanket of snow to keep it warm and comfortable, but it would probably not object to the heavy load on its roof being removed and replaced with warm sunshine. (Halprin.)

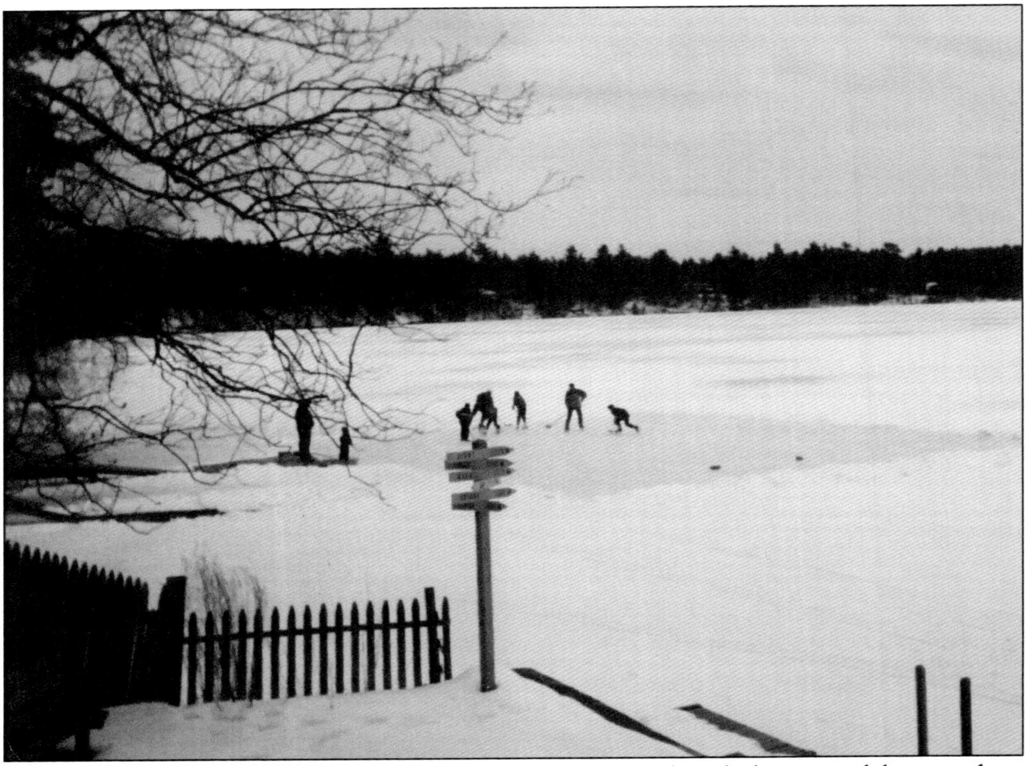

PLAYING WITH A BIG STICK. After a little work with a snow shovel, the winter lake provides a perfect ice rink for playing ice hockey. Here a group of kids get together on the lake after school to have a quick game. (Halprin.)

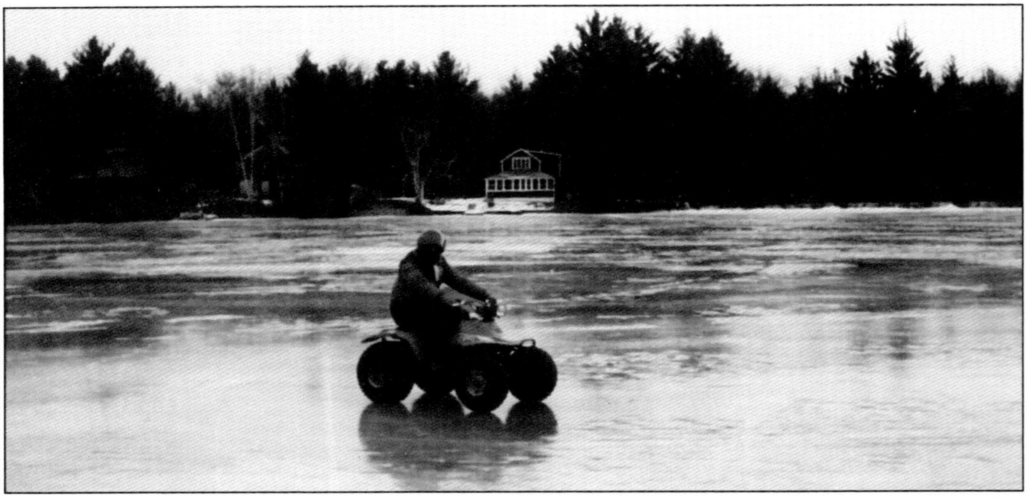

ICE RUNNING. Iceboats are not the only "vehicles" that take advantage of the winter lake. Here a four-wheel recreation vehicle zips over the wide expanses of clear ice on a cold sunny day. (Halprin.)

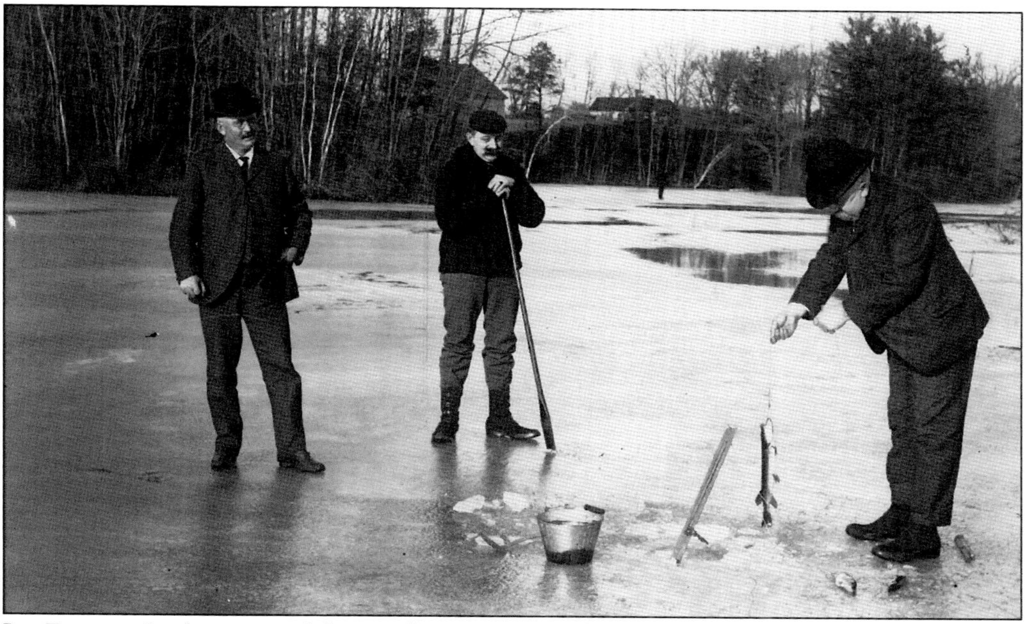

Ice Fishing. In the winter, fishing still continues on the lake, only it is necessary to cut a hole into the ice and tempt the lethargic fish to try out your treat. It is slow and cold work, but when a bite occurs, the reward seems much greater then summer fishing. (Berry.)

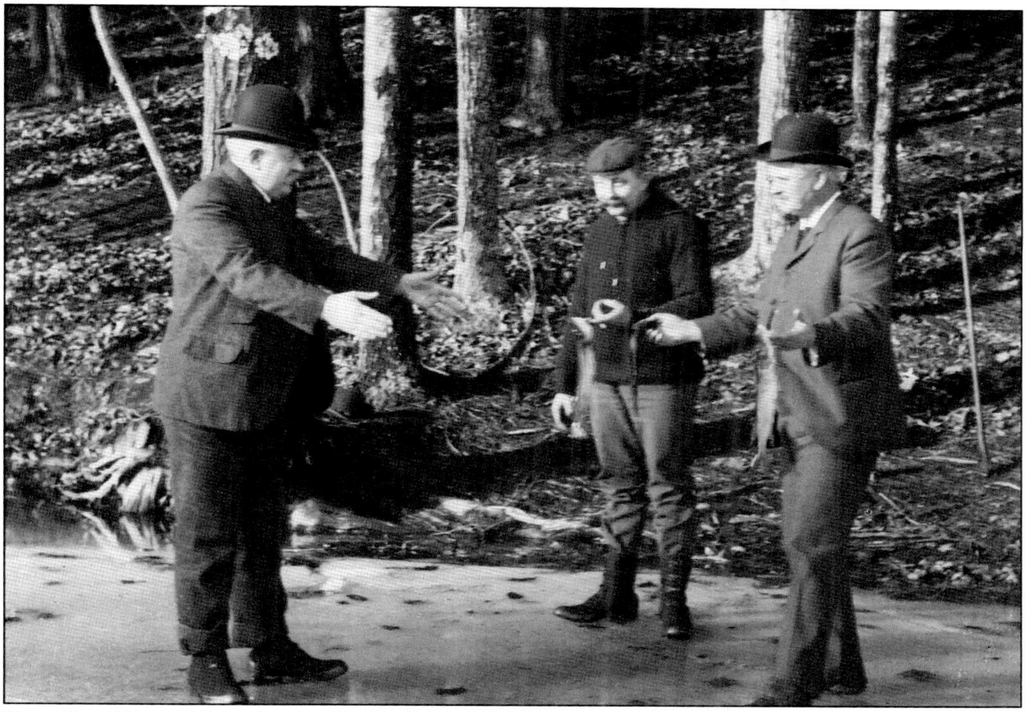

The One That Got Away. Two of the fishermen are showing off their meager catch from under the ice, while the third is describing how big the fish was that got away at the last minute. (Berry.)

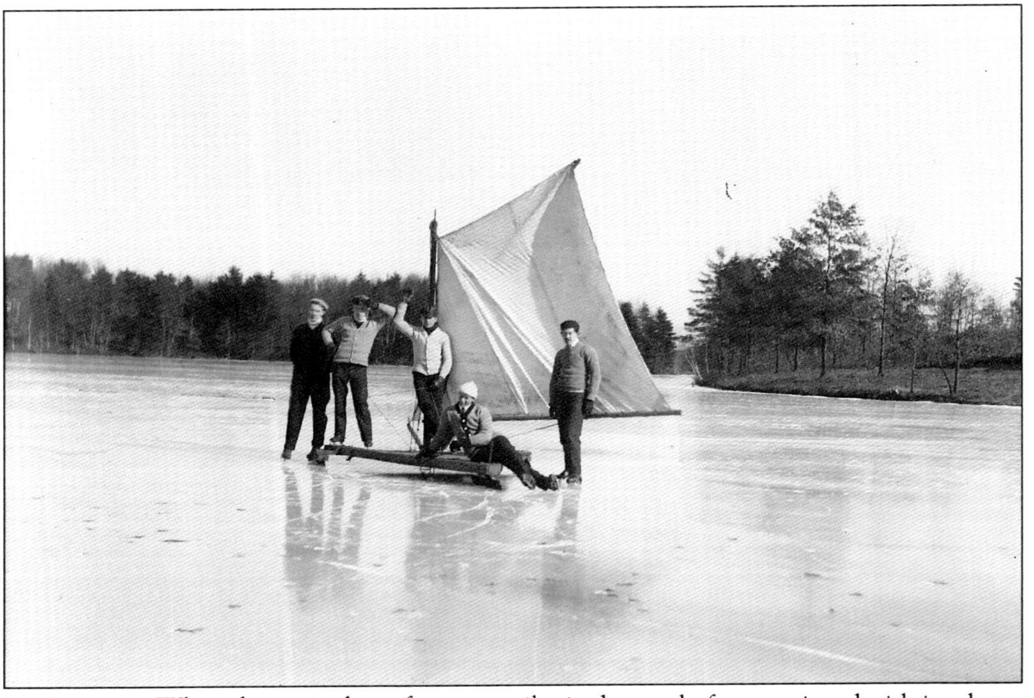

Ice Boating. When the ice is clear of snow, a sail raised on a platform equipped with ice skates becomes a great iceboat. With the right wind, such a boat can travel from one side of the lake to the other in just a few minutes at a very high rate of speed. (Berry.)

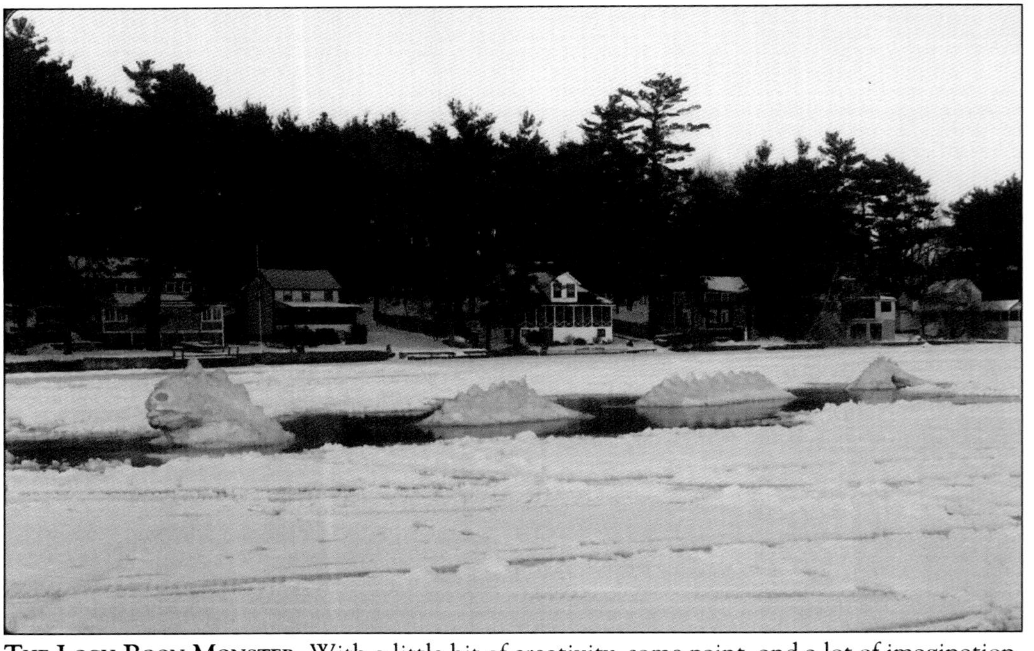

The Loch Boon Monster. With a little bit of creativity, some paint, and a lot of imagination, one is able to get the Lake Boon Monster to rise and show itself during Christmas Day. (It also helps when the lake has several ice sculptors as neighbors.) (Halprin.)

Eight

Modern Times

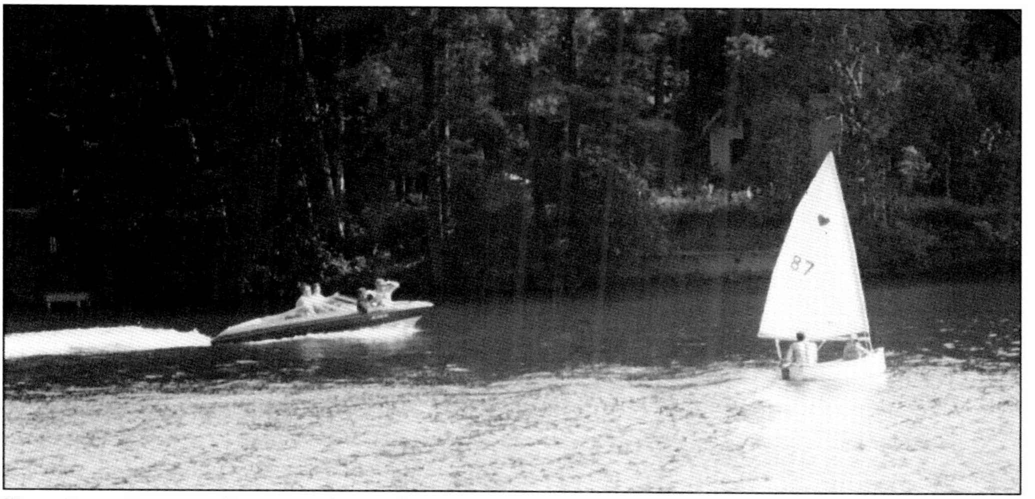

Tiny Sail. Some sailboats are big, others resemble a bathtub with a sheet for a sail. But the fun is just as good and maybe even better if the boat is small. (Halprin.)

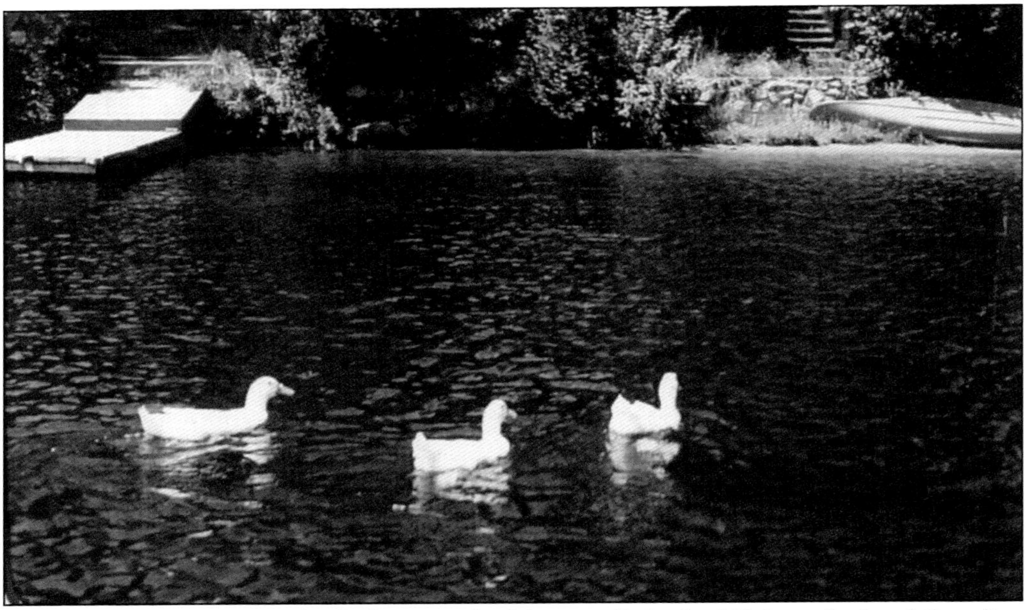

THREE DUCKS IN A ROW. The ducks enjoy the lake as well. In the fall, large flocks of Canadian Geese are also visitors of the lake. (Halprin.)

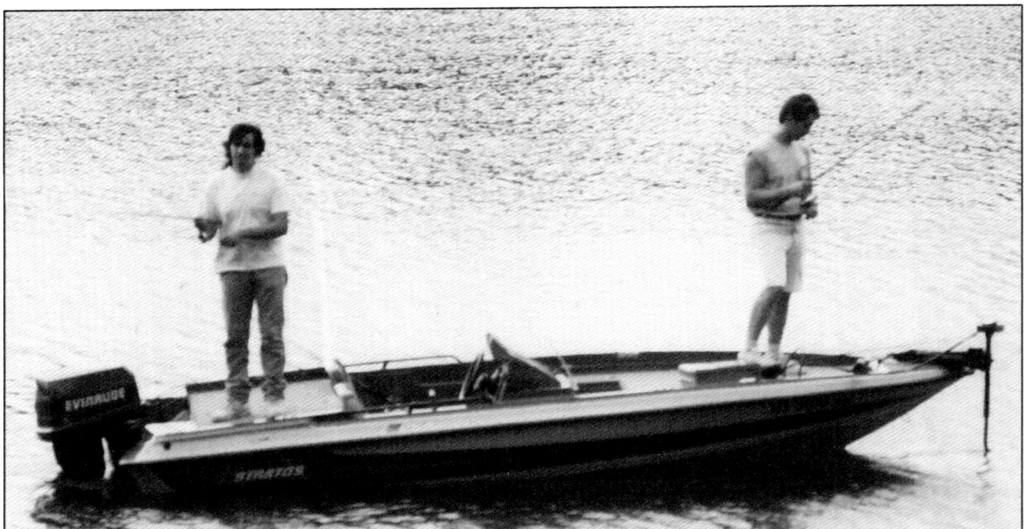

CATCH ONE FOR ME PLEASE. Fishing is still a popular sport, especially during the week and the early morning, when very few other people are around to disturb the fish. The fishermen probe and check every nook and cranny of the lake looking for the hiding place of the elusive and wary fish. But they are there! (Halprin.)

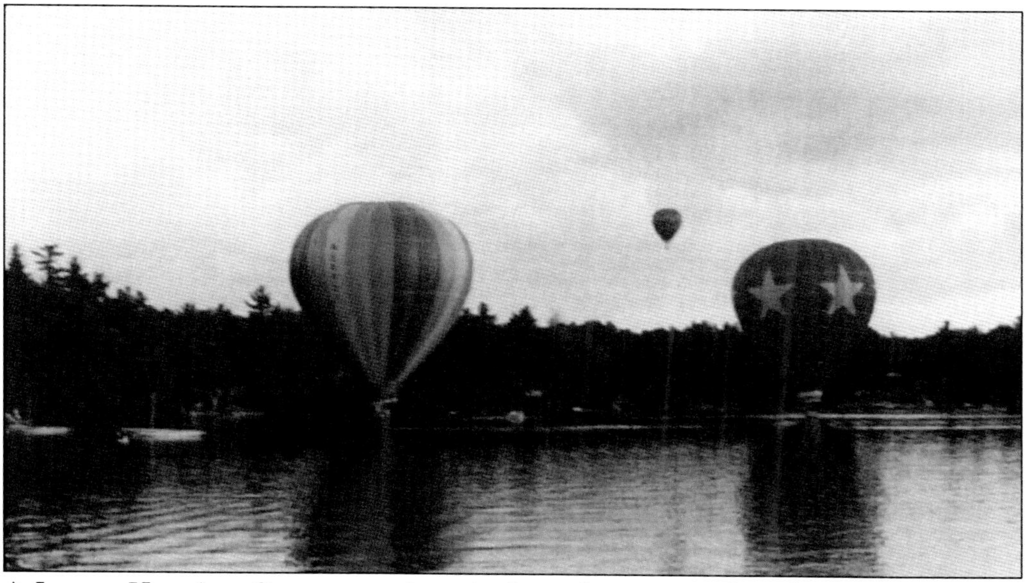

A Lot of Hot Air. On rare occasions, in the early morning when the wind is calm and everything is just right, colorful dots appear in the horizon, then as they get larger, they show their pear shape and their delightful coloring, and one hears the whooshing of their hot air burners as they gently maneuver themselves to just touch the lake. Having playfully kissed the lake, they rise again high into the air then go on to other adventures. (Halprin.)

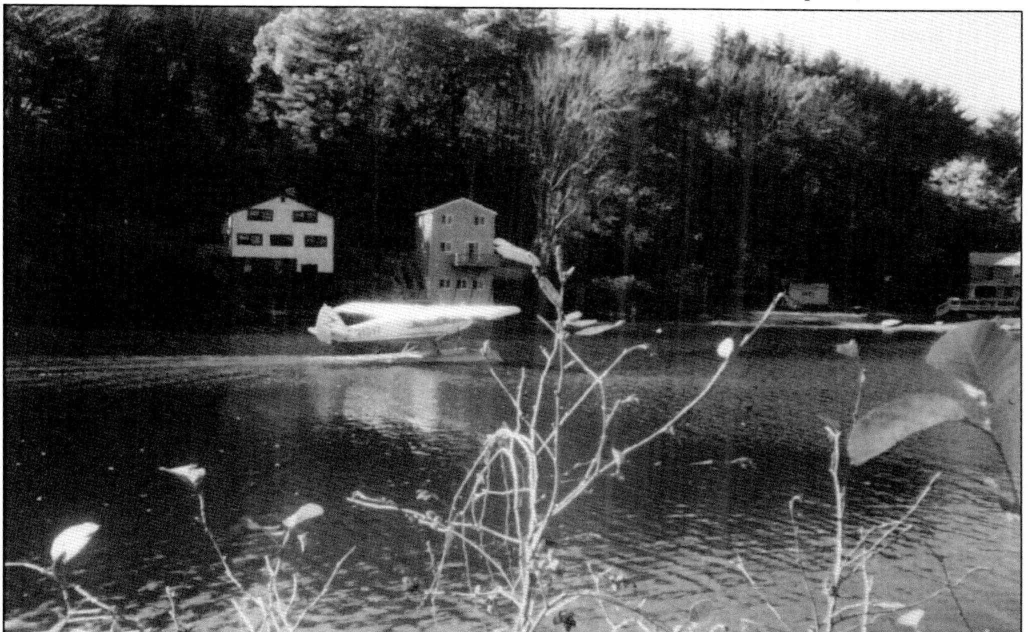

Just Dropping In. Although airplanes are not allowed to use the lake for landing or taking off, except in an emergency, occasionally a light plane equipped with aircraft floats will circle the lake and drop in for a short visit. This Cessna landed on the lake in 1995 near the old Hanson's Beach area.

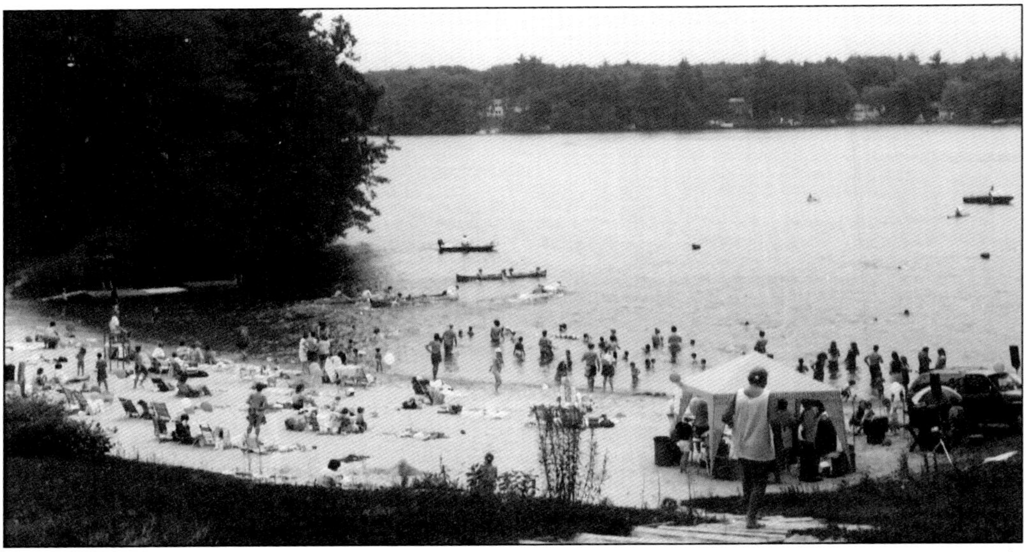

A GREAT BEACH DAY. A sunny warm day brings out a good crowd at the Stow Town Beach (dedicated in 1977). This is the very spot that the first tent was raised on Lake Boon for recreational purposes in the late part of the 1800s. This was quickly replaced by a small cabin, then an elaborate cottage called the Lincoln Club. The area was purchased by the town from the Parker family with a generous and anonymous donation for use as a town beach. The beach was dedicated in 1977 and is now used by many during the summer. (Raina.)

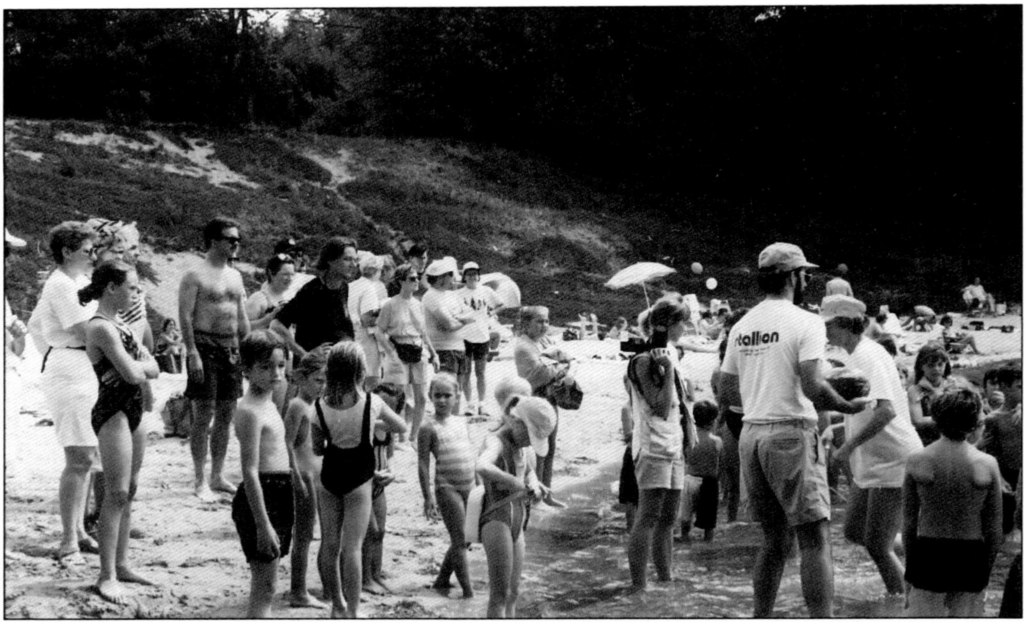

LOTS OF BEACH GAMES. It's never too hot or humid to keep the kids of all ages from playing games and enjoying themselves on the town beach in Stow. (Raina.)

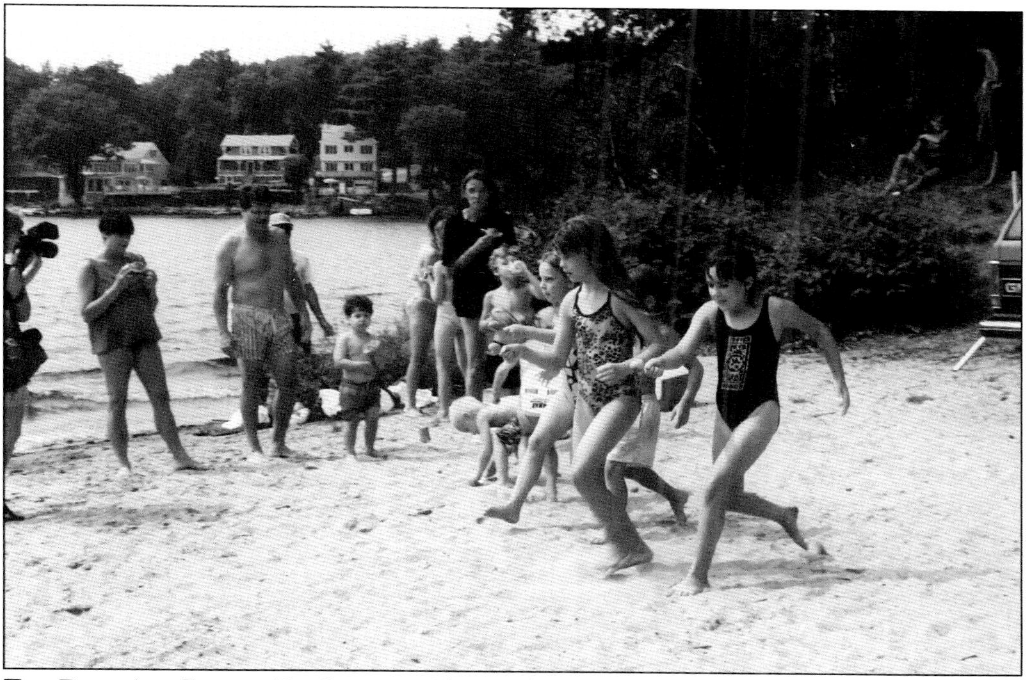

The Days Are Racing By Quickly. These girls enjoy a foot race at the Stow Town Beach during a recent warm sunny day. (Raina.)

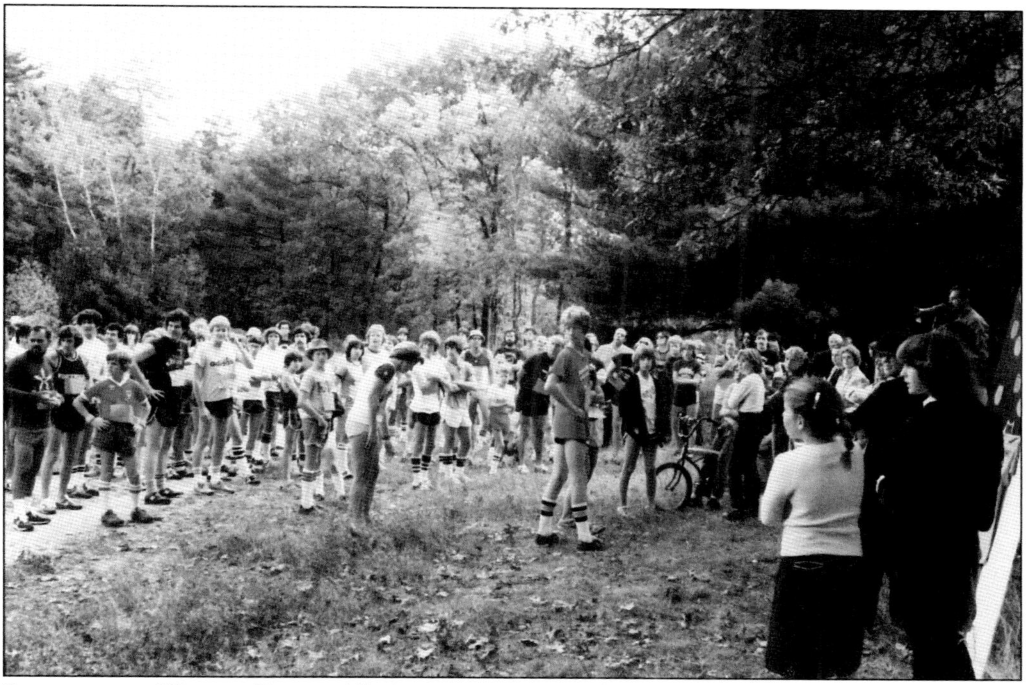

Ready for a Walk-a-Thon. All the contestants are lined up ready to go at the start of the Lake Boon Walk-a-Thon. It is about 5 miles around the lake, and the walk-a-thon starts and finishes at the field next to the Stow Town Beach.

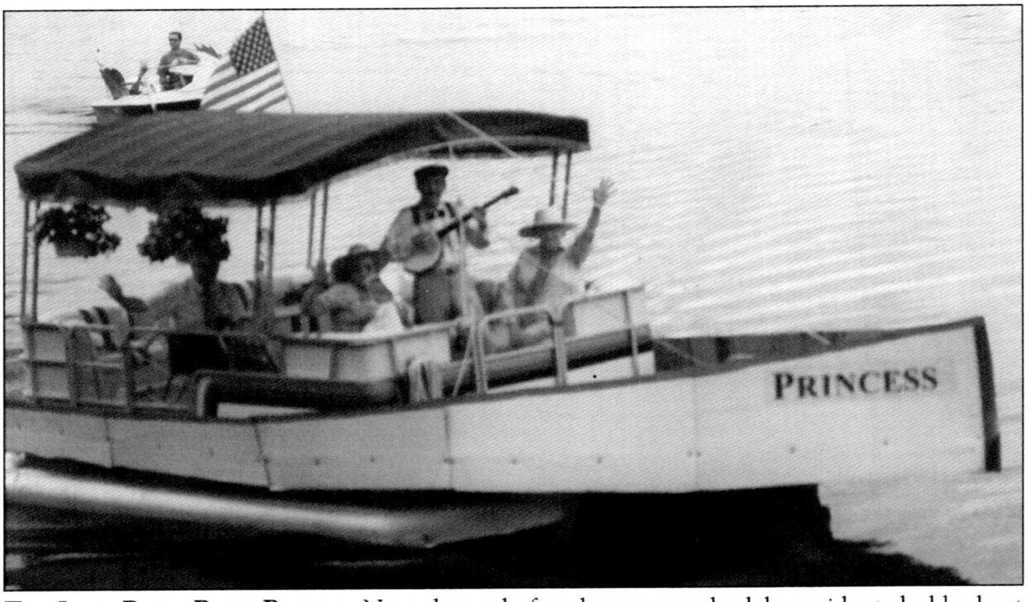

THE LAKE BOON BOAT PARADE. Near the end of each summer, the lake residents hold a boat parade in which all are urged to decorate their boat and bring it to a parade that tours around the lake. Various prizes are given. Above is the lead boat, a pontoon boat owned by Don and Lori Hawkes and converted by John Ketola into a replica of the *Princess* that used to provide transportation around the lake in the "old" days. The gentleman with the banjo at the front of the boat is Alan Kattelle, whose father was a pilot for the real *Princess*.

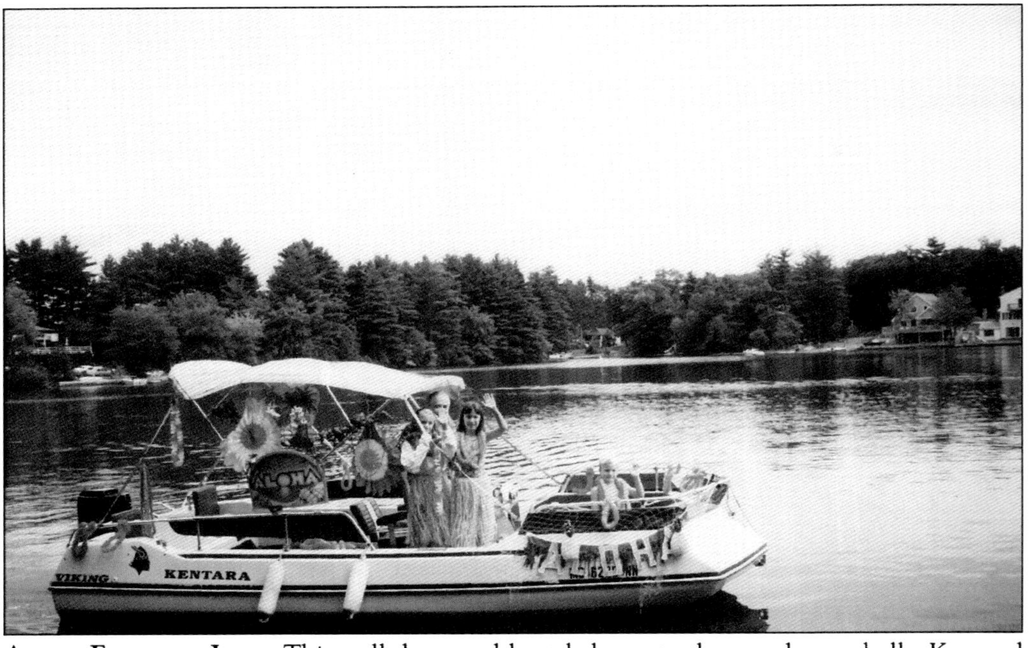

ALOHA FROM THE LAKE. This well-decorated boat belongs to the parade marshalls, Ken and Tami Raina. (Raina.)

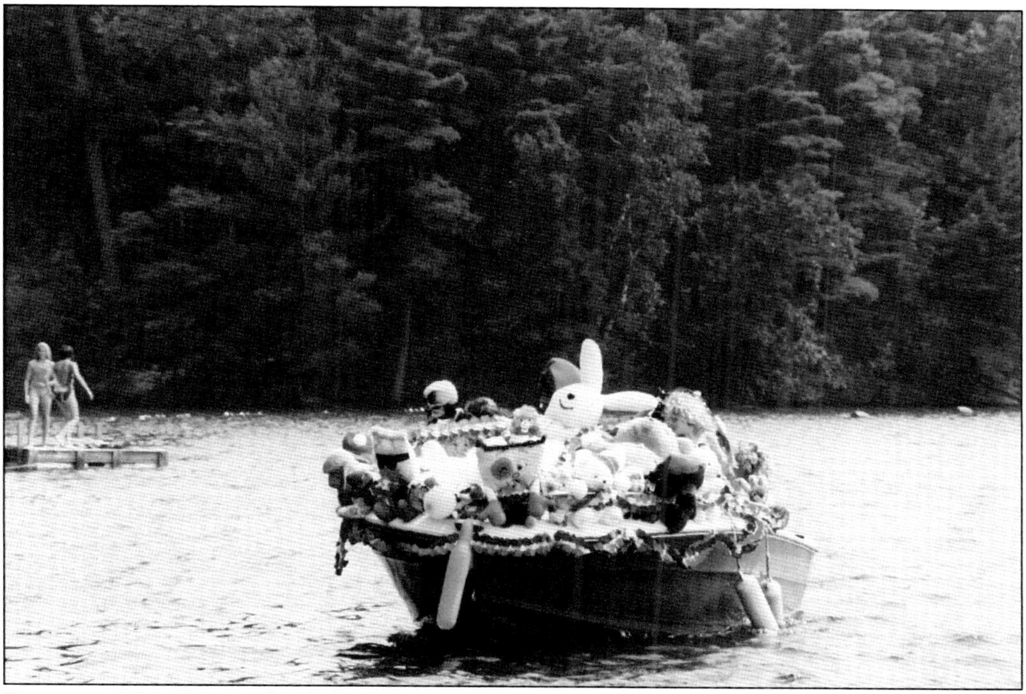

Toys and Us. This toy-loaded contribution to the 1989 Lake Boon Boat Parade was given by Tom Morgan, a Lakeside Avenue resident. (Raina.)

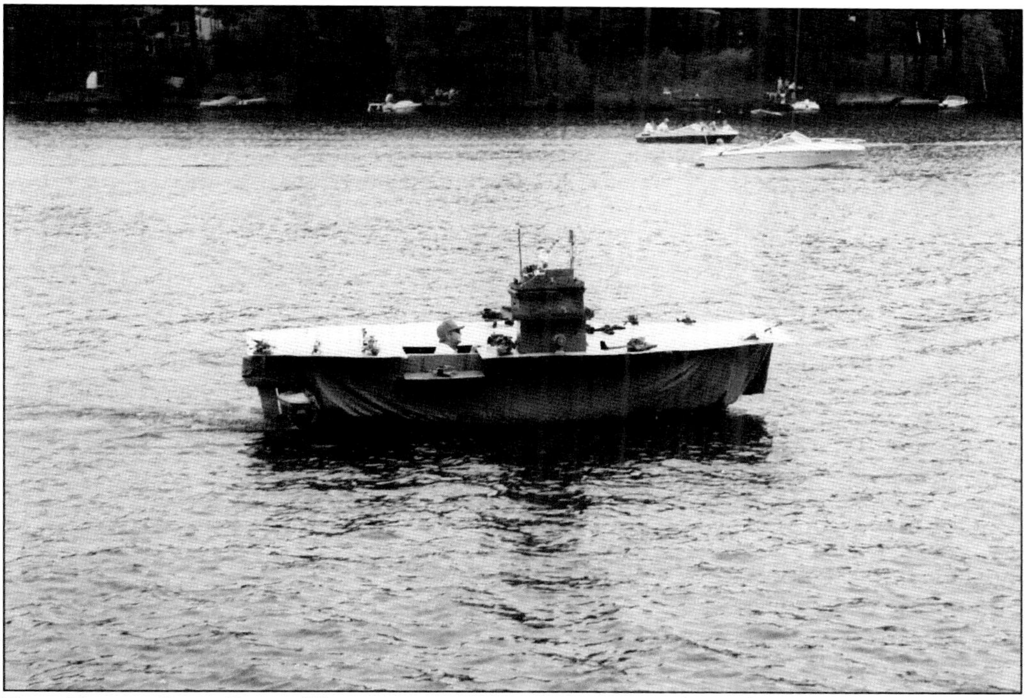

Flat Top on Lake Boon. This very ingenious entry was made in the 1988 Lake Boon Boat Parade by Dennis Forsmo. (Raina.)

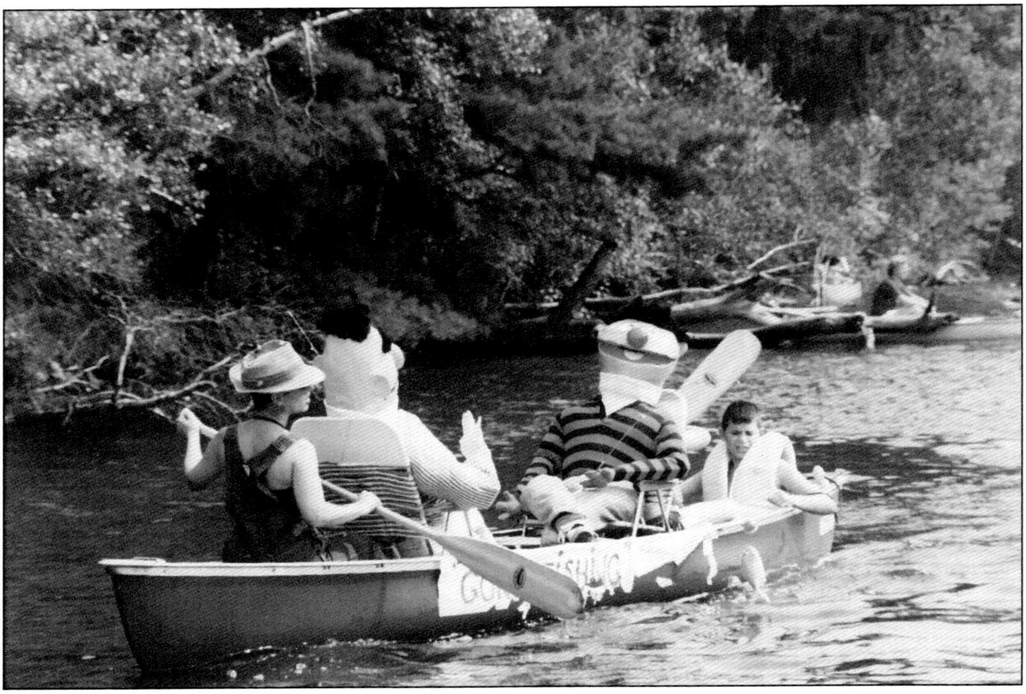

Bert and Ernie. This 1988 entry in the Lake Boon Boat Parade was made by Mary Ellen Forsmo. (Raina.)

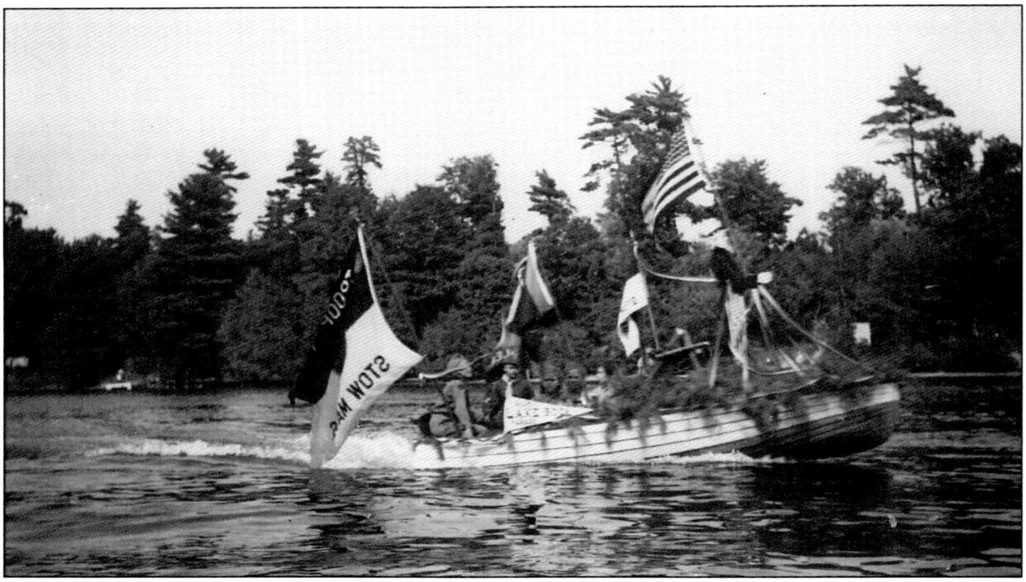

Monumental Float. An entry in a very early Lake Boon Boat Parade was a floating monument to American veterans. (Raina.)

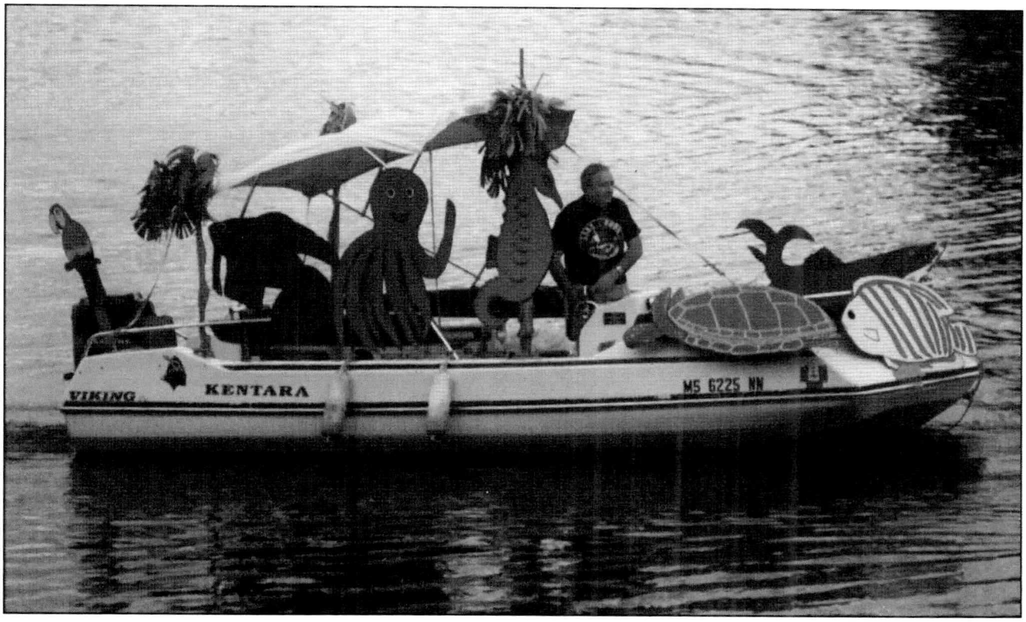

Floating Monsters. Pictured is a seaworld luau on Ken Raina's boat. (Raina.)

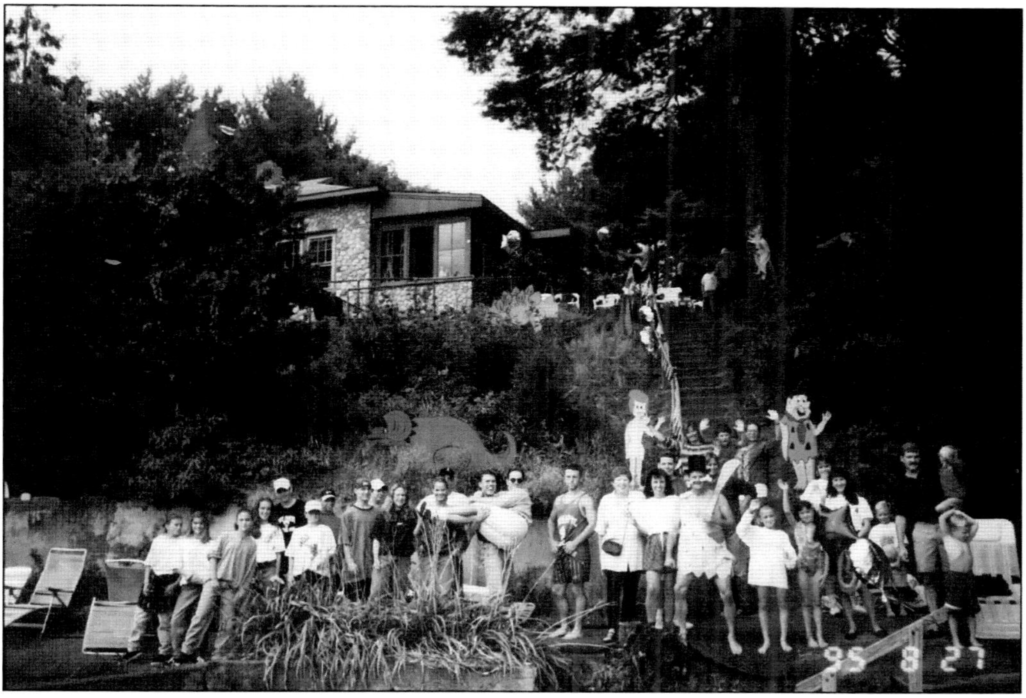

Really Big Shore Party. While the boat parade is going on, besides judging for the best decorated boat, there are also prizes for the best shore parties. Here is the best shore party for 1995 put on by John and Mary Ketolla.

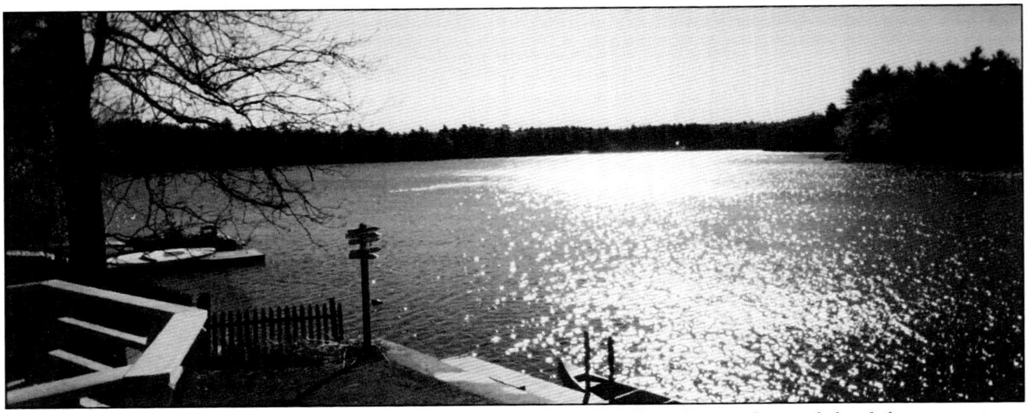

A Shimmering Lake. When the light and wind are just right, the surface of the lake turns into a million sparkling diamonds that shimmer in an unfathomable pattern that is impossible to ignore. (Halprin.)

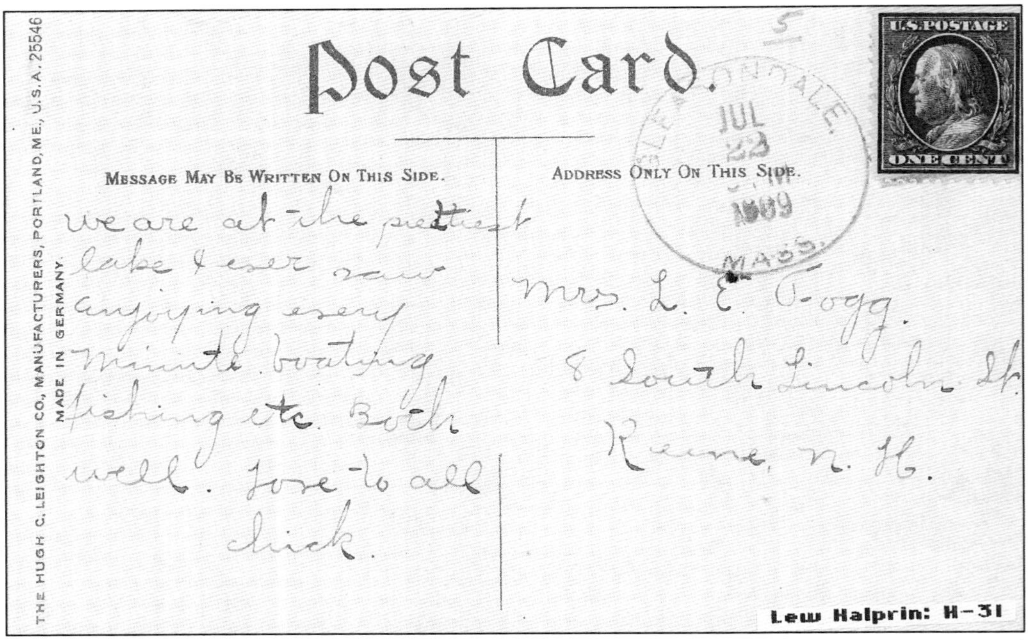

Postcard Chatter. In the early part of the century, telephones were not very common around the lake because of its summer-only nature. However, postcards were a very popular way to send little messages to your friends and family, not so much to say anything important, but as a means to brag that you are on vacation. Pictured here is a typical message. The postcard reads: "We are at the prettiest lake I ever saw enjoying every minute boating fishing etc. Both well. Love to all. Chick" (Halprin.)